She Inc.

A woman's guide to maximizing her career potential.

Kelley Keehn

INSOMNIAC PRESS

Library and Archives Canada Cataloguing in Publication

Keehn, Kelley, 1975-
She Inc. : a woman's guide to maximizing her career potential / Kelley Keehn.

Includes index.
ISBN 978-1-897178-64-5

1. Women--Vocational guidance. 2. Career development.
3. Self-actualization (Psychology) in women. I. Title.

HF5382.6.K43 2008 650.14082 C2008-904291-3

The publisher gratefully acknowledges the support of the Department of Canadian Heritage through the Book Publishing Industry Development Program.

Printed and bound in Canada

Insomniac Press, 192 Spadina Avenue, Suite 403
Toronto, Ontario, Canada, M5T 2C2
www.insomniacpress.com

Canada

Disclaimer

This book, in part, is designed to provide accurate and authoritative information on the subject of personal finances. While all of the stories and anecdotes described herein are based on true experiences, the names and situations have been altered to protect individual privacy. Neither the author nor the publisher is engaged in rendering legal, accounting, or other professional services by publishing this book. As a precaution, each individual situation should be addressed to an appropriate professional to ensure adequate evaluation and planning are applied. The author and publisher specifically disclaim any liability, loss, or risk that may be incurred as a consequence, directly or indirectly, of the use and application of any of the contents of this work.

The material in this book is intended as a general source of information only and should not be construed as offering specific tax, legal, financial, or investment advice. Every effort has been made to ensure that the material is correct at time of publication, but its accuracy or completeness cannot be guaranteed. Interest rates, market conditions, tax rulings, and other investment factors are subject to rapid change. Individuals should consult with their personal tax advisor, accountant, or legal professional before taking any action based upon the information contained in this book.

To Kathy & Ruth

The unexamined life isn't worth living.
Socrates

Table of Contents

Preface

The genesis of this project was the intention of empowering women in the corporate arena. I originally wanted to title the book, *Be The Man Your Mother Always Wanted You to Marry*. When I mentioned this working title to women across the country over the past few months, they usually chuckled and lamented that they didn't marry rich. They would sigh and look off into the distance thinking for a brief moment how much easier life might have been if they'd married a rich spouse.

In the new millennium in North America, many women have walked before us courageously changing the landscape and society's perceptions of what women are truly capable of. They endured ridicule, humiliation, isolation, and more. They took a stand so that you and I would have a new world to embrace decades later. I wonder if they had any idea that this insidious concept of a woman needing to marry rich would still be prevalent in our society. Marrying rich is seen as winning a spousal lottery: the prize is the knight in shining armour and the ticket to freedom.

I adore my mother. She equipped me with a solid foundation at an early age. By forcing me to perfect my math and English skills months or years before my peers in elementary school, my mother allowed me to excel with teachers marvelling at my advanced knowledge. My mom cheered my successes into my adulthood and was there every step of the way to dust me off after my failures. When you're raised and blessed with such a champion of your abilities, you truly believe there's nothing in life outside of your control.

During my early twenties, something curious started to occur. As I tested my abilities in the real world, failed, endured, and persevered, during those times of struggle, great cheerleaders such as my mom and other men and women I admired encouraged me in one breath and in the other, suggested it wasn't too late for me to find a rich husband.

This paradoxical view exists today and I'm not sure if it's ready to be slain by society let alone the average woman any time soon. This notion of the fairy tale of the knight in shining armour that will one day save us, or that we even need saving, is all around us.

Today's woman can earn more than a man, can find nearly everything she needs emotionally from her friends, and is accepted in society if she chooses to be single, divorce, raise children on her own or forgo child rearing altogether.

The TV series, *Sex And The City* has reinforced the idea that women can, should, and will demand more from themselves and each other. We deserve to stand on our own, support each other, stand up for our rights as sexual beings, and more. However, at the end of the recent *Sex and the City* movie, the fairy tale perfection of Carrie and Mr. Big is still there.

Throughout history, men for the most part have been defined by their wealth, their career, and their position in life. Women? Well, we're defined by the man we have and thus his wealth, his status, and his position in life. When writing I started the last sentence with "we used to define" ourselves by our men, but I don't think we're quite there. I've heard the complaints of hundreds of women striving for success and achieving it. Yet, that knight has eluded them and their quest has left them empty.

What if we were our own knights? What if we aspired to be that ideal being, that man if you will, that our mothers wanted us to marry? I'm not suggesting for a moment that a woman become more manly, masculine, or even aggressive. Think metaphorically of what a "man" affords the female gender. He is someone to save us, to take us to the theatre, buy us flowers, wine, dine, and eventually, be invited (often begged and demanded) to mark his territory with the coveted engagement ring (and the larger the better).

What if we could be all of that to ourselves? What if we sought the companionship of a man to complement us, but we were whole individuals capable of standing on our own two feet. What if we entertained ourselves, purchased our own jewellery and diamonds, and stopped waiting for someone to complete us?

I can assure you that this book is not a feminist manifesto or a soap box speech supporting or denouncing the idiosyncrasies of our genders, or an analysis of what society has formed as acceptable norms.

Rather *She Inc.* is an empowering journey to female independence, which, I believe, is only truly achieved through financial independence. To be sure, there will likely be many times in a woman's life when she simply can't be independent—financially or otherwise—due to child rearing or other family priorities. However, the foundation, the strength, and the personal power that is achieved by knowing that she *can* be independent is the point of this book. And, with her ability to earn an income, this book will teach her, and I expect you, to reach her maximum potential with that skill.

She Inc. isn't for a woman looking for the easy way out, but one for who's searching to leave her own unique mark on this planet. She's not looking to get ahead by putting others down nor is she seeking someone to rescue her from life's problems. She's ready to tackle them head on and is willing to start the journey of self-discovery.

I know that you are such a woman. That you are ready to take a leap of faith knowing that independence can and will be yours. Should you encounter a prince along the journey, he will complement not complete you. You will benefit from all that many women before us have fought for: our ability to obtain equality in life and within ourselves by taking action, control, and responsibility now.

Welcome to the voyage of *She Inc.*

Chapter 1

You Inc.

What do you want to be?

I was never one of those lucky individuals who always knew what they wanted to be. Quite frankly, some days I still don't think I've figured that out. But in hindsight, that's also worked to my advantage. I absolutely love what I do today. I wake up every day feeling blessed to do what I do and the "what" I do seems to change weekly. Perhaps not having a definitive goal of what I would be (a doctor, lawyer, painter, etc.) has assisted me in being open to careers as they present themselves.

I was a financial professional for twelve years, and am now an author, writer, columnist, speaker, faculty member, media personality, and tomorrow, who knows? Not one of these positions is one I ever directly wanted, set out to earn, or had envisioned for myself. To be clear as well, none of these roles simply fell in my lap. While I was diligently on road A, road B presented itself. Sometimes I took the journey; sometimes I stayed my current course. Not being sure about what exactly I wanted from life allowed me to entertain alternative paths.

So what do you want to be when you grow up? I say that tongue-in-cheek, but even as adults, many of us don't really know what we want to be. If we attended university or college, we may have had a counsellor to assist us in identifying our skills and the industries with which we could best align our natural talents. The likely reality is that most individuals never really received such specific counsel or were so lost during their early adulthood, and I might add many for life, that they never thought out what career path and position would best suit them. Plus, in our ever-changing world, industries exist and flourish today that were only an ideal just a short decade ago. We can only imagine what the future will bring. What industries and jobs will be obsolete and which will be created that don't even exist yet?

Even if you are doing exactly what you always wanted to and still enjoy it, the chances are, statistically speaking, that you will either make several major career changes in your life or your company or industry will force change upon you.

If you do decide to make the change within your working career, you won't be alone.

Statistics show that you're likely to change your career path a number of times in your working life. A study was published examining the number of times baby boomers (those born between 1947 and 1966) changed jobs between the ages of 18 and 36. Shockingly, the boomers held an average of 9.6 jobs in this short span of their lives. (Source: The Bureau of Labor Statistics. August 2002, "Number of Jobs Held, Labor Market Activity, and Earnings Growth among Younger Baby Boomers: Results from More Than Two Decades of Longitudinal Survey.") According to James C. Cabrera and Charles Albrecht Jr., authors of *The Lifetime Career Manager*, in today's employment environment, most Canadians change careers at least once and change companies at least four times in their lifetime.

Even though you might not make as many career or job changes as the average boomer, you're still likely to make a few in your lifetime. You're also statistically likely to not enjoy your job at all, and possibly the stress or lack of inspiration could affect your health. If you're not doing what you absolutely love, then why aren't you?

If you truly love what you do or can't see yourself changing careers like the numbers suggest, the marketplace might force you to do so. I think back to the banking industry where I started working in 1996. By the time I had joined the bank, the landscape had already changed dramatically. Bankers across North America faced a massive change forced on them by the market. Traditionally, banks made money by lending it to others. Of course they profited from other areas, but for many decades they enjoyed a lending boom by serving the bulk of what the population wanted. The baby boomers were buying up homes and cars and building their lives and families in the 1980s and 1990s. By the late 1990s, the banks realized a major shift was about to happen. The bulk of the population was aging. Their mortgages were paid or being paid off. Their need for lending was quickly being reduced and their retirement and investments were now their main priority. The generations to follow will still require lending in mass, however, their size and impact isn't as substantial as the baby boomers.

Within a few short years, the banks realized that to win over the boomers and offer more of what they were focused on receiving, they needed to specialize and expand their investment expertise, and offer financial, retirement, and estate planning. This transition was just on the cusp of starting when I joined the bank. I was able to witness the industry change dramatically over the past decade. The Royal Bank of Canada rebranded to RBC; The Bank of Nova Scotia became a friendlier Scotiabank; and even the Toronto-Dominion Bank became TD Waterhouse. Many at the time of my employment also constructed wealth management divisions and provincial banks such as the Alberta Treasury Branches became ATB Financial. Lending will always be a mainstay of a bank or trust company, but all are still on board to cash in on the needs of the boomers.

Think about the implication of moving from being primarily a "lender" to being a "server." When I joined the bank as an outsider with a financial advising background, I had no preconceived notions as to what to expect from the banking world, other than my limited personal banking experience. In our society bankers have always been seen as Godlike, dispensing money (a loan or mortgage) to those who are "worthy" and saying "no" to those who aren't, almost like a parent. I'm speaking of the industry as a whole, throughout the time that formal banking has existed. Customers were always asking the bank for something. Bank employees had power, prestige, and authority. A bank position was coveted by many with its advantageous "banker's hours."

Fast forward to the 1990s. Many factors including technology have changed the banking landscape, but to be sure, the boomers have had the greatest impact on the industry. A huge chunk of the population as a whole didn't really need the bank anymore. If they were getting a loan, it might be for a car that they could pay cash for anyway or a cottage that wasn't a necessity. Their affluence as a group started to take away the lending power from the banks. Additionally, with their excess savings, large pensions, and higher discretionary spending (since their debts were being paid off as they aged), they were now seeking advice from the industry about how to manage their cash flow and assets. Today, competition in the financial industry is fierce. It was already overcrowded in the 1990s and has grown as the boomers have aged. Banks, insurance companies, private companies, and more have jumped into the ring to offer products and services to those looking for advice and a decent investment return.

All of a sudden, the boomer was in charge. Not needing anything from the bank or these financial institutions, they were now being wooed and the rivalry began. Bank employees and executives had to shift from a "you need us" mentality to "how might we serve you?" It was a tough struggle for many. Customer service wasn't a necessity before the 1990s in the banking industry. Today, it's paramount.

With a changing marketplace and customer, the banks had to change too. Gone were the banking hours that worked for the employees. Branches advertised being open late, in the evenings, and allowing access around the clock, with the advent of telebanking, Internet banking, and, of course, ATMs.

Bankers too have had to change their personal approach. Mortgage lenders and those specializing in investments no longer dictate when customers can come in to see them. The banks, that previously had a "you'll see us on our terms" attitude, started advertising that mortgage and investment specialists would see you on "your" terms and would fit into their customers' busy lives. They now want to earn their customers' business. These specialists will not only meet customers in the evening, and on weekends and holidays, but they'd come to the branch, client's office, home, or even take them for lunch or dinner. Many bank specialists today work from their home, may earn 100% commission (where a decade ago virtually no bank employees were on commission let alone 100%) and in a way, are almost self-employed, but with the bank as their end employer.

For hundreds of years (if not thousands), the banking industry has remained consistent in the perception of the public. They haven't had to change, innovate, or compete. Within an extremely short period of time, one generation has forced the entire industry to revolutionize how they do business.

Think about your industry or the one you'd like to work in. Is it solid and impermeable like the banking industry used to be? Are you an employee and wish to remain that way forever with a steady income, benefits, and seniority? What if you were the mortgage broker at the bank and within a few years went from a set salary and bonus working in a branch to now working from home with an uncertain salary? To having your job shift to include business development and marketing as much as execution of paperwork?

If you're currently a business owner or self-employed, examine your industry carefully. Is it possible that the product or service you offer might be forced out by the market in the future? Consider the independent book retailer for a moment. It seems that the closing of the Shop Around the Corner in *You've Got Mail* has become the norm in North America. Two of my all time favourite stores have recently closed their doors in Canada and I wonder how many of the remaining independents will survive? I was an avid bookstore connoisseur my entire life. It was a weekly ritual to visit a local bookstore each and every Saturday. Their advice and recommendations kept me coming back. Then, the big guys moved in and I was hooked on the selection and the convenience that my local bookstore couldn't fulfill (they could always get a book in, but it sometimes took several weeks). As I examine my book buying habits, it's shocking and disappointing how they've declined and changed in just a few short years. I believe, in large part, the Internet has served as my number one source of research. It is only if I can't find what I need surfing through the litany of data on the net that I will leave the comforts of my laptop and venture to a bookstore or, less likely, a library. Furthermore, with the ease, convenience, and discounts offered by the online retailers, I, a one time devoted fan of the "little bookstore around the corner," have opted for expediency, much to the detriment of the merchants I adore and admire.

Is it possible that your business too might be forced out of the marketplace by the needs and whims of our ever-changing society? Of course, specialists may survive. There will always be a portion of the population, albeit small and diminishing, who are willing to drive for the advice of an independent bookstore with staff passionate about the content they stock and willing to recommend the read of a lifetime. The average small retailer in that industry, however, will likely be squeezed out.

It's possible that you may have to wear many hats even though you are currently employed in a secure position. Or, as the business owner, you will have to become a shrewd marketer and trend forecaster. A guidebook to empower you to do both is in order. And that's precisely what *She Inc.* will do!

If you know it, they will come

Job dissatisfaction is rampant. It has become socially acceptable to dread Monday morning and celebrate the freedom from the work shackles on Friday. But what if you could do what you truly loved? The type of career or position that has you excited on Sunday evening, raring to start the week? If you're ever going to find that ideal position that fills your life with excitement and fulfillment, you first need to analyze your current employment status.

Self-Assessment Questionnaire:

Rating Your Employment Satisfaction Level

1. Do you currently enjoy your job? Rate your satisfaction on a scale of 1-10 (10 being highest) and detail why.

____

____

____

____

2. Do you enjoy the field that you work in? Explain.

____

____

____

____

3. What do you enjoy the most about your current position?

____

____

____

____

4. What do you enjoy the least about your current position?

5. Would you like to work fewer hours? Why or why not?

6. Would you like to work more hours? Why or why not?

7. Are you being fully challenged? Explain.

8. Are you being paid to your expectation? Are you being paid to your full potential? If not, why?

9. What would be your ideal compensation? What would it consist of (salary, bonuses, other perks)?

10. What first attracted to you to your job?

11. What first attracted you to the field that you work in?

12. Have they changed? Have you changed? Explain.

If your primary career consists of staying at home with your children or taking care of your home, or both, please fill out the above questionnaire anyway. The job or field doesn't matter. What's important to understand is that no job has to be a life sentence. You have the freedom and flexibility to entertain employment options that you've actively considered.

If you've never attended a workshop or read a book on choosing the ideal career, it's essential that you take a few moments to determine what's really important to you. When we set goals, we sometimes don't look at them in their entirety and wholistically in contrast to the other goals in our life. The same is true when we think a job or field is ideal only to later be disappointed with some aspect that we hadn't fully considered beforehand. Take a few moments to daydream about your ideal job and what that means to you specifically, even if you're not considering a career change at the moment.

Determining Your Ideal Job

1. What time of day would you like to go to work?

2. How many hours in a day would you like to work?

3. How many days per week would you like to work?

4. Where would you like work? (i.e. at home, in an office, in a huge office tower)

5. How would you get to work? (i.e. as a passenger, as a driver, taking the public transportation system.)

6. At home or another workplace, what would your ideal office be like? Would you have an office?

7. Would you have a boss or would you be the boss?

8. Would you have employees or an assistant?

9. Would you like new challenges from your work? Explain.

10. Would you like less stress from your work? Explain.

11. Would you like flexibility or consistency in your schedule?

12. Would you like flexibility or consistency in your income?

13. Would you like benefits and bonuses?

14. Would you like more responsibility or less? Explain.

15. How would you like to be acknowledged at work (more pay, advancement, etc.)?

I was surprised to learn from a 2005 Ipsos-Reid survey for RBC Financial Group that about 3.2 million adult Canadians, or 13.5%, said that they would like to start their own business. Roughly 950,000 of them hoped to do so within one year.

I believe that the entrepreneurial spirit is more alive today than ever in history. As a business owner myself, I've had several people express their interest in owning their own business. I would always have these individuals complete the above questionnaire for consistency and likelihood of success.

Let's say, for example, that you completed the above questionnaire and would like to open your own business. You've identified that you'd like the flexibility and freedom that comes with being an entrepreneur, would like maximum challenge, and don't mind the extra stress that comes with starting a new business. But let's assume that you desire a regular paycheque and cannot handle variances in your salary. Let's also assume that you have children and definitely cannot afford to put in evenings or weekends. If you had answered this way and had come to me for advice on opening a financial planning firm, I would carefully caution you to do otherwise. So often the allure of owning a business, with its freedom and absolute control, is overshadowed by the long hours, grunt work, and lack of certainty or security regarding income or time spent at work.

It would be just as defeating for someone who is interested in unlimited flexibility, pay, and advancement to take a position such as a teacher. We know that the education field usually requires a regular schedule and has fairly set salaries without bonuses or commissions. There are, however, exceptions to every rule. Nevertheless, why create more obstacles for yourself at the outset than necessary?

If you'd like to work in a posh office tower, wear a suit, and punch a clock, go downtown one day and look at the companies that are listed in the towers' directories. It will give you a good idea as to the type of position that might exist for you if that lifestyle is of interest. Start to interview your friends, family, and associates. Find out what they really do in a day at work. If their job title or field sounds intimidating or unfamiliar, just ask them to describe what they do in a typical day. That should give you an idea of what that position might encompass. Further investigate by asking such questions as: Who are your customers? Who are your wholesalers? What do you enjoy most/least about your job? What did you do before this job? What education or training was required?

If you completed the above questionnaire and realized how much you really do need a job change, but for whatever reason you cannot or are just not ready for a change, there's great news for you too! Think about all of the activities that you're good at, enjoy, or love and figure out a way to capitalize on them. They could be hobbies or skills that come particularly easy to you that you could try turning into a side business for fun.

Assuming that you love filing taxes and enjoy working with numbers, why not take a tax-filing course and offer to file the returns of your friends and family members for a discounted rate? If you love painting or are a consummate artist, why not take a course on creating your own web site and market your wares world wide and in your free time. Better yet, teach a beginners how-to course on your craft.

Nothing is really work unless you would
rather be doing something else.
–James M. Barrie

If you don't have any hobbies or interests that you feel could generate a side income, try volunteering. Though it was never a goal of mine to enter the financial industry, early in my career I found that I missed the excitement of the marketing and communications training that I received in college. I did have some opportunities to market the overall firm, but not to the level I would have liked. Understanding that I had no real experience in advertising and marketing, I would likely be turned down if I applied for such a position. But they were my corporate passion and forte, so I decided to apply and expand my skills on a volunteer basis.

I volunteered for a number of committees and within a year, I was chairing a committee and soon served on a few boards. During my volunteering years, I learned what school and my current jobs could never have taught me. I networked with city councillors, the mayor, and countless other prominent business people in my city at only twenty years old. Wearing the hat of a volunteer position can open many wonderful opportunities that could easily lead you on the path to a new job or career.

Are you ready to shift?

With an ever-changing world and marketplace coupled with the likelihood of your holding many positions during your lifetime, one thing transcends all of this: The ideal of thinking of yourself as a corporation—You Incorporated! Get ready to open your new business.

Right now, please write your full name in front of the Inc. below.

________________________________ Incorporated.

Congratulations! Whether today you have only one client (your employer), serve many (as a business owner), are a student, or are getting ready to get into or back into the workforce, thinking of yourself as the President and CEO of You Inc. will change your life. Your boss and co-workers become clients you serve and they'll notice. If you're a business owner, you'll understand the importance of not only the many hats you wear, but also the most important one, that of a CEO—the driving and definitive force behind any successful venture. And if you're getting back into the workforce, you'll soon be aware of how every life action and person you meet defines your new venture.

This concept of thinking of yourself as a corporation isn't new, however, my approach and experience with living the ideals of it is new. Shortly, I'll share my story of how this new way of thinking revolutionized my life, tangibly opened doors, created opportunities and "lucky breaks" and how it can for you too if you're willing to apply it. Designing You Inc. is not about aggressively seeking more, working harder or focusing on the pursuit of capitalism. It's an ideal. A way of holding yourself to a higher standard and conveying that standard to your marketplace—whatever and whomever they may be. It's an empowering journey of self-discovery and a manual for consciously creating the map and blueprint of your life. You deserve to be in charge of your present and future now. You can set up the rules of life to win, if you first know what they are.

We'll explore these rules together with the knowledge that there are some laws of life and nature that can't be ignored in doing so. We'll accept as well that the world is not black and white (although we might wish it to be) but is instead various shades of grey. As such, there isn't one definitive solution for you or me. There isn't one way, path, or destination that works all of the time, every time. That is why you're reading this and I'm writing it. If there were a guidebook on life or a human owner's manual, self-discovery would be stricken from the dictionary. But how boring and predictable would life be knowing what each day would bring and the story of your life before it began? Invariably, you'll read through these pages and find many "exceptions to the rules" or find yourself thinking, "Yes, but what about xyz?" That's terrific. I want you thinking and I'd be delighted if you'd share. As unique as you are, you will have different takes on various subjects and materials. I want to hear from you. I want to share your interpretations with other women and theirs with you. Please jot down these thoughts as you come across them, as they pop up, or when you're done the book. Please e-mail me and I'll add them to my Web site or blog and we as women can grow together by combining our interpretations and insights. Within the confines of just one book, I cannot explore every life alternative. Plus, I want you to extract what you will and hopefully take action from the words on these pages.

Paradoxical View Point

When there are glaring contradictions, those light to dark grey spots, you will see a *PVP*. The PVP is the *Paradoxical View Point* to consider and my intent is to open your mind to other views you might think of. To be sure, people must stand for what they believe in or they'll fall for anything. However, so many of our beliefs were formed without our conscious permission. Life isn't black and white any more, if it ever was. Embrace the grey, the duality of both sides—the contradictions and paradoxes. Being uncomfortable with uncertainty keeps our minds sharp and our options open for opportunities. You get to write the pages of your life book now and it's my honour to take you on that journey.

Sidebars

You'll also see throughout these pages my "sidebar" comments. These side thoughts expand the concept and give you greater insight as to the workings of that story, a definition of the content, or some piece of information that doesn't clearly fit within the normal text.

Part of the shift is about distancing emotion from your major decisions and designing the roadmap for your life. Often, decisions made within a business context are easier, quicker, and more thought out. Of course, we're humans not companies, so emotion can never be eliminated. Emotions can be downplayed as long as you don't take it personally—it's business. An individual can be hired or fired based on the facts. But, when was the last time you hired or fired a friend or spouse based solely on the facts? Emotion is necessary, but often clouds our judgment. There is, however, a fine line that can be drawn when using the processes of the corporate world for gain in our personal lives without becoming an unfeeling android.

Employee vs. Owner

You needn't look past our country's airline industry for a classic example of the perspective shift of You Inc. Consider Canada's two largest airlines, Air Canada and WestJet. Air Canada is the largest in our country. Founded in 1937 it has not been without its troubles. Although in 2001, it was rated the world's twelfth largest airline, by 2003 it had filed for bankruptcy protection and later emerged from it in September 2004. Meanwhile, the new kids on the block, WestJet, a regional low cost carrier opened up shop in Calgary in February 1996 with only a fleet of three Boeing 737 jets. As Air Canada was filing for bankruptcy protection in 2003, at the same time WestJet expanded their service to much of Canada. By 2004, the company kept growing and announced expansion to a number of US cities. Today, WestJet has grown their fleet of three jets to 75 and are flying to 49 destinations.

As I write these pages, Air Canada is back in the news with waning customer confidence due to rising flight prices from high oil costs, which are forcing them to slash jobs by the thousands. And WestJet? During yet another Air Canada crisis, they're pretty much business as usual.

Even if you haven't flown in Canada at all or recently, you're likely aware of the overall reputation of Air Canada and their employees. Simply tune into the Comedy Network and you're bound to hear a stand-up comedian slight the company for their lack of customer service, flight delays, and unapologetic attitude. The opposite is the attitude of the WestJet employee. I'm sure you've seen the commercials. A happy WestJet employee smiles realizing that one of the flight guests has forgotten their cell phone, briefcase, or some other article. The WestJet employee overcomes great obstacles to return the item the passenger didn't even realize they had forgotten, and it's all done with a smile. And the tag line at the end of the commercial—"Why do WestJet employees care so much? Because they're also WestJet owners."

Are WestJet employees really owners? Technically, with the profit sharing offered, I suppose they are. In reality, they're not in the boardroom voting on the future of the company. But aren't Air Canada employees owners too with their stock options? Is it as simple as the executives telling, reinforcing, and advertising to employees, the public, and customers that they empower and expect their employees to act like owners? With WestJet, this perspective shift from the top has helped in the tremendous success they've achieved in a relatively short time in the industry. Plus, their reputation for service and friendliness is well known. WestJet is also a rarity in the airline industry with their employees being non-unionized. To be fair, I have encountered many lovely Air Canada employees over the years and true, not every WestJet employee is bubbling and merry, however, generally, they seem to have a lot more fun than their competitors. If you get a chance to fly WestJet, you'll see their airline staff cracking jokes as they read the safety features of the aircraft before takeoff and when taxiing to the gate. Often the pilot will welcome the passengers with a joke or two before thanking them for their business and for choosing WestJet.

Although WestJet began with a simple perspective shift, it had a profound and powerful end result. When a company and their employees truly think as business owners and convey that message to the public, it does have a tangible impact that we can all witness and take note of. Whether you're an employee of an unionized company or a true profit sharing staff member, shifting to look at yourself on a higher level, like as an owner (even if you truly aren't), not only increases the chance for greater success for the company you serve, but will lead to personal gain as well.

But I'm owed: A look at corporate culture

One definitive trait the President and CEO of You Inc. needs to closely consider is the notion of being "owed" within your work. Now that you're a CEO, you see business and work with new eyes. No longer is just showing up or "doing the job" acceptable. You have a reputation to protect and develop. You now see your place of work or company in a larger sense. You see corporate culture more as an agrarian process than that of instant gratification. Sometimes you'll plant seeds that may take a decade to mature. But you know the laws of nature are on your side. You have faith and trust in the planting and nurturing of those seeds and know that to reap a harvest one day, the planting and tending of You Inc. can only be executed by you.

Many of the frustrations with the youth of today stem from their sense of entitlement. These new generations are often criticized for getting out of school and expecting a job, house, and more without necessarily earning it. Perhaps it's true. But in fairness to our youth, many employees through years of bitterness, corporate tightening, and higher shareholder demands on profits have come to feel owed by their employer or customer and thus pull back on their level of participation and service. This feeling of entitlement and being owed is insidious, crippling, and will take down your corporation and its reputation and chances for success with lightning speed.

The July 2008 issue of *Toronto Life* magazine featured a story entitled, "Breaking the Bank." It's a report about Dara Fresco, a CIBC bank employee "who earns in one year what the president makes in a day" and details her recently launched class action suit against the bank for unpaid overtime. Dara is paid an annual salary of $31,000 for her 37.5 hour workweek as a branch head teller. Her beef with the company is that she's been volunteering her time past her scheduled hours, and over the last decade, and estimates that the amount owing to her is $50,000.

I did work for a major Canadian bank during my career. It wasn't CIBC, although I'm sure their structure is similar to the bank that I worked for. The average reader skimming through this article might feel pity for Dara and think that her plight deserves the press she's attracting. Plus, she's not alone. She's attracted over 1,000 tellers to join her in the class action suit. As a former bank employee, my issue with Dara's case is three fold. Situations like Dara's stand in the way of progressing if we are to buy-in to the concept of You Inc.

There are a number of curious details within Dara's story that the average reader might not be aware of unless they have actually worked in a bank. First, when Dara took the position with CIBC, she was likely told up front that she would periodically need to work overtime without pay. Surely, if she weren't told this, within a short period of time on the job she would have realized the probability and could have quit.

Second, it is true that unionized employees have the union to ensure that they are fairly paid for overtime, given the required breaks during a shift, and more. Although I'm certainly far from an expert on the intricacies of a union, I'm quite sure that many unionized companies don't offer stock option plans, extensive profit sharing, and employee investment contribution matching along with the plethora of other benefits an employer such as a bank offers. During my time at the bank, I was shocked by the number of tellers that had amassed hundreds of thousands of dollars in stock shares from their contributions that had been matched by the bank's. If one were to weigh the benefits of these matching and incentive programs offered by CIBC against a unionized job, one might assume that $50,000 over ten years in overtime is not that significant compared to the other benefits offered by the bank, if the employee decides to take advantage of them.

The third point of curiosity to me is that Dara doesn't appear to have looked around at the variety of opportunities the bank and the financial industry made available to her over her decade of service. She might have moved up the corporate ladder. Perhaps if Dara wasn't so busy feeling owed and bitter from missing out on $5,000 a year, she could have been earning twice her salary, if not more by now. A tremendous benefit to working for one of Canada's major banks is not only their fairness policies for women, minorities, and those with disabilities, but also their willingness to educate their employees. Bank employees often have opportunities to further their financial education should they show initiative and expressed interest in moving up the ranks. My boss at the bank started out in the financial industry at an entry level and without the university degree that the bank required then and now. Through years of hard work, dedication, and upgrading his education on the bank's dime, he moved up to Regional VP, Senior VP, and today is the head of the International Wealth Management division of that bank. He too worked unpaid overtime. As I remember, when I worked under his authority, our set hours were 8:30 to 4:30. I always arrived early, usually around 7:00 a.m., but my boss was always there earlier. To this day, I'm not sure what time he actually arrives. The earliest I made it in was 6:30 a.m. and my boss was already there working away. Perhaps that's why the head of a bank can earn in a day what a teller earns in a year. It's not about the time you put into a company or You Inc.—it's the results produced.

Dara could have used the platform of the bank to propel her career into high gear, but instead, it seems she chose to fuel a mentality of animosity and resentful expectation. In an interview I conducted with Patricia Lovett-Reid, she provided the classic example of what a teller can become.

Patricia is the Senior Vice President of TD Waterhouse Canada Inc., author of several books, host of BNN's *MoneyTalk* and a sought-after media authority and speaker across the country. I assumed that Patti joined the bank late in her career and surely had an elite business education behind her to support her senior position in an industry that is still very much a man's world at the executive level. Her story was quite the opposite of what I had expected. Patti informed me that she did not have a university degree and started with the bank right out of high school as a teller. She worked her way up the corporate ladder and today is highly respected in her industry and community.

Simply focussing on what you're "owed" can not only affect your ability to succeed, it can cause you to ignore all the opportunities available. Dara's lawsuit is hurting the industry and CIBC. Boo hoo you might be thinking—the big banks make enough profit and should pay for this oversight. If you perhaps were thinking that, it would behoove you to realize that Canadian banks, unlike those of our American friends, must be owned, in large part by Canadians. If you invest in an equity mutual fund, there's a good chance that you too own a part of a Canadian bank. Those profits allow investors like you and me to benefit from the success of the bank. To complain about their profits is to complain about our own. Dara's move to sue CIBC hurts not just some nebulous corporation, but regular everyday folks too.

Unions absolutely have their place and have served countless employees well over the history of industrialization. However, it's the "union" mentality that frightens me and I question its validity today. The "I'm on my coffee break" mentality as opposed to, "how can I serve?" As one grows and strengthens the company they work for or the client they service, they too increase their chance for success and profit.

Tyson Foods had a factory in northern Alberta that hit the press a few years ago. It was a disgusting story that demonstrated that unions are still needed, even though the working conditions in this country are luxurious in comparison to many others. These factory workers were immigrants; many could barely speak English let alone assert themselves and stand up for their rights. The media reported atrocities such as factory workers soiling their pants because they weren't allowed to go to the bathroom outside of their scheduled breaks. The union came to the rescue and fought Tyson Foods successfully, standing up for the rights of these workers who couldn't stand up for themselves. I applaud the union for their efforts.

On the opposite end of the spectrum, due to consumerism as well as choice and competition in the marketplace, unions and the focus on the workers don't always work any more. General Motors recently shut down a major factory in Ontario, which has hurt the industry. There were many factors as to why the plant was shut down, however, some media reported that with large employee wages and benefits due to unionized rules of seniority, some workers were earning over $50 an hour (including benefits). How can GM compete when other auto manufactures are outsourcing to countries willing to do the same work for $10 or $20 an hour?

Is it fair? No. Are these companies, their unions, or the employees to blame for plant closures? Someone must be to blame. Could we look at the consumer (you and me) and ask if the responsibility lies with ourselves? Think about the purchases in your home—where were a good majority of them made? Without knowing your taste, style, or budget, I can almost guarantee that a good chunk of them were made in China. Last year I purchased an outdoor, weatherproof marquee. Think of something that would be used at an outdoor wedding or party: It's open on the sides with four steel posts holding up a steel roof brace. The entire structure is covered with an extremely durable, rainproof type of plastic. I picked it up on sale for $20 at Home Depot and you guessed it—it was made in China. It came in a large box, but I had no idea the breadth of this structure until it took four people to assemble it. It spans at least 15 square feet. As I sat back and marvelled at the amount of steel, plastic, and cardboard contained, the design of the box, the effort to ship it from China, and all of the other steps necessary to get it in my back yard, I was in awe of how this unit could cost a mere $20. I know if that same product were made in

Canada or the US, even factoring in a equal cost for materials and omitting shipping, but looking at what a North American worker would demand for a wage, there's no way that same structure could be manufactured locally for the same price.

I ask you, if you had the choice of purchasing that exact same structure (assuming you were in the market for it) for $20 knowing it came from China or say $42, knowing it was made locally by fellow Canadians, which one would you buy (all else remaining equal). If we were honest, we'd all buy the one for $20. Sure, we might not mind paying a dollar or two more for a pound of coffee we know was Fair Trade certified, but when it comes to hundreds or thousands of dollars, would you spend more to buy locally? I find it interesting that those disgusted with outsourcing, the evilness of consumerism, and corporations seeking to eke out every dollar of profit possible are often the same people shopping at Wal-Mart or other discount retailers who fill their stores with foreign-made products and pay their staff the absolute minimum wage. If there were a Union Mart—a replica of Wal-Mart, but all of their goods were more expensive across the board because all of their employees belonged to a union and were paid a higher wage than Wal-Mart employees—would you shop there? Likely not. If RBC's bank fees were twice that of CIBC but they paid employees like Dara overtime for every minute of extra work expended, would you bank there? Doubtful. The point is that the next time we think of criticizing the big, mean corporate monsters for their mistreatment of their workforce here in Canada, perhaps we should further investigate at whom the finger should be pointed. And if we find ourselves feeling owed as Dara did, consider that if she raised her bar, opened up Dara Inc., and started thinking like a CEO, she just might start earning what she truly deserves instead of suing for it.

In 2007, just as summer was approaching and the weather was heating up, workers at the Edmonton Molson plant decided to go on strike. Being aware of the short Canadian summer season and the popularity of Molson's with Edmontonians and their affinity for a "cold one" during the summer months, they leveraged the time of year to strengthen their negotiating power. However, Molson's didn't come to the table to play and after months of the strike and millions of dollars lost, Molson's decided to shut the plant down. A landmark in the off downtown area of Edmonton, the locally famous Molson house will likely be torn down as well. Companies, like people, have their breaking point. At what point, if we're not working in substandard conditions, should unions force companies to unionize in order to have their demands met? Isn't it better to have a job, even if the pay could be better than to force the company to shut its doors and cut positions? You Inc., paraphrasing the famous words of John F. Kennedy, is not about asking what your company, client, and the world can do for you, but what you can do to better serve your company, client, and world. Start with the belief that holding yourself to a higher standard and defining and living by the standards of your personal corporation will produce results, not necessarily immediately, but eventually, commensurate with the position of CEO that you now hold.

Stop the insanity

You're likely all too familiar with Albert Einstein's definition of insanity—doing the same thing over and over again and expecting different results. Much lip service is paid to this notion, yet, most of us feel pretty insane at the end of the workweek. Many of us have the same complaints, troubles, and problems day after day, year after year. If we haven't declared insanity yet, then we're likely to concede that we've at least identified it in others. Think of the problems of your friends, family, and co-workers. Have any of them fed you the same problem for years and yet they still haven't changed? Is your company or industry preaching innovation, but as soon as you recommend something different you're shot down?

For us to achieve what we desire, it presupposes that we don't have "it" yet. Whatever it is for you—more money, freedom, happiness, a better relationship, a house, more children, early retirement or the work flexibility to serve your community—to move from where you are to where you want, you need to do something different. Do the same thing and get the same results. It's the simplest and most easily understood concept in the world. Yet, for many of us, it's doing something different that is the most difficult. Sameness equals comfort. Difference can mean change, innovation, courage, risk, fear, and rejection. These are small prices to pay for our personal growth and fulfillment, however, the average person will revert back to comfort when given the opportunity.

We can't simply "think outside the box." Most of the time, we have no clue we're in a box. We're like Jim Carrey's character in *The Truman Show*. We have no idea we can break out of the bubble until we realize we're in one. Einstein also said that a problem cannot be solved by the same level of thinking that created it. What that means is sometimes we need someone to come along and knock on the top of our box, look down at us, and say, "Hi there. Did you know that you're actually in a box? Here, let me help you out."

It's my sincere honour and privilege that you've chosen to pick up and read this book. I'd like to assist in helping you out of your box, and mine too for that matter. I know that learning the principles of She Inc. and thinking as a corporation will fast-track the time that it will take you to realize you're in a box and determine how to get out quickly. Throughout these pages, I will be sharing my personal stories with you—a few about my successes, but mostly about my failures and insights into them. I'll provide you with some business theory, but mostly the lessons of the school of hard knocks. I'll share real life examples, from my own life and others that might seem at the onset to have nothing to do with your life. As you read this book and these stories, know that everything relates. For you to truly think differently, you must do something different. By using examples from different industries than yours, and their related situations, goals, and priorities, I hope to illustrate opportunities that you haven't thought of before. Your mind will naturally extract what it needs from each account to tangibly change your individual situation and life.

Please be willing to stop the insanity. Be open to how each illustration can be applied to your life, how they can better help to define what you want more of in life, and what you can do without.

The Power of You Inc.

The concept of thinking of yourself as a corporation is not unique or revolutionary, though it is life altering. I present the concept to you in the following pages from my unique perspective having lived and, I believe, having perfected the execution of this notion. I first learned of the concept of thinking of oneself as a corporation as an 18-year-old working part-time apprenticing for a financial planning firm (really, I was a receptionist learning the ropes), studying for the industry exams evenings and weekends, and working odd jobs in between to pay my mortgage. I had no clue what I wanted to be in life and never in a million years thought or hoped I would be in the position to impart what worked for me here on these pages for you to read today.

I was young, broke, disenchanted and didn't have a clue what I was going to do with life. My motto early on was: when in doubt, hang around someone smarter than you who can show you the way. Since I didn't have much to offer to anyone wiser than me, I quickly learned that you could buy the time of the most brilliant thinkers and the most innovative business leaders and learn the secrets that fueled their success. How? For under $20 or with a library card I could buy their books or listen to their audio programs. I was hooked on these personal coaches who belted out advice, motivation and strategies each morning while I drove to work and I took every opportunity I had to listen to their words of wisdom. My first series of audio programs was Les Brown's *The Power Of Purpose*. I had visited my brother one day and he was watching Les Brown on a public television station. You could feel the energy of Les pounding on the pulpit encouraging his audience that "you could do it." I was hooked and immediately borrowed the series from the library. I later bought every tape Les put out and was at one point going to contact his office and inform Mr. Brown that if he ever couldn't make a speaking engagement that I would gladly fill in, as I could proudly recite every one of his lectures word for word.

Be careful who you trust

After finishing my brief education at a marketing and management college, it was time to find a company that would provide me with a practicum. I convinced a local and very successful billboard company to allow me to spend three months of my time, for free, to learn the advertising and billboard industry. It was indeed a lesson in patience and persistence as they basically used me as free labour. I was performing the duties of a receptionist (plus, office cleaner, coffee fetcher—basically the office gofer) and was offered little to none of the mentoring that I had hoped for.

Totally frustrated and nearing the end of my three-month term, I literally begged the co-owner to teach me something, anything, about the advertising industry.

The PVP

No matter what position you hold, even if you absolutely despise it, there's always something you can learn if you're willing and take the personal initiative. Even though the billboard company owners wouldn't take the time to teach me anything, through those three months of witnessing how a corporation works (it was my first white-collar position) I observed and recorded what companies in my city had the money to buy advertising, who the owners of those companies were, and did my all to make the dreadful task of filing and organizing the office for months a ground-up education on the inner workings of the industry.

Seeing that I was a dedicated yet unpaid employee, showing up every day of my practicum early and staying late, the co-owner finally agreed to take me on a "drive by." He drove me around to a number of their billboards in the city and described how each "face" works, traffic count and how that applies to the price of each face, the less desirable faces, and so on. It was simply fascinating!

Doing my best to use some of the teachings of my marketing training, I offered thoughts and ideas for growing the company. I was shot down immediately; the co-owner informed me that there was no possible way for them to grow further. He told me that every possible billboard that could be erected in Edmonton had already been done by them or by their competition. When I inquired further, he educated me on the municipal process that a new billboard must go through. The by-laws were specific. Many parts of a city do not allow advertising of that sort at all. The parts that did had rigid rules, such as the number of metres required between signs and much more. He was resigned, saying that there wasn't a spot left in Edmonton in which to place a billboard. Since all of their current billboard faces were already sold out months in advance, the only way for their company to grow would be to find more opportunities to erect signs, However, by his account, the city's space was tapped out.

As a young, energetic, and naïve practicum student, I wouldn't take no for an answer. I thought there must be some spot in this huge city that one could work within the by-laws to find. My boss gave me a bunch of books and manuals that listed the criteria and I meticulously studied those pages looking for some overlooked opportunity.

I scoured the books, each day at work presenting a possible spot, idea, or way to approach the city. All were shot down. After several condescending pats on the head, I stopped looking.

I left the billboard company and went about my life and career. However, I can't help but notice billboards in my city and every city I visit. It's not something I'll ever be able to ignore.

One day, driving downtown in Edmonton, I noticed new signs on the streets. They were about eight feet tall and about three feet wide. They were hard plastic signs with large, poster-sized advertisements. It was curious to me that the city allowed this new company and type of billboard to pop up all over town.

Months later, again driving downtown, while paused at a red light, I saw a new form of advertising: a mini billboard in the centre of a series of bike parking stations on every other street downtown. Hmmm. For a city that wouldn't allow further traditional billboards to be erected, there certainly were a number of creative companies that found a way to work around the definition of a "billboard."

Then, a few months ago, after finishing a workout at the gym, I had a visit to the ladies room. On the back of the stall door, what was starring me right in the eyes? You guessed it, a mini-billboard featuring an advertiser and I was the captive audience.

It took me over a decade to realize that the co-owner from the billboard company, who I trusted, admired, and looked up to, was absolutely wrong! It's true that perhaps the real estate for a conventional billboard was full at the time, however, it was my belief in what this individual told me that blinded me to the opportunities that would later present themselves. Had I believed in the possibility of expanding the billboard company, I could have made a career in the advertising industry. Other individuals believed there was another way and they found it in a bike advertisement, and direct selling to retail businesses by using their unused spaces as successful alternatives to the big signs.

Who have you listened to and believed in your life that told you it couldn't be done or that you couldn't do it? Usually, it's someone we think is smarter, wiser, our mentor, or is an individual who is more educated or experienced. Be cautiously selective when listening to those who tell you something can't be done. And be extra careful to weigh the advice of those that you consider smarter or brighter than yourself when they espouse a limiting belief. You could be keeping yourself from an adventure by buying into their opinion, which may or may not be accurate.

How thinking like a corporation worked for me

My story

In my late teens, I thought I'd try my luck in the modelling industry. I'd had some decent offers and since I didn't know what I wanted from life, it seemed like a good idea to me. Once I had a small taste of the industry, I knew very quickly it wasn't for me. The lack of brain power that was required along with the misalignment of the sexual nature of the industry didn't mesh with my values.

With a humble yet extremely loving upbringing by a single mom with three kids, there wasn't an education fund waiting for me at the end of my high school diploma. I desperately wanted to find myself, my skills, and get out into the workforce. It seemed more prudent to bring cash flow into my life as opposed to expending it via a university education, so I opted for a condensed local college marketing and management diploma. I fell in love with the material and excelled in every class. Finally, I had discovered my talents and love and would finish college and seek a career in the advertising industry.

Much to my dismay, I quickly discovered that Edmonton didn't have much of an advertising industry, and the small firms that did exist either weren't hiring or were looking for skills more advanced than mine. They required a university degree and years of experience.

Needing to do something, I took the odd jobs I could find. After working for a week as a receptionist at the college I attended, a contract position came up. The college placement officer urged me to take the position. I was adamant that the last thing I needed was another odd job. I wanted a career already! I had a burning desire for a job with advancement opportunities to show what I could do. Reluctantly, I took the five-day contract position.

The job was with a financial planning firm. The owner needed someone to perform non-selling telemarketing for a volunteer organization that he was president of. I showed up, was given a long list of calls to make, and had five days to make them. Being in a white-collar environment seemed right to me and I instantly fell in love with the company and staff. Although I had lightly studied the stock and bond markets during my teen years, I didn't really comprehend what a financial planner did.

I diligently went to work happily making my calls. I arrived early and stayed late and, to my recollection, finished the five-day job in fewer than three. The incentive was there as I was being paid a flat fee for the work independent of the hours put in. After finishing early, the President was thrilled. He commented that he overheard me making the calls and appreciated my cheerful and professional attitude and tone. He was further delighted that the job was done in record time. I was just having fun. It was the first job that I wasn't working my tail off physically. (Generally, in my teen years I was a waitress, dishwasher, and any other restaurant job that was available.) For the first time in my young life, I actually felt appreciated for the job that I did.

The President informed me that if there were a position open at his company, he would gladly hire me. Unfortunately, there wasn't. But he did offer to write me a letter of recommendation, which was a thrill for me. And if I didn't need it for copying later, I'm quite sure I would have framed it.

A few months later, a phone call came in from the President offering me a full-time position at my then dream office. Treating them as a client, getting the job done early, and maintaining a cheerful attitude kept me foremost in their minds and as soon as a position opened up, I was the first and only call they made.

I spent a number of years with that firm, apprenticing under the watchful eye of my boss, whom I greatly admired. I was extremely lucky to start my financial career with this man who became my mentor for many years. Should I have landed a position with a firm lacking in ethics, I'm quite positive my career would have turned out much differently.

When I started in the financial industry, it was still predominantly an older man's industry. I recall attending mutual fund briefings at 18 where 300 grey haired men were in attendance and just a few women were in the crowd—most of them assistants to the men.

Although entering the world of finance was not my intention, goal, or dream, I enjoyed my years apprenticing while getting my financial education in the evenings and holding down two jobs on the side to pay for the condo I bought at 18. One day my boss pulled me into his office and informed me that he could no longer pay me a salary. I was shocked to say the least and terrified as he informed me that within 30 days, I would be on 100% commission, responsible for finding my own clients, and out of the nest of the apprenticeship.

It was a turning point indeed. Still a kid in the industry at around 20 years old, I knew I couldn't compete against those with more education, skill, and decades of experience. I was just a rookie. Who was going to invest their money with a small unknown financial planning firm and a young woman to boot?

One day I was downtown running errands. I stopped at an ATM to grab some cash and saw someone I recognized sitting behind glass doors in one of the bank's offices. I hadn't formally met him, but had seen him a number of times in the halls of my office building when he was attending a course there for a few months. I noticed he didn't have anyone in his office and, sheepishly, I knocked on his glass door. As a shy young kid, this introduction wasn't easy for me, but I did it anyway. His name was Jim and he recognized me and seemed happy to meet. He handed me his card and told me to keep in touch. I thought nothing of the encounter and went about my day.

Months passed at my firm and any money I had saved while on salary was running out. I was still working night jobs to pay the bills and wasn't making much progress building my own client base. I was terrified of failing and the pressure to make ends meet forced me to see what other opportunities might exist for someone with my limited skill set and experience.

Not fully appreciating or understanding the vastness of the financial industry and the many facets and positions within it, I wondered if one day a bank might consider hiring me. I completed the questionnaire that I had you do at the beginning of this chapter. What little I knew about how a bank worked at that time seemed to align with what I was looking for in a career. I always dreamed of working in a tower downtown, having to get dressed up for work, and living the corporate lifestyle. My current firm at the time was very laid back, on the edge of town, and not a bustling type of office.

However, I had no idea what positions existed at a bank or how I might convince someone to hire me. I had no knowledge of what they required. The Internet was at its infancy and research couldn't be done as easily as it can today.

Then it struck me. I had a very valuable resource in my Rolodex. I pulled out Jim's card and called him up. Although I was totally intimidated, Jim seemed like my only resource. I told him I was thinking of getting into the banking industry and asked if I could take him for lunch. He agreed and shared as much as he could with me at that meeting. I'm still friends with Jim to this day and am thrilled when he calls on me now to provide resources and references for him.

I was armed with a little more information, but still viewed the banking world as a huge, vague machine. I constructed the best cover letter I could and called every bank in Edmonton during my lunch hours for their mailing addresses and the branch manager's name (remember, it was the old days without the Internet). I sent out dozens and dozens of résumés and hoped and prayed someone would see some skill of mine on my résumé that would align with a position they had at the bank. This is precisely what every job-hunting expert tells you not to do—not to leave it up to the employer to figure out what you can offer—you have to clearly tell them. I was desperate and didn't know what I could offer.

The phone started to ring and I had interviews with nearly every major bank in town. How could this be? I had only a few short years in the industry, little experience and direct education, and was lacking a degree. However, I did have a skill that the banks were eager to capitalize on. Financial planning firms are all about written recommendations, or at least were at the time. The sell and lure of the independent financial counsel like the planning firm I had worked at was that it came with a written report and analysis along with personalized advice. It doesn't sound like much today, but back then, the banks were terrified of giving investment advice. I remember visiting my personal banker when I was 18 and asking about which mutual funds were best to invest in given the market at the time, where interest rates were, and other cyclical factors. I recall that she explained the bank's limited offering of mutual funds, presented me with a brochure, and wished me luck making my own picks.

As I detailed earlier in this chapter, the banks were desperately seeking employees, from the inside or out, that could give investment advice and now serve the needs of their fastest growing market—the baby boomers. I lucked out on timing indeed and didn't realize that my few years at the planning firm would be worth so much to the banking industry when I came calling.

Of all the interviews, it came down to a trust company and a major Canadian bank. The trust company was paying nearly twice the salary and benefits as the planning firm that I worked at. And the bank was paying twice that. It was a simple choice for me and I couldn't believe how lucky I was to even be considered. I waited to see who would call first and make a solid offer. Dave, the person in charge of hiring for the bank, called. He informed me that he really wanted to hire me and that he thought I'd do a great job in the role, however, the bank had pulled back the decision to go ahead with new investment positions. I was devastated but not surprised. Really, who was I to think I could make such a corporate jump in status, position, and income? The choice was made for me and I called the trust company and accepted their offer.

Sidebar:

I've had a great deal of lucky breaks in my life. However, I can trace back each and every one to a controlled event, which I was ultimately responsible for initiating. That's great news for you and me—as the old sage saying goes, luck happens when opportunity meets preparedness. I am telling you the details of my career path as it's only in hindsight that I'm able to see for myself how each person, detail, and action led to the next, to better and greater opportunities, and not one was insignificant. I'm also sharing these details with you not because I think I've achieved any overwhelming success as far as the average person might be concerned. What I can extract, and hope that you will too, is that things worked for me and luck happened, I know in part, from continuing to think of myself as Kelley Inc. as opposed to the many roles and positions I held. Each problem that presented itself in my career path provided the opportunity to find a solution for a better life—a life I could never have known without these "problems."

Very quickly after I accepted the position at the trust company, I knew I had made a colossal mistake. They were not prepared to do what they had promised for the position to succeed, provided no training, and since I didn't have an ounce of banking experience, I knew I was doomed. I was hitting my targets and some months even exceeding them, but I was miserable. My learning curve was steep and the effort I had to expend was far greater than that of my colleagues, who all had a banking background. I made the best of it and kept trying harder to convince my bosses to give me the tools to excel in the position. They wouldn't. By the way, the trust company is no longer around and was bought up years ago by a bank.

Sidebar:

In thinking as a corporation, I made it a policy to network as much as I could. I didn't see any tangible benefits to doing so early in my career, but soon realized that it was logical to meet as many people as I could. I also hated networking alone and wouldn't go to an event unless invited or had someone to talk to me in case no one else did. I put in practice a personal system of keeping the business cards of everyone I met. I didn't have database software at the time and just typed in everyone's contact information into a Word document file. I sent thank you notes or "nice to meet you cards" in the mail whenever I could. I knew they were seeds but most of the time it felt like throwing rice on the wall and never seeing

> any of it stick. I kept at it nonetheless, convincing myself that keeping in touch, standing out with a small detail such as sending a card didn't take a great deal of effort and maybe one day it would. I also sent Christmas cards regularly to everyone on my quasi database.

Even though I didn't get the job at the bank, I still sent Dave a thank you card in the mail. He was so kind to me and didn't have to call me personally to explain why I didn't get the job. He could have just sent me some form letter in the mail, but instead took time out of his life. I also of course had him on my Christmas mailing list.

After about six months at the trust company, I was disappointed, immensely frustrated, and fed up with the financial industry. I started to look in the classifieds for yet another employer that might find some tangible skill of mine that would fit their company. However, I fretted about making a career move too quickly. After all, I only had a few years of the financial firm on my résumé, previous to that a bunch of odd retail and restaurant jobs, and now, only six months at the trust company. How could I make a move? A prospective employer would think I had no dedication, loyalty, or that I was fickle and immature. Plus, many employers in the past told me that I was at a disadvantage since almost every position I was after required a university degree, which I didn't have. (A great number of employers view a degree as a form of dedication—even if the degree doesn't apply to the specific position, they still may require one to prove that someone has perseverance.)

I stayed put at the trust company. I convinced myself that a move would be unwise and would be a blemish on my résumé. The Christmas holidays were approaching at the time and at least I'd have a few days to forget my misery. Over the holidays a call came in on my cell phone. I couldn't believe it—it was Dave from the bank on the other line. He thanked me for my Christmas card and asked me what I was up to and if I was happy at the trust company. Thinking again like a corporation, I've also been careful not to criticize other organizations. After all, if someone is quick to negatively comment on their past company, they're likely to do the same with yours.

I told Dave that it wasn't quite what I had hoped for. Even thought I was withholding the true details, I'm sure he could hear the actual dissatisfaction in my voice. He then said what I couldn't have thought of in a million years: he told me the bank had agreed to the new positions, could I start right after the holiday season? Needless to say, I was elated.

Sidebar:

Did I get the bank job simply by sending Dave a thank you and Christmas card? Of course not. But it did keep me in his mind for when the bank was ready to hire. Dave also had confidence in me based on my transferable skills built advising clients at the financial planning firm. Not only was a business degree required for the job, but an MBA was preferred as well. It certainly helped that Dave himself didn't have a degree and saw some raw talent in me. Thankfully Dave was willing to give me a chance and bend the hiring rules.

For the sake of brevity, I'll skim over the rest of my career. I loved my time at the bank and had the opportunity to oversee $300 million in assets, educate my branches on investments, and meet with affluent clients who had hundreds of thousands of dollars, or even several million to invest. Starting at the bank at the young age of 21, as an investment manager, I was able to witness the successes of the ultra wealthy (and the seemingly wealthy), had an executive position, and learned a great deal about working for not only a large corporation but also one of Canada's most international banks at the time.

I saw the position of investment manager start to wind down at the bank. Most of my fellow investment managers had taken alternative positions within the bank after sensing that that role was coming to a close. Dave worked hard to present many options for me, but again it was difficult, as I didn't have a banking background per se. I could have gone international with the bank, but I knew early on that I valued my family above all things, and that moving wouldn't make me happy. Few executive investment positions existed in Edmonton and my only option left with the bank was to climb back up the banking ladder (as opposed to the investment one I was now skilled at), or work for one of the bank's subsidiaries in a fully commissioned environment.

I chose to make one final move in the financial industry and opened up my own independent financial firm. What I didn't know throughout my career was that with each client experience I was actually doing research for the books that I didn't know I would later write.

Building my practice from scratch was definitely the most challenging role I had had to date. Forgoing a great salary, benefits, and a cushy expense account to pour every dime into defining and building that business was taxing to say the least. So many individuals go into business for themselves thinking they'll finally play by their own rules, have ultimate freedom, flexibility, and unlimited potential for upward income. That can be true, assuming that you stay in business long enough to find out. A plethora of books are written each year convincing, luring, and describing the ideal lifestyle of the successful business owner. Focus and attention are drawn to the potential for greater things than a single employer could ever offer. Again, maybe true, if one can make it past the critical first two or three years when most businesses fail. Like any overnight success story, when you actually hear the truth and details of people who start their own business, you usually learn that it wasn't overnight at all but usually it took years if not decades of pounding pavement, working much longer hours than a regular job (plus evenings and weekends), and still many small business owners aren't taking home more than their staff.

I enjoyed my time running my firm, and if it wasn't for the ideas, insights, and opportunities presented by my business coach, I'm quite sure I'd still be content at my office today. I was in acquisition mode—buying up other advisors' clients and growing in any way I could. I loved my clients and my job and truly thought and believed that it was my last career move ever.

One day I decided to form a group of friends and acquaintances. I had done a great deal of research over the years, really just for my own edification, as to why the rich are wealthy, why some people have lots of money and don't enjoy it, why some people look ultra rich but are one step away from bankruptcy, and how to win at this game we call prosperity. It was an extremely informal gathering and lasted a few months. It forced me to develop my material that I was to present to the group weekly and I gained valuable feedback and insight as to the practicality and application of my theories.

When mentioning this group in passing to my coach, he convinced me that this would be a valuable course to teach my clients. I had complained in the past to him that I simply didn't have the time to sit down with my clients to delve into their psychology of money in addition to the tangible investment meetings we had to have. I expressed concern that many of my clients, as a whole, weren't living as prosperously as they could. How could I help them? I had never thought of developing a course before and that idea from him was the impetus to create The Prosperity Factor for Women course, write a book, and sell my firm. Now I'm writing my sixth book.

I have no idea what the future will hold for me. I have a sense of it and will be sure to go after more and grander goals. Thinking of myself as a corporation, treating each person, challenge, opportunity, and position as if I were the CEO of Me Inc., dealing with the uncertainty of never knowing who will be my client tomorrow, boss next year, who I'll call upon for a favour, or sell an idea to has served me well.

There are so many more details to this story. My boss at the financial planning firm bought my business when I sold it later to pursue my new career of writing and speaking. The girlfriend of my boss during my practicum at the billboard company bailed me out of a marketing campaign for my first book that was going horribly wrong. A colleague from the bank that I've reunited with during my touring travels suggested that we could change the way our kids are educated about money in our school system after reading my book, *The Prosperity Factor for Kids*. I could go on and on about how the people and happenings that I thought would never serve or affect me in my life were the seeds I planted that I had forgotten about. The rice I threw on the wall was starting to stick—ten, fifteen years later. Had I operated as an employee along the way and not shifted to and carefully designed Me Inc., I know those seeds would have dried up and never matured.

What seeds could you be consciously planting, tending to, and then trusting will bear fruit one day down the road? Are you ready to be the owner, president, and CEO of You Inc. and hold yourself and life to a higher standard? Will you realize that when you think at a high level life provides a high level offering as well? If so, read on. I have an investment that I'd like you to consider.

Your million dollar ticket

Let me ask you if you've ever purchased a lottery ticket? Likely, you have. Why? The obvious answer is that if you won the lottery tomorrow, your life would likely change. Whatever the jackpot, $5 million, $10 million or even $50 million, if you won it tomorrow, would all of your money problems be over? Many I ask this question to will say no, their money problems wouldn't be over. Then why purchase the ticket in the first place? We as a society must assume that our financial woes would disappear with such a windfall. After all, we don't go about town just throwing loonies on the sidewalk—we spend the dollar or more on a ticket thinking that a sum of money would benefit us somehow. Another question for you—would you feel better about yourself if tomorrow you truly won the lotto? Yes? No? Most individuals again would answer no, that they really wouldn't feel better or different about themselves if they won a windfall tomorrow (although, there's always a resounding yes from some ultra honest soul).

The bad news is, with the extremely low probability that you'd ever win the lottery, you really might as well throw those loonies on the ground with the intent of sprouting a money tree. The great news for you is that statistically, nearly all lottery winners not only lose their winnings within three years of receiving them, but are actually worse off financially than before they won the money. How is that possible? To actually be in a less advantageous financial situation after winning thousands or millions of dollars? The found money syndrome plagues not only lotto winners, but also those that have inherited assets. The effect is compounded as the latter is often thought of as "blood" money in addition to being "found."

The self made millioniare has years if not decades to amass their wealth: It didn't happen overnight. Incrementally, as their bank balances and assets grew, so too did their gradual comfort with their wealth and the energy it brings. Likely, their financial IQ and emotional ability to accept, grow, and hold on to this money grew as their assets did. Their self-esteem adjusted over time and one day, some don't even realize that exact day, they became a millionaire. It was a process, and during that time span, it was part of their identity and life.

The lotto winner has no opportunity to gradually become accustomed to their new-found wealth. You might think it absurd that someone winning such a large amount of cash could blow it all and actually be in the red after the fact. You might think that you would never make such a mistake. It's possible, if you're in that very small percentage of people that aren't as affected by or already had a great relationship with money before receiving more of it. But the likelihood is, you'd fall within the statistical average.

What's great about this anaysis is that I hope you've learned that throwing more money at someone's money problems won't necessary solve anything and might even exacerbate the exisiting money issues. So then how does one deal with their money problems since even if they won the lotto, it would be a potential detriment? The solution? It's an internal game. We must look to the millionaire: How she feels about herself, how she holds herself, what she knows about money and finance, how comfortable she is with the energy of her wealth, and learn to emulate her financial well-being.

Your greatest asset

Although I'm no longer in the financial industry, I do have an investment to sell to you within these pages. It, if you choose to capitalize on the notion, will instantly have you transformed into a millionaire. For no money down, no interest, and no payments ever (I know—the offer sounds like your local car dealership's advertisement) you too can own this asset free and clear. Are you interested? Do I have your attention? Seriously. If you're not excited about this, I really need you to grasp my offer. In the next paragraph, I'm going to tell you how you can put this book down and become an instant millionaire.

I hope the suspense is intriguing you at least. Okay, here it is—your million dollar investment. Ready? It's You! I know, that's not exactly what you were hoping to hear, but bear with me. Think about this. If you were to earn an average income of, say, just $30,000 per year from the time you were 18 years old (I know, that's a little more than the average 18 year-old would be earning) to the time you were 65 (and most 65-year-olds earn much more than $30,000 a year) you will have earned over $1.4 million in your working lifetime. Have you ever considered that? And I'm only using a modest salary to illustrate this concept.

Still not impressed? Are you thinking, Alright, so I'm "worth" over a million dollars in my working lifetime, I can't sell myself (in an ethical way) to cash in on my value. This is a fair point and brought up by many I teach.

Let's pretend for a moment that you had a rich aunt pass away in Europe. You just found out and didn't even know she existed. You're the only heir to her estate and she has willed you an orignal Chanel suit. It arrives and it's exquisite. It's still in its original casing and housed in glass. Even if you're not a brand label kind of girl, you know this is going to be worth a mint. You open up a picture frame that was also sent along with the suit and you see it displays a certificate of authenticity stating the estimated value of the outfit to be in excess of $1.4 million. The caveat is, you can't sell this suit for two reasons: First, your aunt stipulated in her will that it must be passed down to future generations. Second, there's no available market that exists in which to sell this suit. There are assets—diamonds, original paintings and the like that are so rare, so valuable, that a direct market does not exist. However, that doesn't lessen the value of the asset. Quite the contrary.

Imagine for a moment how you would feel. Really put yourself in the picture of inheriting the valuable heirloom. You now, right now, are a millionaire. It's true that it's not a liquid asset (one that can be sold easily), however, your insurance agent is urging you to insure it and assures you that the extra cost is nothing to think about considering the value of this suit. You tell your banker about this inheritance and they now add it to your net worth statement (your worth after your liabilities are subtracted from your assets). Everyone recognizes the value of this rare gem even though it can never be sold.

You, yes you, are that rare gem—a metaphorical original Chanel suit worth in excess of $1.4 million. Try this on for a moment. Feel, for even a flash of a second, how it would really feel to be an actual millionaire. Would you sit up just a little straighter in your chair? Would you stand just a little taller, with more confidence and strength? And what if tomorrow you were to purchase a new car? It's a Saturday and you've dressed down and comfortably. The sales guy seems to be blowing you off as a viable prospect and you say or think to yourself, "Hey, do you know who you're talking to? You're talking to a millionaire here!" And, if one day you ventured into Holt Renfrew, Tiffany's, or some other extremely upscale store totally unexpected, in your worst outfit after, say, a work out, and the saleswomen are looking you up and down with judgment—you're secure enough to know that you can dress any way you damn well choose. After all, you're a millionaire! Who do you need to impress?

There are a few important points to the explanation and my convincing you (I hope I've done an adequate job) that you are actually worth over a million dollars—even if your bank balance couldn't be further from the truth.

Million Dollar Lesson #1

Relationship experts often offer the sage advice that if someone doesn't really love themselves, they can't possibly fully love someone else. The same is true in understanding your true worth. When you understand what your potential is, and I mean, really *get it*, not only does your life change, but magical things start to occur and you turn around and realize that everyone has the same inherent worth as well, not only as valuable human beings, but tangibly in a financial sense. (I'm a financial geek—what can I say. Only my kind would break human worth down into dollars and cents.)

If you came to my main workplace, not my office but the place where I'm "on," it's wherever in North America I'm presenting for some group. If you sat in my audience as I described the million dollar concept to you, you would see me wearing my best suit, my favourite and most uncomfortable shoes (I get a great deal of compliments on them), my nails would be freshly manicured, and my hair straightened as well as possible. What you wouldn't have seen is all of the work that I went through before getting up on that stage. It's likely I hit the hairdresser if it was time for a root touch up, and definitely woke up four hours before I had to be at my presentation to ensure that I was polished, professional, and fresh for you, my audience member. You wouldn't know that I spent hours the night before tweaking my PowerPoint presentation and consulting my coach on new material in case you'd heard me before. And, to top it all off, even though I was in a pantsuit, I would have shaved my legs for you (more information than you needed to know).

The reason I go through these many rituals and tell my audience about what I've done for them that they can't see is because I didn't come to speak to a bunch of people from some company, or some conference. I'm not writing these words for some abstract person on the other end of the page. The reason I arrive at my absolute best for the day and now as I write these pages (yes, I dressed up for you too even though I'm writing at home and no one will actually see me today) is because, and please read this carefully, because I am writing this for you, my millionaire. If you were at my presentation, all of that work would be for you and my other millionaires.

Think for a moment if someone supremely powerful, wealthy, or famous were going to be coming into your workplace tomorrow. How would you dress knowing this information? Your workplace might be ultra casual with a uniform of golf shirts and jeans. Perhaps you might not put on your best, especially if that were an evening gown, for example. But whatever your normal style of dress, wouldn't you kick it up a notch or two? Would you ensure your nail polish was fresh, your shoes were shined, and if you were wearing something casual, would it at least be ironed and tucked in? Afterall, someone very important will be coming in.

That very important and special person is you! If I knew I was meeting you tomorrow, based on the context of that meeting and location, I would be at my best for you. And the reason is, you are that very wealthy, powerful, and famous person to me. You might not feel that way or think of yourself as lacking the hard, tangible investments to support my analysis of you, but that is truly what I would think of you and would prepare for even before seeing you.

Once I really "got" this concept of thinking of myself as a millionaire independent of cash flow and bank balances, then I was fully able to treat everyone in the same light. True, you will not see me in a suit at every meeting and yes, there are times that for whatever reason I can't be at my total best, but in those rare circumstances, it's not a reflection of the person I'm meeting. It's a reflection of me at that time.

If tomorrow that billionaire or celebrity really were to pop into your office unannounced, knowing how you usually arrive in a relaxed, controlled, and known setting, how would you feel about that? Would you be caught off guard? Feel embarrassed by your appearance? Worse?

I have met Mr. Jimmy Pattison, one of Canada's billionaires. I was lucky enough to have the opportunity to interview him while I was a columnist with Sun Media. I also had the privilege of visiting my province's premier recently. I was his special guest and had the opportunity to meet and chat with him in his private chambers. I have also met numerous celebrities over the years in my travels. I can assure you that I arrive to meet these individuals with the same level of preparation as I would for you. Again, given the context of the situation, I might not be sporting business attire, but I would be prepared. I think this rule of mine has afforded me many "lucky breaks," as some might call them. The essence of my conviction here is that when you treat others with respect, perhaps more than they even hold for themselves, and view them as the millionaires they have the potential to be, magical things start to happen. The question I ask you is, if Mr. Pattison, Tom Cruise, or Bill Clinton were to be dropping by your office tomorrow, would you be ready and prepared for that situation? What about your boss and co-workers? They too are millionaires and have the potential to be even more. How prepared are you for them? If they became famous or influencial ten years down the line, would they remember you as someone that treated them with the same awe and respect when they were a nobody?

The PVP.

Although I attempted to paint you a picture of how I might look and prepare myself for you, I must clarify an important point. I dress not to impress, but to respect my audience and the people I meet with. What's the difference? If I were to try to impress you, it would be about me. To respect you is about you. As an audience member, for example, knowing my background in the financial industry it wouldn't matter that I'm a writer now. You would likely expect me to show up in some sort of business attire. If I were a novelist, it might be totally acceptable for me to arrive in a tattered t-shirt and jeans. Furthermore, as I tried to convince you that I thought of you as a millionaire and dressed for you as I would Mr. Pattison or a superstar, it wouldn't be too congruent if my shoes were worn, my hair unwashed, or my appearance disheveled.

An essential element to treating others as if they too were millionaires is to understand the difference between "respect" and "impress." *The Canadian Oxford Dictionary* defines "impress" and "respect" as follows:

Impress: to evoke a favourable opinion or reaction from (a person). E.g. *a child's behaviour intended to impress.*

Respect: deferential esteem felt or shown towards a person, thing, or quality. E.g. *I have great respect for her judgment.*

I suppose I can't help impressing some by respecting them according to the above definitions. The key, though, is that my motive and drive for my actions is not to impress, at its core. If it's a side benefit, then that's a bonus. My intentions and yours are purely to show our respect for another person. No matter what our usual work uniform is or the type of clothes we wear within our comfort zone, if you and I were to attend someone's wedding or funeral, it would be disrespectful to don certain attire, no matter who you are. It's in part about the context of the situation and leading with admiration, not about garnering accolades for our ego's sake (although, it's a likely a side benefit).

Million Dollar Lesson #2:
The Red Cloth

Dr. Deepak Chopra tells a Vedic story of the red cloth. As it's told, a white cloth was dipped into some red dye. It then sat out in the sun for a time until it just about returned to its original white state. However, a little bit of dye remained that left it a pale, soft pink. The cloth was again dipped into the dye and sat out for a time in the sun. It was faded, but a little more of the dye remained. The cloth was dipped again and again and each time placed in the sun. Eventually, when the cloth had been dipped in the dye enough times, the ink was so deeply permeated into the fabric of that cloth that it could sit out in the sun for any amount of time and not lose its colour again.

You are that cloth. You must be willing and patient to dip and dip. Focus on thinking of yourself as a millionaire, feeling it periodically, trying it on, and practising how you would be if you were in such a position. Over time, bit by bit, the feelings, thoughts, emotions and unconscously knowing would be so solidly planted that you would transform into that millionaire. The dollars might not be there right now, but your potential is. Perhaps that's why the lotto winners can't hang on to their instant fortunes. Since they didn't have any time to dye their metaphorical cloth and establish their identity as a millionaire, they find a way to push the money away in any form they can. But not you. Your practice, your dipping, your belief in your worth will ensure that when your millions do manifest into tangible assets (and I'll be waiting for that e-mail from you to share in your success), you'll know and be ready to hold on tight and claim your fortune, whatever that may be.

Million Dollar Lesson #3:
Law of Attraction

You've likely seen or at least heard of the wildly popular movie, *The Secret*. I haven't seen it myself, but I have heard from the countless fans and devotees, the princples explored. I am a fan and huge supporter of the Law of Attraction (the thought principle, as opposed to the scientific idea), which is the main theme of the film. If you're not familiar with the Law of Attraction, its basic premise is "like attracts like," or, "you get what you think about; your thoughts determine your experience." (Source: Redden, Guy, *Magic Happens: A New Age Metaphysical Mystery Tour*, Journal of Australian Studies: 101.)

What was an airy-fairy type notion not long ago has now entered the vernacular of the general public. After all, the concept of attracting that which we focus on is logical, hopeful, and I know from personal experience, does work.

However, I do have a slight bone to pick with those who focus only on the positiveness of the law of attraction. It is a law which presupposes many elements that need to be in place before that law can be fullfilled. Isaac Newton's first law of motion outlines that an object in motion will stay in motion unless acted upon by an outside force. This presupposes a number of factors that the law doesn't address when applied to human nature. There are subconscious factors that a human can use to manipulate or mess up this timeless law. There are some outside forces that might be weak and barely affect the moving human. The law after all was not identified to describe human nature, but we so often quote it. For example, think of a time you were raking a huge yard of leaves in the fall and sat just for a moment to rest your weary back and bones and thought, "I'd better get up now or I never will—object in motion right?"

In Michael Losier's very successful book, *The Law of Attraction*, he details many tangible applications of the law of attraction. One though irritates and frustrates me: With a relatively short description, Losier mentions that if someone truly, with all their being, were to act on the principles of the law of attraction, they could actually influence their winning of a lottery. Critics of *The Secret* and the law of attraction question the occurrences of car accidents, misforture, or illness (especially the sickness of a child, for example). If the law of attraction works to attract that which you wish, does it always manifest that which you don't wish as well? (e.g. How can a child who doesn't know better manifest cancer?) As for winning the lottery, I'm curious why the author describing the process hasn't already done so? I do think that believing that all you have to do is think and focus on what you want, will make it happen. There are some caveats and presuppositions for that to occur, otherwise, disappointments and failure are imminent. If you truly, with all your heart, being, and soul knew you would absolutely win the lottery, could you affect the universal powers to favour that belief? I suppose that could be true. I don't doubt that. But the question then becomes, *how* do you go about doing that? If I or Losier or anyone else had the answer, we wouldn't be working and would be rich beyond our wildest dreams.

I do, however, believe that the law of attraction does work in our favour, whereas magic and coincidence are more common experiences on our journey to achieve that which we desire. When I'm focused on a goal and am studying to reach it, volunteering my time, attending every function possible to attain it, and so on, it is there that things occur serendipitiously. Sometimes the one person that can expedite the journey to my goal happens to be at the party of someone I met at a networking function. I get the goal and success is achieved.

Did the law of attraction make that happen? Not clearly. Did the concept assist in meeting the right people, being in the right place, and therefore increase the chance of me attaining the goal? This seems more logical to me.

I can't think of a goal that I'd have a chance of reaching by sitting at home on my sofa and simply "focusing" on it. I'm not sure the proponents of the law implied that it's that simple either. Losier's easy ticket to financial freedom should be followed up with a few disclaimers. I know the law of attraction has worked in my life and can in yours as well, so long as action—specific and strategic—plus focus is applied.

Million Dollar Lesson #4:
Don't kill the goose laying the golden eggs

If you're still skeptical and are one of those women who's hard to convince of the importance of their worth, consider Aesop's fable of "The Goose That Laid the Golden Eggs." From Wikipedia:

A man and his wife had the good fortune to possess a goose which laid a golden egg every day. Lucky though they were, they soon began to think they were not getting rich fast enough, and, imagining the bird must be made of gold inside, they decided to kill it. Then, they thought, they could obtain the whole store of precious metal at once. But when they cut the goose open, they found it was like any other goose.

The morals of the story are listed as:

Greed destroys the source of good.
Think before you act.
Those who want too much lose everything.

The many morals are valid indeed and the story and its meaning likely are not new to you. What is new is a further insight I want you to extract from the story. Think of the goose as an annuity investment for a moment. If you're unfamilar with an annunity, they're investment vehicles that are often purchased in retirement and offered by life insurance companies to provide a guaranteed stream of income to the investor. There are many reasons for purchasing an annuity and a plethora of options along with bells and whistles. For simplicity's sake, I'll describe the most common. An investor gives the insurance company a lump sum of money, let's say $100,000, to invest and lock up on their behalf. The insurance company then provides the investor a monthly or annual amount that they will pay as regular cash flow, guaranteed, for as long as the investor is alive. The company would factor in the sex of the investor (women typically live longer than men), their age, and a few other details to determine the amount they're willing to agree to pay this person until they die.

You are that goose and that annuity. Your golden eggs are your ability to earn an income over your lifetime. Your mind, body, heart, and soul produce those eggs each year. And, if you, the goose, are killed (metaphorically of course) in the pursuit of just a few eggs, that annuity stops paying dividends. Period.

Are you taking care of your most valuable investment?

When you now think of your million dollar investment and your true worth, and if you were given an annuity that was valued at $1.4 million when you turned 18 that was promised to pay you $30,000 a year, every year, sometimes a little more, some times a little less, how likely and interested would you be in protecting and looking after that annuity? What if your Chanel suit weren't just worth $1.4 million, but also paid you an annual income or had the potential to? Let's say you were able to take it around to galleries and fashion focused events with the projected income each year of around $30,000 for doing so? With such potential for lucrative cashflow, would you even hesitate to take the finest care of this suit? Would you complain about the $1,000 bill to have it cleaned periodically, the extra house insurance cost for protecting it from theft, or the marketing costs for telling others about your ability to showcase it at their gallery for profit? Of course not. Think about yourself for a moment: You as a lifetime annuity. You as a multimillion dollar investment. How have you been taking care of your rare asset—you? Do you get regular massages after working overtime? When was the last time you took a 48-hour break just for you, without guilt or complaint or an illness such as the flu forcing you to? Are you preventative in taking care of your most valuable asset, treating it (you) with the respect it (you) deserves? Or, are you constantly performing damage control, maiming the goose until one day it will die or no longer lay any golden egga?

It's essential that you're absolutely convinced of your ability to produce golden eggs and the necessity of looking after the goose first. This is so often the most difficult idea for women to grasp. If we have conditioned ourselves to accept a lifetime of putting others first; how do we now do the opposite? In reality, we can't. However, we must know that if we don't put ourselves first when necessary, the goose, and us, will stop bearing those eggs. If you don't buy into this concept, you'll never get others to understand it as well. You may have teenaged children demanding your time, a spouse who doesn't appreciate why you need a day away from the family, or a boss who can't understand why you need an extra long weekend here and there. You must fully buy into this concept and be the champion of taking care of your goose for the integrity of its long-term production. If you don't, everyone loses out. But as the owner of you, no one is going to look after your investment for you.

If you're a mom, I can almost guarantee without knowing you that you put your children first. I fly a great deal and have almost all of the flight attendants' pre-take off speech memorized. I find it interesting that they state, each and every time, that in the case of emergency, if the oxygen masks drop down and you are travelling with children, to always affix your own mask before helping others with theirs. Most moms would agree that it's instinctual to help your child first. Yet, if there were an actual emergency and you're not alert (or alive) to help those around you, helping them first isn't the logical solution. As difficult as it is for so many women, there will be times in your life that you absolutely need to save yourself first and look after your needs ahead of others, for the long-term success of both you and them. It's not easy and it needs to be initiated by you. It will likely take a great deal of practice and strategy to not only put yourself first, but to cast any guilt aside for doing so. Remember the goose. Repeat it to others and yourself if necessary and take care of your annuity. It will pay you handsomely if nurtured.

The self-made millionaire or successful individual, knowingly or not, likely thinks of themselves as a corporation. Whether it's the teacher simply making a humble salary, but saving prudently and building a small real estate fortune or the worker with a restaurant on the side that turns into a respectable chain, thinking of yourself as a corporation opens up a world of possibility no matter where you find yourself today or how limited you might think your future is. Your future is brighter, more rewarding, and more attainable than you might have ever considered. Now, let's build the foundation to that future in the next chapter.

Chapter 2

Who's navigating your life? Developing "You Inc."

The importance of corporate policies

Why do companies expend all of the resources, time, and energy they do to design policies? It's because they know that advanced thinking formed into structured procedures equals success—if implemented and monitored. And when these policies are examined and improved, a company's employees will have a successful plan to follow.

It's been said that rules are like eggshells, they're meant to be broken, but if you don't know what your rules are, how will you know when you've broken them?

If you were an employee, why would you care about thinking of yourself as a personal corporation? First, there's the strange phenomenon that I've experienced in my short twelve-year professional career. It's the experience of bumping into someone you knew from school, past jobs, or other areas of your life; somehow, you cross that person's path again in an unexpected way. No matter what size your city is, you've likely experienced this "it's a small world after all" situation. It sometimes comes out of Murphy's Law, doesn't it? That person you've just flipped the bird to in traffic might be attending the job interview or client meeting that you're scheduled for later in the day.

What are your rules for life and when do you break them? Do you even know if you've broken them? If rules are meant to be broken, shouldn't you at least know when you've broken your own? Do you think some much-needed clarity could come into your life if you actually knew what your rules were, if you had a corporate policy statement that is flexible enough for the corporation of You Inc.? And when do you break your rules? Do you have a different set of rules for business conduct than for your personal life?

Love him or hate him, we all remember the moral debates in coffee shops and around water coolers on the subject of former US President Bill Clinton. Many conversations I overheard went something like this: "Yeah, maybe he is a dog in his personal life, cheating on his wife all those times and then being caught in sexual misconduct with his intern, but he was a great president. He fixed the economy, helped the environment, and his personal life should be his personal life."

What do you think? Have you ever bent the rules because they didn't apply personally or within your work situation? Do you consider yourself to be an honest citizen who would never cheat or steal, yet you find some way to justify fighting a speeding ticket that you know darn well you deserved? And having discovered, after arriving home from a long night of Christmas shopping, that the sales clerk didn't charge you for a $50 purchase, would you convince yourself that they'll never miss it because they're such a big store anyway? Do you give any of these issues any thought at all?

I was blessed enough when I entered the financial industry to have a boss who was willing to take me under his wing. He truly had a heart of gold and he led a life of impeccability. I knew he was respected in his industry but it wasn't until I left his financial planning firm that I truly understood the importance of living by your own personal policies and knowing when you've broken them.

My boss had a quotation that he truly lived by and would often say out loud during our meetings or when making difficult decisions: "Act as if the entire world is watching, especially when no one is watching." He would go so far as to call another financial advisor whose client wanted to join our firm.

Whenever I have mentioned to colleagues in the industry that my first apprenticeship was with Wayne, the response is always: "Wow, you were lucky to have worked with such a great man." This is what his competitors were saying. Can you imagine what his friends and family say about him? He knew somehow that even if no one is watching, it all counts because someone is watching—you. And each time you commit a personal "crime," no matter how big or small, it has a significant impact on that tiny voice inside your head that says you're a great person, you're worthy, and you are a person of your word. You deserve to hold yourself in high esteem. Each simple and small act works towards building your self-esteem at many levels, even though "no one" is watching.

What you'll need

Before we get started, you'll need two very important tools as you design your own corporate rulebook. First, I'd like you to purchase a blank writing book, ideally one small enough to fit in your purse. Ideas will spring forth at the most unusual times of day and during your life—record them or risk losing them forever. Second, and we'll discuss this further, you'll need a file folder for documenting valuable feedback you'll identify while putting your policies into practice.

Your macro policies

When designing and thinking about the rules for You Inc., you'll need to create both macro and micro policies. The first, macro, are your larger ideas that you'd like your corporation to stand for, those you're striving for, and some that may take you a lifetime to achieve. Your micro rules and policies are more tangible, every day guidelines for your life and they need to be clearly communicated to others. We'll explore both. Let's start with the macro ideas for You Inc.

Holding Yourself to a Higher Standard

It is not how much we do,
but how much love we put into the doing.
–Mother Teresa

So now that you're the president and not just some employee who follows someone else's rules, you make the rules! What's your stance? How do you dress for work? What goals and dreams are you making happen? What's your plan?

After creating a great plan that includes clear and defined policies for their employees to follow, many companies make the mistake of allowing it to sit in some drawer or cabinet and never look at it again. This should be a work in progress. It might take you six months to a year to discover many of the rules you need to move on to the next stage of making your personal policy statement. Start today! On a fresh pad of paper begin to jot down your observations about your own behaviour and that of others. This will begin the process of creating rules that will allow you to live a freer and more effortless life.

How do you start such a seemingly daunting and obscure task? Begin by noticing your upsets. Each time you're upset with something you've done or something someone else has done or failed to do, you've broken one of your personal rules. It might be obvious or it might take a little digging, but with each upset, you'll discover a new ideal to live by in the future. It's been said that a mid-life crisis occurs when individuals decide that they're now going to live by their own rules. After a lifetime of being told by parents, teachers, employers, and others how to live and what to think, and having decisions forced upon them, the light bulb goes on.

Now, you might be thinking that more rules are the last thing you need in your life because you have enough to follow already. I agree. You probably have many rules imposed on you on a daily basis, but these are going to be your rules, and with these clear rules and your personal policies, I guarantee that freedom will follow.

Personal policies

This above all:
to thine own self be true.
–William Shakespeare

How do you view your employer? As an employer or as a client who is buying services from You Inc.? Do you treat your employer as a client who is supporting your company or do you show up five minutes late and leave ten minutes early? Did you know that just 15 minutes per day of downtime at work adds up to over ten days of downtime per year? Your employer might pay for this time, but life will not!

If the company you worked for were a ship and it was sinking, the priority of the ship's captain (your boss) would be to save the ship. The captain would get rid of all unnecessary cargo to lighten the load until smooth sailing was once again achieved. Only what is absolutely necessary would be kept. Are you valuable and necessary cargo at your place of employment? Are you a vital crew member on your employer's ship or are you just "showing up" or putting in time? If pink slips were handed out tomorrow at your workplace, would your name be anywhere near the top of the list?

It's not enough to be busy,
so are the ants. The question is,
what are we busy about?
–Henry David Thoreau

Now let's flip the situation around. What if you worked the 15 minutes per day that most people waste? So now you're showing up on time and maybe even leaving 10 minutes later than everybody else. Now you might be saying: "Hey, I already work hard enough for my boss, with low pay and little to no recognition for the contribution I'm making. Why would I want to give my boss one minute more than I'm being paid for?" This thought is why it's vitally important to think of yourself as a company.

If you took on only one major client (your employer) and from time to time you put in more work than you were paid for (many would assure you that such efforts are required and should be thought of as paying your "dues") just as the owner of any start-up company must do, you could create a name for yourself and your company and build your reputation in the community. You could be certain that when the demand for your company's product or service had risen, your own profits would increase accordingly.

This new thought process works regardless of whether you're a server at a restaurant or a vice-president of a national corporation. Treat your employer (or prospective employer, if you're now looking for work) as a client of You Inc. and you will experience amazing and profound effects in your life.

As if you could kill time
without injuring eternity.
–Henry David Thoreau

What if you despise your job? Have you already started looking for another job because you can't stand each moment that you spend in your present one? Have you at least thought about it? Well, first off, you have some major decisions to make. Why are you still there? How long will you allow yourself to live like this? Now, if you're thinking about using those 15 minutes per day to look for a new job on the boss' dime, you might want to think again. The reputation of You Inc. is on the line and if you are going out, then go out with a positive bang!

If you were your boss, what would you think about an employee who spends office time looking for a new job or idly chatting with friends via e-mail? Maybe this is why you don't enjoy your job, you aren't paid what you think you are worth, and you aren't receiving the recognition you deserve.

What if you spent that time doing that little extra that makes all the difference? How about doing some extra filing for the entire office? (Especially if that isn't your job—remember, you're pleasing a client.) Why not make a couple of extra calls a day, e-mail the boss with a new idea or an alert about what the competition is up to, or just make your shop a spotless place of business? What type of valuable cargo would you be then if rough seas should arise?

And if for some reason these new efforts go unnoticed at first, don't be concerned, life will eventually notice them. Furthermore, this is the new level of excellence that you've committed to, whether someone is taking note or not. Your goal should be to wow your boss regardless of whether this is your last week on the job or part of your journey to a ten-year position. If you owned the company that you now work for and you knew what type of employee you are, would you keep you on?

Paying attention to simple little things that
most men neglect makes a few men rich.
–Henry Ford

The customer comes second

Are you a person who over-promises and under-delivers? Why do you do it? Do you find yourself trying to please everyone and end up displeasing yourself the most? As the most important person in your corporation, you now have a duty—a duty to look after yourself for the sake of the overall viability of your corporation.

A couple of years ago, I was at a corporate conference and was lucky enough to hear a talk given by one of the executives of WestJet. His stories were fascinating and the one that resonated with me the most was that they never put their customers first. I was shocked by this statement. What did he mean they didn't put their customers first? From the beginning of sales school, we are taught that the customer always comes first.

WestJet's story is a little different. The employee always comes first and the customer second. The reasoning for this unusual policy is that it's easier to find a new customer than it is to find a new employee.

I found this to be one of the most profound business statements of my career. Of course, we've had it backwards all along. Companies spend millions of dollars on hiring, training, and finding ways to keep their employees happy and to profit the overall corporation. If that employee is made to feel in the wrong for the sake of one customer, the company loses so much more in the long run. In addition to potentially losing all of its investment in that employee's training and education, it also weakens employee morale and leaves the impression of an uncaring company.

As the sole employee of You Inc., how often are you sacrificing your corporate self-esteem for the customer? If you're a salaried employee of one company, you have one major customer. Is that customer worthy of you? If you're a business owner, figure out the "wince factor" of each of your customers or clients.

The wince factor is simple: each time you see that customer or hear the person's name on your voicemail or see it on the screen display, do you wince at the very thought? Perhaps it's time to pass that client on to someone who can relate better to that individual and free you up to meet with the customers you truly love. But what if this client represents a large account for your firm? Certainly, the importance of the customer and the size of the customer's account make this decision more difficult, but imagine a work environment that you love and that loves you.

I'm not suggesting that every time you have an issue with a client, you immediately try to cull the account or pass it off to someone else, but I am suggesting that you look at those customers who drain your energy and imagine what it might be like to deal with only your best customers. After all, with all of the energy you're spending on the wince-inducers, you might have little left over for those who truly deserve your time. And if you're a salaried employee and your largest and only account happens to be your employer, perhaps now is the time to entertain the idea of finding a new employer.

Creating your micro personal policies

It takes less time to do things right
than to explain why you did it wrong.
–Henry Wadsworth Longfellow

Here are some useful questions to ask yourself in order to determine the rules that work best for you:

What do you wear when you're working?

Whether you work at home or in an office, it's important to establish a work uniform. This might seem like a simple notion, but a corporate uniform will allow you to mentally focus when wearing it and to relax when you take it off. In my field, the rules are fairly blurred on acceptable work attire. There's quite a mix between suits and sweaters, with the latter chosen by those who do not wear a formal suit. I remember a lesson that answered this question for me very early in my career.

I was running my first trade show. It was in a suburb of Edmonton and the attendees were mostly farmers. I thought it would be appropriate to dress more casually and wear a sweater and casual slacks because it was winter and the attendees would mostly be wearing jeans. I was overwhelmed with comments such as, "Oh, you city people can't even dress up for us farmers!"

I was shocked at their attitudes and since it was a two-day trade show, I arrived the next day in a suit. I had obviously read my crowd all wrong. Again, I was shocked at the comments. "Oh yeah, you city people in your suits, thinking that you're too good for us farmers." I couldn't believe it. There was no pleasing these people, but the truth is there's no pleasing everyone, so why not start with pleasing yourself?

Then and there I decided that a suit was my personal and ideal work uniform and, for the last decade or so, I have always worn, at the very least, a jacket or formal suit during my work hours in the financial industry. After I sold my company and re-branded Me Inc. with the new roles of writer, speaker and more, I used to wake up each morning and put on a suit even though I had winded down my office and most days don't meet with anyone.

Sidebar:

As we'll discuss, your rules are not set in stone and in perpetuity. As you refine You Inc. and develop new markets and distinctions, you'll need to review your policies. Think of it as a guidebook and when something isn't working, even something as simple as being uncomfortable in your uniform, for example, it's time to review and update your policies.

What's your ideal work uniform? What's your current uniform? What do you wear when you're not working, on holidays, when you're totally relaxing? If it's the same clothing, I suggest you examine your choices.

Consider a few distinctions. First, like a uniform, your work clothes should be like a type of armour. When you put on a set outfit for work, you should anchor that to working. Focus on what's needed from your work and how it improves your power, courage, and focus. When you take that armour off, you're off. Now when you put your jeans on for example, it's not just that you're psychologically off, your jeans feel different than say heels and a skirt. Think of the last time you dressed up for an important event. Perhaps an award ceremony at your child's school, a wedding, or work function. Did you feel better about yourself? When you feel better it shows. I might also suggest that on those days, say a gloomy Monday morning, when you just don't feel inspired or motivated that you put on something extra special for work and notice how you feel throughout your day. Did you walk a little taller, enjoy the compliments on your extra effort, or simply liked what you saw in the mirror—that you dressed up for you?

I had a friend who worked from home and stayed in his jammies until noon most days, had no uniform at all, and wore clothes he'd never wear out in public. When I spoke with him on the phone he sounded just as he looked. He actually had a closet full of dress shirts and a lovely wardrobe, but since he worked alone from home he stopped caring about his appearance unless he was going out. I asked him if he'd try an experiment. I had him shower and dress first thing in the morning even if he wasn't going out at all that day for just one week. He had to put on dress pants and a dress shirt—even if it was the same outfit all week (but preferably he'd change). He agreed. When I called him during the week, he sounded fantastic. From my end of the conversation, although I couldn't see him, I could guess that he was sitting straighter in his chair, spoke with a more professional tone, and seemed happy. By the next week he'd forgotten about the experiment and told me the week before was one of his most productive ever. Will simply dressing up change your life? Perhaps.

I can tell you that if the only thing it does is make you feel better about you, that's the most important element. And I'm quite sure you'll see that it will transform your life by changing how you feel when at work and how others treat you.

I know when I dress as though I'm going to attend a business meeting (even though I'm not) when I'm flying that I get better treatment. More people make an effort to talk to me on the plane, ask me for help in the airport, and the flight staff is more accommodating. The question becomes though, is it my outfit or is it how I feel in my outfit that encourages people to treat me better? Whatever the case, I know the value of the little extra effort it takes and I, as well as you, deserve it!

A second important element to your work uniform is that it is identified with your profession. When you think of a navy outfit, with a hat, gun, and shiny gold pins, what comes to mind? Likely a police office or security guard. But in your line of work, you might not have a clear uniform, such as a firefighter, nurse, or pilot does. What would you like your uniform to say? What do you think your marketplace expects your uniform to be? Ignore the casualness of society today. I'm surprised when I enter a prestigious office and see less than cared for outfits worn by the staff. They might have lavish offices and multimedia equipped boardrooms with no design detail overlooked, however, their own staff and their dress do not show the same attention to detail. Just because your workplace or client might not have a set guideline for what should be worn during working hours, don't ignore the importance of creating this policy for You Inc.

Sidebar:

When I first opened my firm and was marketing for new clients, I thought it would be a great prospecting idea to give seminars to upscale retirement homes. Since I was still relatively young and wanted to develop my senior client base, I thought aligning with other professionals (preferably older men) would lend credibility to my offering workshop and would convince the retirement home owners to let me in the door. I convinced a very successful naturopathic doctor to conduct these seminars with me. He was senior in his profession and was looking too to expand his practice and bring in new patients for the junior doctors on staff. He was well spoken and an experienced public speaker. He always dressed in Giorgio Armani suits and presented himself well.

We held three workshops for one retirement home and it was well attended. I called up the person who ran the facility and asked if she'd like us to run another series of seminars, since our past ones were so well attended. The woman was thrilled and said she'd be delighted for me to run more, but asked that I not bring the doctor back. I was stunned. When I asked why, she told me that the residents didn't like him and didn't trust him. I couldn't believe it. I had wanted the doctor to present with me to increase my credibility—not bring it down. When I inquired a little further as to why the residents didn't like or trust him she painted a very clear picture. You see, the residents of the seniors' home have a medical doctor visit them on a regular basis. He wore a white coat, a stethoscope around his neck, and carried a black bag during every visit. The woman had shared with me that the residents didn't think my fellow was a real doctor. Yes, he was dressed immaculately, but he didn't dress the part of "doctor," in the way that the residents had become accustomed to.

The third distinction you'll want to make in selecting the ideal work uniform for You Inc. is the message it projects based upon what your corporation stands for. We'll explore branding our corporation in the next chapter and our dress is absolutely an extension of that brand. It's also the easiest way to stand out and set us apart from the crowd.

The PVP:

When looking at how you dress for work, keep in mind that context is the key. You may enjoy wearing the latest fashions, and be bold and stylish, after all your uniform should be an extension of you or it won't seem authentic, but keep in mind though, it should also be respectful of your audience, market, and workplace. If you're a home design consultant, for example and your work outfit is young, hip, and somewhat sexy (low cut tops, short skirts, and boots) and you're now branching out into corporate office design, you may need to rethink your uniform in order to respect your market. If you were pitching a law firm tomorrow, a mini skirt and too low-cut a top might not mesh well with a conservative law firm even though it's your style. They might extend some latitude due to the nature of your business, expecting you're not going to dress like a lawyer for example, but it might be the deal breaker if you come in without knowing your market. There's a fine line between wearing what's an extension of you and what's respectable to your customer (boss, client, co-workers, etc.). You needn't change your style and wear a baggy suit and turtleneck, but you might consider being more conservative while at the same time keeping fresh and fun if that's your image.

As mentioned, when I was in the financial industry and had my own firm, my uniform was pretty much the same year round. I wore a somewhat conservative pant or skirt suit and was rarely business casual attired. One day I was meeting with a client of mine who owned a very successful trucking firm. I was taking him for lunch of a warm sunny Friday and wondered if I should alter my uniform as I might make my client feel out of place or uncomfortable. Considering so many companies today subscribe to the notion of "casual Fridays," I wondered if I should break my uniform rule and relax my outfit. I decided not to as I had learned that lesson once before (remember my farmer tradeshow story?). My client showed up in a three-piece suit and was, without a doubt, the best dressed in the entire downtown restaurant. I was dazed to say the least. I can't imagine how embarrassed I would have been if I dressed "down" for this client who was better dressed than me, even though I was in my standard suit. I inquired, "Doesn't your company subscribe to casual Fridays?" I didn't say it, but he knew where I was going with my line of questioning, being surprised that someone who owned a trucking firm would be so dressed up. He told me his personal policy that I'll never forget. "Absolutely not," he said. "I don't believe in casual Fridays and never will. Furthermore, nor would I allow my staff. No one in our office is allowed to wear jeans." This last part is permanently etched in my memory and personal policy book. He ended saying, "just because we're a trucking company, doesn't mean we need to look like one." Wow! Was his company so successful in an extremely competitive market because he held himself, his drivers, and staff to a higher level starting with their uniform? It can't be measured, but it can't be discounted either.

My last lesson on the notion of creating a corporate uniform came from when I had given a morning kickoff presentation to a group of extremely successful realtors. I was invited to speak on the subject of defining You Inc. and got to this part about creating one's uniform. I thought this was especially important since realtors have such great latitude with what they wear. I should note that before presenting this section, I asked the 100 or so realtors that were in attendance how many of them would likely be seeing one of their clients later that day. Every single one of them put up their hand.

In the audience of this morning session, with all realtors agreeing that they were likely going to see a client that day, there was only one person wearing a suit. Only a handful were dressed in what I'd consider business casual attire, most were dressed ultra casually, and a handful were dressed unacceptably casual in sweats and hoodies. As you can imagine, there was some resistance and closed body language when I started talking about their uniforms. The group held themselves out to be "professionals," yet their style of dress didn't convey that at all. I asked each of them to give me one of their business cards and as I thought, nearly every single one had a picture of themselves on the front of their card. Also as I assumed, nearly every picture of the realtors depicted a very professional, well-dressed image.

I asked the group about this and the room became very quiet. I asked them to consider the client they were going to meet later in the day. When they handed their client a business card with a photo of them dressed in a suit and arrived as if they were going to the gym or golfing, how special would their clients feel after *not* being dressed up for? If they'd dressed up for the picture on the card, why didn't their valued customer deserve the same? The arguments, as I guessed, started to come. What if my market is farmers, or fitness buffs, etc? My answer? Don't put that picture on your card then. It sends an incongruent message. If your main clientele were, say, rural veterinarians and you lived a similar lifestyle and loved getting out in the country with animals and such, then the picture on your card might show you with a horse or dog posed in the country in a dress jacket and jeans. When you showed up in a similar outfit, it would be just what your customer expected. But if you're wearing a three piece suit holding a briefcase in your photo and you show up with a jogging outfit (even if your customers are fitness buffs), carrying your marketing materials in a plastic grocery store bag (this is what I actually witnessed from one realtor), how does that make your client feel? That you're usually professional and dressed appropriately, but they're not important enough for you to extend the effort for them?

The PVP:

I'll repeat that context and congruency are paramount. Your uniform should be an extension of you. Sometimes you might dress it up or down slightly, but it's part of your brand and sends a positive, consistent message about you and how you present yourself to the public and your marketplace. I have a good friend that had a very similar position to mine when we both worked for the bank (hers, a competing bank). Her clients were exclusively farmers in rural areas around the province. She also had a love and natural affinity for the farming community and the animals many of them owned. She was extremely successful and earned a high six-figure salary. Her "dressed" up uniform consisted of jeans, nice hiking boots, and layers of tops and coats depending on the weather. She drove a 4x4 and never carried a briefcase. Her dress was an extension of her and her market and she excelled at it. She was true to herself and respectful to those clients she was meeting. Although we had nearly identical jobs as far as investment advising was concerned, I would have failed miserably within her territory. Could you imagine me driving up in my Mercedes, wearing high heels that would get stuck in the mud, and wearing a skirt suit and having horses and sheep rub up against me?

I couldn't do it and if I did, I'd be miserable or wouldn't stick around in that position for very long. The same could be said for my friend if she were to trade spots with me. She'd arrive at my downtown high-rise office with her hiking boots full of mud, knapsack in lieu of a briefcase, and likely wouldn't last long either. She could conform as much as I could, but we'd lose our authenticity and would probably hate our roles.

When you examine your uniform, be true to yourself. Understand your marketplace, your workplace, your clients, and their workplace and adjust according. However, if you have to adjust too far, it's time to examine what makes you, you. If you can't be your true self, consider changing markets.

When do you handle the most challenging task of the day?

Do you wait until the last hour of your day, fretting about it for hours? Handle the most difficult task of your day first thing in the morning and you'll find power and strength in doing so.

How are you going to get everything done?

Write down the six things that you need to accomplish each day. Start the night before or first thing that morning and write down only six. Then, list them in order of importance and keep that paper with you all day. Start with the first on your list and stay with that task until it's completed or for as long as is possible. Then go on to the next, and so on.

If you can't get your list completed in a day, you wouldn't have been able to do it anyway. By writing down only six tasks, you greatly reduce the chances of feeling overwhelmed or that you have a hundred things to do in a day. Once your list of six is complete, you can go on to the next. I encourage you to keep a separate log of secondary to-do's and if, while focusing on your primary list, you think of other tasks that are important, write them on your secondary list. This way, you will keep focused on the tasks at hand and will know that when they're done, you will not have missed any details. You will handle the rest later.

Do you play the sex card?

Whether it's a style of dress or innocent flirtation, when it comes to work, there's no room for sex. Playing the sex card reduces the validity of your talents. As a strong woman who knows what she's good at, why imply that it's only your femininity that got you to where you are?

How's your timing?

Do you arrive early for work and appointments and allow for traffic and weather-related delays, or are you the type of person who is always late, who rushes out the door desperately in need of a cup of coffee at work before you become human in the morning? If you were to arrive 15 minutes before any appointment, you would be able to relax and focus your efforts so that you could enter your meetings calm and poised. If you work for one employer, remember that this is your client. Waking up a few minutes earlier will ensure that you make a great impression each and every morning on your employer and co-workers.

What are your rules regarding social interaction at work?

Is it okay for you to consume alcohol or drink to excess at the staff holiday party? Do you agree with dating on the job? How about letting loose with clients or co-workers?

The great thing about thinking of yourself as a corporation is that you make the rules. Although at times the questions above might seem unnecessary, and possibly you won't always follow your own rules, it is important to know when you've broken a rule that you have set for yourself. And how will you know if you've broken one of your own policies if you've never taken the time to identify them?

Work like you don't need the money.
–Mark Twain

As Les Brown says in his *The Power of Purpose*, "Wherever you find yourself in life, you made the appointment to be there." All of the choices you made in the past have led you to where you are right now. The great thing about realizing this, whether you like where you are or not, is that you have the power to change your situation by changing the little steps that move you in the direction of your desires. Do you wish you had a different relationship from the one you currently have? Then what are you doing now to change it? In five years, what will your relationship look like? The same as it does now, but with more bitterness and resentment, or will it be filled with passion and love because of the steps for change that you identified?

You have absolute control over where you are and where you're going because if you don't have control over you, who does? Is there a higher outside power over your life? Absolutely! What's the mix—50/50, 60/40? We'll never know. But so often in our lives, we're not happy with something we create. We make the choices and blame God or the universe. We ask why this has happened to us. It happens to everyone. Generally speaking, you have the ability to change your surroundings. There are people who had a lot less and did a lot more!

Words have power

The words we speak have great power, as do the words we think. Words and phrases referring to money, such as "filthy rich" and "too rich for my blood," have power. Did you know that it's been said that people who use the phrase "[So-and-so] is a pain in the ass" are much more likely to develop hemorrhoids? While that's somewhat amusing, and whether or not it's an old wives' tale, when we say a word, we are sending a command to our nervous system and are focusing on that word, even if we think it has no bearing on our lives.

How many positive words do you have to describe a wonderful experience? When was the last time you felt elated or filled with bliss? Do these words exist in your vocabulary? Take a moment to write down five positive words. If you need to find a thesaurus or go on the Internet to look for some, do that now. I would suggest you check out *www.dictionary.com* because this site has a wonderful thesaurus feature. Just type in "happy" or "fantastic" or any of the usual words you use to describe your positive experiences, then write down some alternatives.

1. ______________________________
2. ______________________________
3. ______________________________
4. ______________________________
5. ______________________________

Over the next few weeks, try to use these words in addition to your regular vocabulary and see what happens. See if your experience changes as you use new words to describe that experience. The same principle works with your self-talk.

What about our negative experiences? I would guess that you can easily think up many more words to describe your less positive life events. When was the last time you were angry, frustrated, enraged, depressed, blue, and on and on?

I have a wonderful friend who often feels frustrated. He uses this word to describe his reactions to his day, his work, his family, and sometimes his friends. And how does he generally feel? Frustrated, of course. He tried the simple exercise of changing this frequently used word in his vocabulary and it changed his life. He decided to use the term "mildly miffed" in place of "frustrated." When he told me about the challenges of his day after using his new word, he would actually smile and laugh a little as he described some very challenging events. This new lightness came from just changing his use of words.

When you ask someone how they're doing, how often will the person sigh and proclaim, "Busy, very, very busy"? Everyone is so "busy" these days, and as a society, we put great emphasis on this word. In the corporate arena, we might want the other person to know how busy we are to gain a spark of empathy or because we don't want more work piled on our desk. But at the end of the day, this simple word, which many of us use to describe our entire day, causes us to go home feeling exhausted from being so busy.

A very good friend of mine pointed out a new phrase to me last year and I've been using it whenever the opportunity arises. These words have totally revolutionized how I think about my workday. He suggested trying the phrase, "Well, it's a bit crazier than I'd like—but I'm still having fun."

I took his advice and the first couple of people I said this to must have been very incredulous because at the time I wasn't just a "little bit busy"—I was frantic and swamped, and I wasn't having any fun at all. But after a while, and I couldn't believe how many times in a day I had the opportunity to use my new phrase, I was able to put my day into perspective. My friend had given me a gift of focus with my new words, and within a few weeks, I found congruency each time I stated this new phrase. I was actually having fun! Just a simple reframing and a few new words changed my entire experience and, at the end of the day, put those inquiring after me at ease as well. After all, who wants to continue a conversation with someone who feels busy, swamped, or frantic?

Also, at a very early age, I chose to completely delete a popular word from my vocabulary, and this too has revolutionized my life. I grew up observing a family member who was often severely depressed. I watched this person suffer many years of this illness and, though still young, thought at a very early age, "Well, what if I don't believe in the option of being in a depressed mood and never use the word depression?" The result? The word depression truly doesn't exist for me. I understand that it is a word that many use to describe their feelings, but it isn't one I would ever use. As a result, I can happily and wholeheartedly report that I have never been in a depressed mood. I've been sad, blue, worried, and experienced a few other less-than-wonderful states, but never depressed; it's not even an option.

Ponder the following words of Ella Wheeler Wilcox, who so eloquently expresses the importance of a positive self attitude for attracting more of what you would like in your life. I would add that both your thoughts and your spoken words manifest an ideal attitude and life.

Solitude

Laugh, and the world laughs with you;
Weep, and you weep alone,
For the sad old earth must borrow its mirth,
But has trouble enough of its own.
Sing, and the hills will answer;
Sigh, it is lost on the air,
The echoes bound to a joyful sound,
But shrink from voicing care.

Rejoice, and men will seek you;
Grieve, and they turn and go.
They want full measure of all your pleasure,
But they do not need your woe.
Be glad, and your friends are many;
Be sad, and you lose them all,—
There are none to decline your nectar'd wine,
But alone you must drink life's gall.

Feast, and your halls are crowded;
Fast, and the world goes by.
Succeed and give, and it helps you live,
But no man can help you die.
There is room in the halls of pleasure
For a long and lordly train,
But one by one we must all file on
Through the narrow aisles of pain.
— Ella Wheeler Wilcox

Try this simple technique. Write down five words you currently use that are not serving you any longer.

1. ______________________________
2. ______________________________
3. ______________________________
4. ______________________________
5. ______________________________

Now, pull that thesaurus back out or pop back on the Internet, and find five new words or phrases that would better focus your mind or soften the impact of the word you're currently using.

If you find that there are times when your old word would more appropriately describe your experience and a substitute doesn't work or you just need to wallow a bit in some mood, go ahead. Be sure to give yourself ample time to feel what occurs in your life—anger, sadness, worry—but don't allow these feelings to consume you. Schedule them when possible, feel their intensity, and set an alarm clock to alert you to when it's time to focus on being more constructive.

Why sometimes I've believed as many as six
impossible things before breakfast.
–Lewis Carroll, *Alice's Adventures in Wonderland*

The dangers of universals

When was the last time someone told you that you never do something right or you always do some other thing wrong? A universal is a word that someone uses to make a statement that makes a sweeping judgment, whether intentional or unintentional.

Universals are dangerous because they don't factor in any reasonable exception. You might tell your spouse, "You never take the garbage out," when this statement is perhaps only true this week. Your boss might tell you that you're always late when it might only be the second time you've been late in months. Have you ever caught yourself using a universal when judging yourself? Have you ever accused yourself of "always" making stupid mistakes or never picking the right lover to be with? Universals can make us and others feel hopeless.

Handling inner and outer critics

To avoid criticism do nothing,
say nothing, be nothing.
–Elbert Hubbard

Handling outer critics can be simple and effortless with this easy exercise. Generally, when someone criticizes us, they'll use a universal word or statement. For example, your boss might say, "You're always messing up." You could simply feed this universal back to your boss. "Really boss, I'm *always* messing up?" And what's your boss most likely to say? "Well, I guess you're not *always* messing up." Then, you must follow up with another extremely important question: "How, specifically?" It's one of the most powerful little questions I've ever learned and used in my life.

When we're extremely frustrated or feeling overwhelmed, one act can often seem like the total sum of a person. You're always messing up—whatever you did specifically to receive the castigation of your boss, might have felt to her, even if it was one episode, that you really were always messing up. What we focus on expands but we can only focus on so many bits of information—a redirect can have staggering results. If you were to ask your boss what she specifically means by your messing up, she might say something like, "Well, you botched that sales meeting we had last week and we might lose the client."

First, she's still talking to you and you haven't been fired, so this is a good thing. Second, she's focused on one specific thing now, not waving a blanket of judgment over your entire career performance. You can now ask more empowering and unambiguous questions of your boss such as, "What can we do in the future to ensure that I handle such a meeting to your satisfaction?" Your boss might realize that you need more training or that you have been under a lot of stress and could use a vacation or an assistant. Whatever the result, you want to stop the sweeping generalization of the statement. This simple shift also works wonderfully with yourself, your family, and friends.

Let's say you arrive home late from work and your spouse greets you at the door (you not realizing pizza has been ordered two hours ago and is now cold) and says, "You're always late; you never think of my needs." Again, repeat the statement back, "Really, honey, I'm always late and I never think of your needs?" You might gently remind your spouse that you called three times last week before arriving home late from the office. This is a great opportunity to set your rules as a couple and determine what's expected when coming home later than usual.

Sometimes when a criticism or an exaggerated judgment is cast, a universal doesn't exist. For example, someone might pick up this book and report to me, "Your book is stupid." How does one handle a response like that, assuming I even care to respond? If I did care to inquire further, I might say, "I understand that you feel that my book is stupid, but I'm curious, which part of my book did you find beneficial?" Again, I'm feeding back a question that focuses their mind on a more positive note. No matter who they are, I highly doubt that they didn't learn at least one new thing from my book that could benefit their life in some great way.

Try this on. Don't think of the colour blue. What did you just do? I can bet you thought of something blue, didn't you? But I told you *not* to do that. Our brains don't truly understand the word *not*. We first have to think about the thing and then not to think about it while it's already thought. Not just confusing, but impossible. Try *not* to think of falling as I say, "careful not the fall as you head out on the slippery walk." We don't do this consciously, but at a laser fast speed. Our mind must first picture what it's not to do, therefore focusing on exactly what we don't want. If someone tells me that my book is stupid (and thankfully no one has), I could simply focus their mind on something else—which part did you enjoy? Which part of my book did you find compelling, inspirational, or enlightening? The likelihood is that their mind will find something positive or constructive to report back to me.

What about those insidious inner critics—you know the ones—your own voice and your own self-talk. Most of us talk to ourselves in negative tones and use disparaging words that we would never tolerate from others but it's somehow acceptable in the solitude of our minds. When was the last time that you blew a speech, yelled at your child, or did something that deserved self-reproach? Perhaps your self-talk sounded something like, "You'll just never get it right. You're a terrible speaker."

I've been a speaker for over a decade now and I can assure you that there are times when I nail a speech and other times when I do not connect with my group for whatever reason, but usually it's somewhere in between. When my critical inner voice is there to meet me after a talk that was less than perfect, it's usually pretty harsh.

The two most powerful words on earth

Negative self-talk and self-criticism are inevitable. There are times when you know you could have done better. In the example of giving a talk, perhaps the sound system was acting up or my audience was smaller or larger than anticipated or maybe I just didn't know my material as well as I could have. There are two magical words that Charles Faulkner points out to us in his audio program *Success Mastery with NLP* that can counteract even the toughest of critical voices—the words are "so far."

Get to know these words. "I'm a terrible public speaker…so far"; "I just can't sell and will never reach my goals…so far"; "I'm an awful mother, spouse, friend, [insert noun here]…so far." By adding these two powerful little words, what does the end of the sentence focus your mind on? For me, it adds hope and encouragement. We're often so focused on being perfect that it is empowering to look at ourselves with some levity. By adding "so far" to a self-defeating thought, you remind yourself that life is a journey and you're a student of life getting better and better every day.

Make feedback your friend

If I have lost confidence in myself,
I have the universe against me.
–Ralph Waldo Emerson

There are no failures in life. We've heard this from some of the greatest minds of our time and of times long past. In life, feedback is a great friend, and failure our foe. Is this simply semantics? Sure, why not? Each perceived failure in life is actually quite exciting. It's a new road map for the future and if we listen carefully, we'll know what to do better next time, what not to do, and so on.

The word feedback is also a wonderful way to reframe our focus—just when it's needed. To explain a failure is difficult and can even be humiliating and debilitating. To examine the facts and determine what can improve our lives is empowering and focuses our minds on improving, by not dwelling on a past that's unchangeable.

As a public speaker, I can happily report that I've advanced over the years. I've had more than my share of bombed talks and have a binder full of areas for improvement. And just like many public speakers, I still get quite nervous before a lecture. But as a seasoned professional, I can usually handle whatever a group or venue throws my way.

Years ago I was invited to speak at a large women's show as one of their main stage presenters. This was quite an opportunity for me and an exciting venue indeed.

Unfortunately, the stage was set up more for a rock band than a prosperity lecture and the microphone kept feeding back an awful screech. I was somewhat paralyzed on the stage but worked my way through a very painful speech. Being so far away from my audience definitely stunted my normal flow, as did the feedback from the sound system.

Don't be too timid and squeamish
about your actions. All life is an
experiment. The more experiments
you make the better.
–Ralph Waldo Emerson

For a while after this presentation, I was horrified and kept reliving all that had gone wrong. How could I bomb like that with hundreds of presentations under my belt and years of experience? My business coach and a very good friend walked me through the powerful re-frame of failure versus feedback.

First, he awakened me to the fact that I wasn't actually as bad as I thought I was—that the audience actually enjoyed my talk. But since he had attended so many other presentations of mine, he was honest that it certainly wasn't my best job to date. What he had me do there and then was to write down all of what had thrown me off. I listed that I hadn't checked the stage, and I didn't make sure that I had a cordless microphone so I could walk closer to my audience and connect with them, and so on.

Just weeks after that, I had another significant talk booked and was extra nervous because I assumed that I was on a destined path leading to more substandard speeches. I stopped trusting myself for a moment and believed that my last "failure" was going to be the norm from now on. Before this next talk, I took my list of "musts" as a presenter and ensured that the room worked for me and my audience. I used the feedback from my last event and others to focus on a better talk this time around. The result? I'm truly thrilled to report that this talk was my best ever. I was still a little nervous at the start but all of my past "failures" and really taking the feedback to heart as a learned lesson proved effective.

When in doubt, act "As if"

Be as you wish to seem.
–Socrates

Socrates knew that sometimes you must act before you actually feel to become what you aspire to be. For example, do you have a challenge in life that requires you to be confident when you're scared silly? Try this simple notion: act as if you're a confident person and see what happens.

How would confident people stand? What self-talk would be running through their thoughts? How would they breathe? You might not feel confident as you handle many of your challenges but this game of pretend can produce profound results and, eventually, you might find that you're not pretending at all. What if you have a problem with depression or are in a rut that you can't seem to shake? Well, try on the thought of acting "as if" you are a happy, joyful, and light-hearted person. Would they have a smile on their faces? Perhaps they would sing or whistle a tune. Try this simple exercise in almost any situation where you would like to change how you're feeling. When in doubt, try acting "as if."

Flexibility equals opportunity

How many times have you turned on the news or read in the newspaper a story featuring someone who has opened a unique business or come out with a new invention and thought, "I could have done that!" It happens so often. A scotoma or a blind spot happens to almost everyone and to some of us on a regular basis. How many times have you opened the kitchen cupboard looking for the salt or pepper and maybe even cursed a family member accusing them of moving it? Perhaps over the mumbles and complaining, a family member hears your dilemma and reaches in front of you pulling out the salt shaker with a look of disdain. Humbly, you apologize and swear on your life that it wasn't there just a moment ago.

Scotoma can limit our successes in life too. We often have blind spots or opportunities that, for whatever reason, we just can't see. Creating more flexibility in our daily life will give us the ability, over time, to create a broader view of life and enable us to see what we didn't before.

We often get stuck in the doldrums of life and forget to appreciate the wondrous world around us. When we try or do something new for the first time, it's always exciting. But after a while, even the most exciting experiences and situations become mundane. Think of the first time you saw the love of your life, walked up to your new home, or entered your office on the first day of work? Everything was a treat: the smile of your lover, the potential of your new home, and the view in your office. Over the years, we stop noticing the little things and then tread dangerously inside the proverbial "box." As we stop noticing the subtleties of our environment, we limit our possibilities within it, not to mention our ability to enjoy it.

The following are a few fun ideas that were adapted from Charles Faulkner's audio program *Success Mastery with NLP*. They're great for expanding creativity in your life and will work your flexibility muscles:

- Dress differently today. If you usually put on your pants first and then your top, change it up. Put your left sock or nylon on first if you usually aim towards the right.
- Do you usually brush your teeth and then wash your face in the morning? Try the opposite for a week.
- The next time you're driving to or from work, take a different path home; even one block off your normal drive will reveal homes not previously noticed.
- Walk down your street with different eyes, as if for the very first time. Take a stroll around your neighbourhood and really try to notice what you haven't before. Be in the present and take in all of the stimuli around you.
- Be someone else at the grocery store. The next time you're shopping or waiting in line, pretend to be a glamorous movie star, model, or hero of yours. Imagine what it might be like to not want to be noticed and who might be looking your way. Feel, if only for a moment, what it is really like

to be that person. Or, perhaps visit a different grocery store the next time you're stocking up. See and interact with the cashiers and other shoppers. Notice how the same chain store is similar but likely laid out differently depending on its location.

- Put yourself in the shoes of someone across from you at a boring meeting. Imagine yourself in their body, what they might be thinking, how they're sitting.

hildren have a natural ability to be in the present and make any event fun and entertaining. Be silly and indulge that still small child within you and look for the wonder in your daily life today and forever. Doing so will clear up your scotoma and unveil exciting new opportunities just waiting to be discovered.

Stop losses and checkpoints

If you've ever purchased a stock with a full-service broker, you might know about a practice called a stop loss. When you purchase a stock, you're aware, or quickly made aware, that there are risks associated with your purchase. You hope that it will increase in value but equity market investments are not guaranteed so no matter how sure the bet might seem, there's always the risk of loss. A stop-loss system comes into effect if the stock starts to plummet.

We'll assume that the stock you're going to buy is selling at $20 per share. The conversation with your broker at the start should include your downside exposure. You might tell him that you're hoping the share moves to $25 and at that time he should sell half of it. But should it start to decline, you couldn't handle a loss of more than 25%, for example, so he must start the selling process if the stock should fall to $15.

Would a stop-loss system have helped your investment portfolio in the past? Has your portfolio ever decreased in value by much more than you anticipated or even knew to be possible? Did you realize that you could only handle a 10% drop in your investment values after your portfolio had already tumbled 40%?

Think about how this simple system in the investment world might be effective in your own life. How simple it would be, for example, to identify at the start a "stop loss" in our relationships and careers? Have you ever stayed at a job or in a relationship you knew you should have left years before? Did you stay for a 40% loss when you could only handle 10%? Have you let an innocent habit get out of control and take over your life?

I remember a time in my life when sugar cravings took hold of me and my appetite for chocolate bars became insatiable. At an all-time low in my health plan, I was up to five chocolate bars every day. Looking back, I can't understand why I didn't at least curb my bad habit to some degree. How much easier it would have been to move past my sugar cravings if I had imposed limits upon myself. How about two chocolate bars a day or even three?

But I just kept sailing higher until finally one day I had had enough. How did I know that five was the magic chocolate bar number, the number that was to determine my limit? Why not ten per day or more? Somewhere within my subconscious, I had determined five to be the magic number. Why not do this process consciously?

We all have bad habits we wish we had under better control. I'm sure that most of us can relate to gaining a few pounds each Christmas season, but have you ever consciously vowed at the beginning of December to keep that gain to less than a maximum amount? We know we're going to gain the weight, so the question becomes how far out of control we are willing to let it go until we've had enough.

Sometime in my teen years, I vowed to stay under a maximum weight. I knew at the time I wanted to lose a few pounds but I also wanted to ensure that I never went over this maximum because I didn't know how far I might sail by it. If one morning I'm even one pound over this maximum, it triggers a "that's enough" attitude instantly and I do whatever is necessary to take myself back under the maximum. I have also changed my maximum weight over time as my body has changed but I have found that having a goal of what "not to reach" is sometimes as important as a goal to aim for.

My example of weight gain and loss is pretty easy to measure and provides a simple example as it involves dealing only with numbers and watching the scale, but how about that dead-end relationship, friendship, or job? We hope for and work towards a better life for ourselves, doing everything possible to achieve it, but at what point will we know it's sliding negatively and that we've had enough? Try the simple mental exercise of evaluating your life and habits in order to determine a measuring system for your own life.

I truly believe that we should monitor our life as we do our investment portfolios—with quarterly reviews (goal setting and life reviews) and stop losses. Imagine how much more on track our lives would be and how much easier it would be to win at this game we call life.

Specialize but never become an expert

When you're an expert at something, there's only a limited number of ways to do it. When you're new to something, there is an infinite number of ways to do it. Furthermore, the novice is not handicapped by ego—you have nothing to defend and so have no sense of your own self-importance.

When I first took up the sport of golf, I couldn't believe how ridiculously difficult it was to hit a tiny ball with that long and cumbersome club. I remember going to the driving range to learn the basics of the swing and grip.

After a lot of practice, I had that all-rewarding connecting hit that made pursuing the sport worthwhile.

Over the years, I have dabbled at taking lessons here and there but since golf takes consistent practice, I've never really improved. My skill is just about the same as it was nearly a decade ago but my ego, with respect to my ability, has certainly increased. Now when I'm at the driving range and someone corrects my swing or suggests a different technique on the course, I greet those comments with resistance and annoyance.

I think that I was actually a better golfer during my first years in the sport. Back then I was willing to take suggestions from anyone because, what's the harm in trying? But now I think I've become an expert and know my own ability and have lost the playful joy a novice experiences.

What's your essence?

As Wayne Dyer encourages us to do in his *Manifest Your Destiny*, "Become like the orange." You've likely never thought about it, but no matter what is done to an orange, whether it's squeezed, sliced, or thrown at a wall, the only thing that can come from an orange is orange essence—what it is filled with. What's your essence? Do you think of yourself as a generally calm person but when squeezed and pressed and stressed, you fly off the handle?

I love being an observer at friendly socials or Christmas parties when individuals partake in the alcoholic beverages offered and often have a little too much. You'll likely agree with me that once the guard of the shy wallflower is down, with the blame placed on the cocktails, that person is often the life of the party. Or what about that timid guy who feels ready to take on the world and fight the entire room after two rum & Cokes? My particular favourite is the live-by-the-book person who never shows any emotion but who, after the third glass of champagne, just loves complete strangers.

Going back to my golf example, I have also found the golf course to be a wonderful venue for determining a person's essence. And I'm not alone as more and more corporations are taking key executives out for a game of golf before hiring them or offering opportunities for advancement.

I think everyone should at least try the sport of golf. The game teaches patience and how to get along with others. You will probably have three other people with whom you will be walking the course for four to five hours but, at the end of the day, it's a game all about you. It's kind of like life!

In life, as with golf, there will be many times when no one is watching and it's really easy to cheat. If you find your ball has landed in a bad lie, you can just kick it onto the green or out of the severe rough or you can forget to count the three swings you took in the sand when no one was really looking. The question isn't about the opportunities to cheat and take shortcuts; the question is whether *you do*. And if you do—in golf or in life—you're just cheating yourself. This particular sport can also reveal a person's attitude when faced with adversity or less-than-ideal conditions. Does the individual remain positive in spite of a poor performance, bad weather, and unruly fellow golfers? Or will three poor holes have the golfer wrapping a club around the nearest tree?

We can blame our poor behaviours and attitudes, whether in golf or in life, on many things but at the end of the day, only we can really control them. We can't control the weather on our wedding day or guarantee that our kids are going to behave this week or that our partner will love us, but we can control our reactions to any situation. So getting back to the example of the orange, what are you filled with? Does it matter how you're squeezed to determine your essence?

There's always someone watching

More people are watching than you think—customers, co-workers, and suppliers. Many times it's not the boss who's noticing your achievements or your slacking or late arrivals, but often someone is watching and it could hurt your future. If all of your co-workers suddenly left and opened up a shop similar to the one where you work now, would you be the first on their list to bring over or would you be dead last? Remember that you might not report to these people, they might not sign your paycheque, but a future employer or someone you might like to have as your own customer one day could be among them. Are you burning bridges without even realizing it?

Take the time and the opportunity to create the policies of your new corporation and watch your success soar. Remember that you have the same 24 hours a day as the billionaires of the world, so make each moment count and start planning to win now.

I want to be thoroughly used up when I die,
for the harder I work the more I live.
I rejoice in life for its own sake.
–George Bernard Shaw

Keep your new rulebook handy. It won't be blank for long. Examine things that upset you or others and start to document them and establish rules that work for you, ensuring that you communicate those rules to others. Are you consistently late, always running into unforeseeable delays such as traffic, your kids sleeping in, and so on? Maybe you need a micro rule of getting up earlier. My rule, and I've tested it over time, is to get up four hours before I need to be "on" for a meeting, media interview, or for a presentation. I need time to relax, get ready, and plan for contingencies and things that inevitably will pop up that I'm not prepared for. I've tried to be more efficient and scale down those four hours and failed miserably. Now, I don't even question it. The night before, it's simple what time I need to get up—I don't have to think about it again and it's just one less detail to worry about and struggle with.

What other rules can you think of that would make life a little easier for your corporation and yourself? How about how long you wait for someone? It could just be coffee with a friend. If she didn't call you on your cell to tell you she was running late, how long would you wait? Mine is 15 minutes. If someone doesn't call to tell me they're running late and to see if I can wait for them, I won't stay longer than 15 minutes in a business or personal setting, and I communicate that rule to others. There's no questioning involved. My time, as is yours, is important. By that person's being late, they're presuming that their time is more important than ours. Accidents and such are sure to happen and this rule will be broken many times, however, it's a start indeed. And of course, if you had a meeting with your boss or your most important client and they arrive late, you might bend and even break this rule. But at least you'd know that you were breaking it in the first place.

Creating your policies and rules

We learn more from our failures or at least, hopefully we do. Each set back, disappointment, or flat out failure gives us valuable feedback on what not to do next time, what to do in the future, and provides an opportunity to create a working policy for mitigating those errors. In theory, one should examine victories as well. I have not had much success personally with the latter. Why was a particular presentation, book, or meeting a hit? It is much easier to learn from the perceived failures. I think of it in terms of my health. When I'm having a great day physically, I feel terrific energy, and nothing in my body pains me, I don't analyze why. However, if I wake up tired, irritable, and with unease of any sort in my body, I quickly examine the evidence. Did I not get enough sleep; what did I eat yesterday to cause this; and so on. The same process is prudent in every aspect of your life. Don't let an upset, failure, or setback go unanalyzed. Be careful not to berate yourself. Create distance and provide feedback—it is an opportunity to construct another corporate policy.

Being in the financial industry for over a decade, I had a solid list of policies. To be sure, they took that long to create, but each year, there was less and less creation of rules and more refinement. When I sold my firm and entered the world of writing and speaking, I had to create a new set of corporate policies for a new world. I had no experience as a professional speaker. What do I charge and when and how should those fees be negotiated, collected, invoiced? What time do I arrive at an event, what's my check list, what details should be confirmed with the client? It was a daunting task with a steep learning curve. And many mistakes were made with an ever-expanding "feedback" file.

Policies

You may have a payment policy, for example. If you are a web designer, you might require a 50% deposit up front. If a client isn't willing to pay this even after reviewing your credentials, you might have a policy not to work with a client that won't pay the deposit.

When I worked for the bank, it was their policy that investment managers, such as myself at the time, would meet clients at their home, work, and in the evenings or on weekends. This was revolutionary for banks at the time. When I opened my own firm, I made it my policy not to meet with clients other than during normal business hours. Another policy of mine at the time was to meet with a potential client at least three times before we agreed to work with each other. That way, I truly knew if I could help someone with their finances, determined if they were someone I'd like working with over a number of years and allowed the client to check me out and decide if they wanted me managing their money.

A corporate policy I have today surrounds travel. First, I make my speaking fee simple. It's all-inclusive other than extraneous travel—flights and hotel are the only extras. My meals and incidentals are my own. Another very important policy I've learned to employ is that I must be flown out the day before a presentation. I can't tell you how often I'm shocked that a client will plan an entire event around my presentation or make it a key element to their conference. They'll spend a great deal of time and money for their event, my fee, and my flight. Then, if it's a short distance, say from Edmonton to Vancouver and I'm speaking at 3 p.m., they'll insist on flying me out that morning with the thought of saving one night's hotel expense (usually less than $200). Although it's only a one and a half hour flight from Edmonton to Vancouver, Edmonton can be a very tricky city to fly out of during the long winter months. I have not flown out as scheduled more than 40% of the time I fly in the winter months. When I point this out to clients, many of them still don't budge. They'd prefer to risk my possibly not showing up at all, wasting thousands of dollars, than pay a couple hundred dollars to ensure I'm there for the event by flying me in one day early. My reputation is on the line. Even though my contract would protect me in such an instance, it's personally essential that I get to my clients' events. Often they don't travel as much as I do, or they don't understand all of the flight delays and what could go wrong. In such a case, it's my policy to pay for the extra hotel stay personally so I can fly in a day early or, with some clients, insist that they do or decline the engagement at the outset.

Your policies should not only be designed to protect you, your interests, and your bottom line, you must also have your client's interestes at heart. You know your job, position, and industry better than they do and you need to educate them on the risk management of some decisions and why you've created your policy in the first place. And remember, when I use the word client that could mean your boss as well. You might have a personal policy that if you work late a few nights in a row, you get to come in late on Monday morning. You may need to communicate this rule to your boss and co-workers, as they might all be leaving work at the sound of the bell and think you're a slacker coming in late on Mondays. You would want to communicate with your boss and let him or her know that you took the initiative to stay late a couple of evenings to get an important job done, for example, and that you don't mind doing this and are committed to the company. As everyone leaves on time, they might not be aware of the extra hours put in.You need flexibility so as not to become resentful, and that might mean coming in late on Monday morning or leaving early on Friday when a job is done. It's in the best interest of your boss and co-workers to not only understand your commitment to the company and projects, but also to recognize that you work best and are most productive when given flexibility. This might not suit the place you've chosen to work and you may need to either break your rule, communicate it better, negotiate with your boss, or consider another client (place of employment).

Breaking policies

A policy can, of course, be broken. This is where it's essential that you know your policies to begin with and let the client know that you're breaking one, this time only, so they don't expect it every time, or when referring you to others assume a policy that you wouldn't normally extend. For example, if a Fortune 500 company or a senior branch of government hires you they might tell you it's their policy not to pay a deposit. You may still want the contract enough, and know that they will more than likely pay your bill, so you break your policy. Nonetheless, you should ensure that you still communicate your decision to break a policy with them.

When I had my firm and met a client on the weekend or in the evening, I was sure to let them know that I didn't normally do so. If they were a very large account and this broken policy was going to become the norm with them, I reminded them often that I normally wouldn't do this for a client. Why? First, it made them feel special and important. Not that my other clients weren't, but the reality is, there are times with a policy simply needs to be bended or broken in business. One can't be too rigid, but don't let yourself be walked on either. The second reason it's so important to communicate to your customer (even if it's your boss) that you are breaking a policy is that you don't want them spreading the word. For example, I wouldn't want that client to refer me to their friend and say, "Kelley's great. Not only will she make you money in the markets but also she'll meet with you any time—evening or weekend." Or, if I relaxed my speaking fee by 50% in a very special circumstance, such as for a not-for-profit group, I don't want it to spread. While I am thrilled when clients refer me, I wouldn't want them telling others about how they too can get my fee reduced.

If you have staff, communicate with them as well the parameters of breaking policy: when, for whom, how they will be held accountable, and so forth. As important as a policy is, it's equally essential to know when that policy can be broken by you, your staff, and when the policy needs to be revised or no longer works and should be tossed altogether.

Rules

Rules are very similar to policies, but not as stringently enforced. It would still behoove you to write them down and communicate them with others, but they're more likely to be broken. I've always had a rule of being happy and having fun for both my staff and myself when we're at work. However, that rule is broken at times. It's not a policy that I'd necessarily communicate with a client as it's somewhat irrelevant to them.

You might have a rule in your office that your desk is always cleaned off before leaving on Friday, that the phone is answered by the second ring when possible and so on. These rules might be more accurately described as guidelines. As long as they're not abandoned or broken continuously, the company and what it stands for won't fall apart, yet, they are still integral.

Processes, systems and checklists

You'll want to create systems, processes, and checklists as you find yourself doing the same thing more than once.

As this is my sixth book, I have a clear process for starting, working on, and finishing a book. My publisher and editor have a system for their part.

If you were in the event planning business, you may have a marketing system in place to help your client fill the seats of the event. The brochure and invite should be mailed on such a date, the e-mail reminders are sent twice and on these dates, and lastly, the registrants are called 24 hours beforehand to ensure they show up. You may have a post-event system of keeping in contact with attendees, offering them products and services from a number of your clients, and so on. Systems provide a clear guideline of what to do when.

Lastly, the checklist can be used within a process or system. When having a staff member or contractor make customer service calls on your behalf, you may have them refer to a checklist that says: remember to smile as you speak, don't eat or drink while on the phone, sit up straight, etc. When I travel, I also print a checklist of items that I need to bring. As I have forgotten so many things in the past, I keep my checklist with me while travelling and add new items as I realize their importance to my comfort and make sure to follow-up.

If you do all of the grocery shopping in your family, creating a master checklist of menu options and items to keep in your car will make life easier at the end of a long day when heading to the supermarket. Creating a list of items, taping it to the fridge, and insisting that your family write down when they've used the last of something will also ensure that you're not making last minute runs to the market or banging on neighbours' doors for that cup of sugar or eggs the kids used up last night.

Leaving things to memory means often forgetting essentials. There's a time to practice your skills of recollection—use those muscles when remembering peoples' names. It does take some time and effort to create and maintain a checklist, however, I can assure you that if you're doing something regularly, it will make your life and the lives of others easier!

That gives you an idea of the importance, but also the simplicity, of creating policies, rules, processes, systems, and checklists. They're what consistent and dependable companies are built on. They seem rigid and time-consuming, but ultimately will reduce upsets in your personal and professional life and will, in the long term, save you much effort. Don't get caught up in semantics and be sure to look up the definitions for yourself. At the end of the day, you want your policies and rules to work for you and your many clients. Their technical terms are not as important as the benefit they need to provide.

Your corporation's personal inventory

I'll bet that you know more about your liabilities than your assets. And I'll also bet that you're really good at pointing out your failures and shortcomings, and, if this is the case, you could be in deep trouble. If your financial balance sheet is out of alignment and your net worth is negative, you need to look at where you want to go and what's going to get you there. Yes, there's merit in understanding and doing some analysis of what went wrong so that you can learn from your mistakes—just don't live in them!

Create a balance sheet of your personal assets. Think of everything you're good at and write it down. You don't need to worry about how you can turn your strengths into profit, just list all of them. Are you a great listener, parent, and personal coach? Do you have a university degree, specialized training, or a wonderful understanding of English or a second language? Are you a master in the kitchen, a superb interior designer? The secret to success certainly starts with understanding your skills and assets. I also encourage you to list a few of your liabilities as well, just ensure that you take the time to detail the solutions and action steps needed to overcome them.

Take a moment now to list your top five or ten assets, and over time add to this list as you realize what you're skilled at and where your strengths lie.

1. ______________________________
2. ______________________________
3. ______________________________
4. ______________________________
5. ______________________________

Fundamentally, there are a limited number of ways for a company to grow and stay in business long-term. Three options exist. Expenses need to be cut, assets need to increase, and a boost to cash flow may be required as well. These core strategies apply to your employer or client and certainly to You Inc. As you practice examining how to cut your expenses and increase your income, you will become more skilled at it over time and it will serve those you work for immensely. It might seem like a small drop in an ocean to care about minor expenses in a large company, but if everyone in that organization didn't care about the drops, it would eventually add up to a large lake. As the CEO of You Inc., you now have a new respect for your assets and costs and as such, respect others' as well. You know that a dollar wasted of a client's resource affects everyone. If that client notices or not, you do and it matters to you.

Your debt inventory

Take inventory now of all of the expenses in your life that you are willing to re-examine and try to determine where the fat can be trimmed. In chapter five, I'll give you an exercise I call my "anti-budget" where I'll walk you through a fun challenge of cutting excess without suffering. But for now, list every major debt in your life that is fixed, such as your mortgage, credit cards, car loans, student loans, and so on:

____

____

____

____

____

____

____

____

____

____

Now, I challenge you, if you don't already know, to find out the exact details of each of your debts. Do you know the interest rate you're paying on your credit card? It could be costing you hundreds of dollars more than necessary. Do you know what the annual fee is? Are the rewards worth it if you're keeping a balance at a high rate? Should you perhaps switch to a lower rate card with your bank or consider consolidation? What about your mortgage? What's your interest rate, prepayment options, or the benefits to increasing the frequency of your payments? If these details are somewhat foreign to you or you haven't always paid attention to the financial details of your life, not to worry. We'll cover all of these concepts and more in chapter five, but for now, at the very least, list all of your fixed debts and find out their true cost as much as you can from your paperwork.

As you examine some of the costs in your own life, be keenly aware of those you work for and with. It might be your child's soccer league, your volunteer organizations, or your employer. Where can costs be trimmed thereby saving more money?

Your asset inventory

The second step is increasing profits, growing assets, and, shortly, we'll look at increasing cash flow as well. Now, list all of the assets you currently have—your home, car, investments, etc. These are what I call your tangible investments.

1. ______________________________
2. ______________________________
3. ______________________________
4. ______________________________
5. ______________________________
6. ______________________________
7. ______________________________
8. ______________________________
9. ______________________________
10. ______________________________

Are your investments performing as efficiently as possible? If you own a home, it's likely your largest tangible investment. What can you do to increase its worth? If you have an investment portfolio or pension at work, when was the last time you requested a review to monitor its growth and ensure it's performing with the average market benchmark or better?

If your asset list was left blank, you're not alone. There are times in a business' life, and within your life and that of your personal corporation, when this part of your balance sheet might be empty. If that is the case for you, you need to pay extra attention to the next section coming up. If your asset list is full, your attention needs to be on not only protecting those assets but also growing them as efficiently as possible.

This section can be a great deal of fun and allows you to flex your creative muscles. I want you to now list all of the intangible assets you have at your disposal. These are resources, people, knowledge, skills, and more that, if exploited effectively, could translate into increased cash flow, opportunity, advancement, a raise or increased fees, and so on.

Let me give you a few examples:

- *Your network.* These are not only the people you know but also the people they know. For instance, you may desire to get into the entertainment industry. A foot in the door is all you might need for a fulfilling and rewarding career. Perhaps you discover that the husband of your co-worker at the law firm you work at part-time is an executive of the exact company where you're looking to intern. List all of the people in your life that you know and who they know and start getting interested and asking them questions about their resources as often as you can. They might provide just the "lucky breaks" you need or will streamline the process of getting from where you are to where you want to go.
- *The demographic/psychographic traits of your network.* Who are the people you know? What do they do for work, where do they vacation, what do they do for fun? How old are they? How many are women, men, married, single, or have children? What issues do they face? What stresses and life concerns do they have? What do they seek most?
- *Their needs.* After completing this exercise, you might determine that you have a number of friends who have exceedingly high incomes (perhaps they're corporate climbers and don't have children, for example). They're extremely busy, have lots of disposable income, and time is their most valuable commodity. Later, when we discuss bringing more income into your life and corporation, you might determine that you have a number of products and services you could offer to this group. You might prepare frozen, healthy meals for the week and have them delivered. What about starting a concierge business on the side for them or a corporate gift shopping service? You needn't concern yourself at this moment with what you'd do with the demographic and psychographic nuggets you've extracted. Simply list everything you can think of that's unique to those in your network and look for emerging patterns.
- *What you enjoy and what you're good at.* As mentioned in the last example, don't worry about why you're listing it. Simply try it. Write down every detail you can about what you're good at, what you enjoy, what you'd likely be good or great at given the time, opportunity to do so, or further training and education.

- *Other intangibles.* Take some time to really think here. You have a plethora of intangible assets that you need to explore and consider. Do you live in a small town? Perhaps knowing everyone by name and growing up there since childhood is a tremendous asset if you were to start a restaurant or open up a shop. Advertising would be easy since word of mouth would spread fast. Or maybe you live in a large city with a thriving IT community. With your natural knack, this opens up opportunities you'd never have in a smaller city. What other intangibles exist that you might capitalize on if your eyes were only open to them?

You'll need more workspace than I could provide in this book to answer the above questions I've asked. Take some time with this exercise and never, ever stop. Revisit all of your assets, hard and soft, often. Ask your friends and network or mastermind group what assets and breaks they see in your life? They might come up with a list of items you've never thought of or didn't really think were assets. Use the book that you purchased for writing down your corporate policies and leave some blank pages open to work on this over the next 30 days and into the future. Once you're aware of the many assets in your life that you didn't even realize were there, you can focus on how best to benefit from them.

Sidebar:

If you are unfamiliar with a mastermind group, it's simply a group of like-minded people that get together to empower, educate, and hold each other accountable. Your group can be comprised of friends, family, strangers, really anyone, but ideally, individuals who think differently than you, are from contrasting industries, or who often can assist in new ideas. The notion of masterminding was first written about by Napoleon Hill in *Think and Grow Rich* (a fabulous read if you don't already have it in your library). A mastermind group can and will absolutely fast-track your career by tapping into the resources, knowledge, and skills of others.

Increasing your assets and cash flow

If you've examined your debts and have structured them as effectively as possible and scrutinized your assets, the next logical step in growing your corporation is to look at all of the ways you can bring in more cash flow. There are times in our lives when we (our companies) have no debts and no assets, thus nothing to improve upon within the "debt or asset" categories on our balance sheet. The only strategy for building wealth becomes increasing income.

First, I'd like you to list all of the possible things you could do to bring more money into You Inc. Please focus on the "could." Simply brainstorm without judgment. I'll later have you choose the best ideas and scale down what you "would" do. As you list what you could do, even if you wouldn't want to, it will open your mind to possibilities you hadn't thought of. If you currently drive, for example, you "could" drive a cab for extra income on your days off. As a woman and considering the possible dangers in such a side job, you likely "wouldn't," but list these ideas anyway. From your cab idea for example, you may determine that driving for some extra income isn't a bad idea at all and possibly something you might enjoy. With the cab idea, you drill down and come up with the thought of starting a seniors' driving service where you drive elders to pick up their prescriptions, groceries, or simply do the shopping for them and deliver the goods. As a woman, this spin on driving for a profit might resonate with you and fulfill your desire to assist this needy segment of your community.

Now list all of the things you could do to bring more cash flow into your life. Here are a few more cash-generating ideas to get you going:

- Ask your boss for a raise
- Increase your fees if you're self-employed
- Hold a workshop on a topic that you have some expertise in
- Teach a class for a community college
- Put on cooking classes in your home
- Sell prepared meals to your busy friends
- Write a book or an ebook
- Sell items on eBay
- Have garage sales for busy friends and take a percentage of the profits
- Clean homes or businesses
- Start a pet daycare/walking service for those in your neighbourhood
- Run a morning shoe shine kiosk in a downtown office tower during slushy winter months
- Become a home inspector (most operate after hours)
- ______________________________
- ______________________________
- ______________________________
- ______________________________
- ______________________________
- ______________________________
- ______________________________

- ____
- ____
- ____
- ____
- ____
- ____
- ____
- ____
- ____
-

Now, list the ideas that you're interested in and likely would do. Write them in order of priority.

- ____
- ____
- ____
- ____
- ____
- ____
- ____
- ____

Lastly, pick just one that you're willing to try. Or, at least that you're willing to do some research on and explore how it might bring more pleasure, joy, fulfillment, and yes, even money, into your life.

By flexing your mental muscles and using your inherent intangible assets and creativity, not only can you increase the bottom line of your personal corporation, but also increase those of your employer or clients.

When possible, and as mentioned previously, consider volunteering your time in a committee or board member capacity for an organization that is important to you or can advance your career. Consider being part of their fundraising efforts. What you'll discover is that the corporate community is often eager to align with non-profit organizations and the goodwill that's expressed when they offer in-kind products, services, or money. If you're not a great asker personally, you might find the task much easier when doing it for a worthy non-profit organization. Plus, your personal benefit is that you'll learn about raising funds and capital from others and in ways you've never thought of previously. Perhaps that knowledge will be just the germ of an idea You Inc. will need in the future.

Sidebar:

I served on a number of committees and boards during my career and have learned more than I could ever have imagined about raising funds, sourcing corporate sponsorships, and writing mutually beneficial sponsorship proposals.

When I was looking to announce and market my first book I ran into difficulty because it was self-published, and the expenses were totally my own. The publishing and editing costs had run double what I had budgeted and I wasn't willing to throw more money into the project. I asked myself how I could possibly market and advertise my book launch while spending little or no money. After all, I had done exactly that to promote a number of events and projects with the organizations I volunteered for. I created a sponsorship proposal that would announce my book and launch and would feature the sponsors in a series of newspaper advertisements. It would showcase their company as a supporter of literacy and so on. Everyone thought I was crazy, saying, "you can't ask for money from companies—you're a 'for profit' business." I gave it a shot and was able to raise enough money and call in a few favours to pay for $20,000 worth of advertising in one of my city's major newspapers. Be creative and have fun. Above all, when someone tells you it can't be done (or you tell yourself this), question the reality and possibility of such a statement and ask yourself if there is a way it "could" be done.

Whenever I've had the opportunity to sit down with individuals or have had workshop participants analyze their assets and expenses and had them fill out a net worth statement, just as you did in the previous pages, no matter how wealthy or how far away from that they were, they've always found (and I hope you did too) that they had more than they originally thought. The fear of looking at what we have and the doubts of whether we'll be in a positive position once the list is complete are completely unfounded. We tend to have more than we at first assume and it all starts with realizing what we do have. Try it; I know you'll be surprised at your personal inventory, too!

Being in service vs. being sucked up

Now that I've written a few books, had a few columns, and am regularly in the media, the number of requests for help, guidance, and free advice can be a little overwhelming at times. I used to pride myself on returning messages, both phone and e-mail, personally and in record time. With hundreds of e-mails alone coming in each day, that's become impossible. It is a frustration that many of us share to some degree.

One day, a woman who's called on me a few times in the past and is now an acquaintance asked me for some free advice on getting her book traditionally published. She holds herself out as a sales guru and one newsletter I read of hers harped on the importance of following up—that your word is all you have and if you break it, basically you're killing your corporate future one failed promise at a time, or something to that effect.

Although swamped with many requests, I gave this woman thirty minutes of my time. In exchange, I made one small and simple request. She was travelling to the US and being paid but didn't require a working visa. I knew there was a particular form that one needed in this situation, but I hadn't had much success in finding it on my own. When I asked her about how she was conducting such travel, as I would like to as well, she was vague and limited her responses. She offered to *try* and find the form and would send it my way. I had given her 30 minutes of my time at no charge. I gave her every idea and resource freely that I could in that time. I shared what worked for me, what failed, and suggested many ideas she could take away. In exchange, she provided me a two-minute, generic response, and a year later, I still haven't received that form.

There will be times that people seek your advice when they can offer you nothing in return. Give your advice freely to them. If you believe in karma or not, it's a good thing to do and will come back to you, trust me on this, in some way. There will be others, though, who can and should reciprocate for your support, knowledge, advice, resources, and such. There will be individuals who believe that they're owed by others, life, and everyone in their path. They're energy-suckers and will do just that to you. If you're like me, you can't spot them initially. So, give your time, energy, and advice freely the first time. If someone can reciprocate and they don't, consider that eventually resentment will set in and it will be your responsibility to communicate that you would like something in exchange.

If you've been an energy or resource "sucker" without offering something back, be honest about it. We all have, some more than others.

If the sales guru calls me tomorrow, how likely will I be to assist her again? I can assure you my advice wouldn't be as free flowing. I use her as an example, but I could cite dozens of episodes that I've had in the last month, not to mention over the years. I must clarify again that there are times that one should not expect anything in return. And it's a natural trait of many women, when others ask for help, as a gender, we usually truly wish to do that. If it's a friend who's going through a relationship problem, a colleague who needs advice, a friend needing your time for something, I'm sure you'll agree, if you can, you're willing to assist.

I wake up each day wanting to be of service. I used to do that by helping people with their finances. Yes, many of them were wealthy and would have done just fine without me, however, when I had a chance to help someone that I could not profit from who really needed my guidance or assistance, it made me feel great at the end of the day. I wanted to help more individuals like that, although I knew I wouldn't be able to stay in business focusing on them. You still have to pay the bills for your office and staff. If you don't make anything at the end of the day, long-term, you're not going to be able to change too many lives. It's great to be selfless, but one needs enough money to do that.

Now, through writing or speaking, I hope I get to impart some story, advice, or nugget of knowledge that could potentially change someone's life. I feel I can wake up and be of greater service than ever in my career. Whereas someone needed a great deal of money to invest with me to receive my financial advice or needed to pay me a large hourly fee for my counsel, now people can buy my book, can read it free at the library, or can hear me speak through a workplace that has sponsored one of my presentations.

There is a fine line, though, where being of service and being emotionally sucked up start to blur. When someone contacts me for my knowledge and experience on getting published, writing a book, breaking in with the media, or some financial aspect of their life, I truly want to assist. There are a few reasons for this. First, I've contacted many people seeking their wisdom offering no reciprocity and many have assisted freely. Second, on my many adventures, I have had people appear out of the blue offering to help me on my journey with no personal desire for anything other than to lend their experience, expertise, or knowledge. As such, I wish to do the same as much as I can. Lastly, why wouldn't I want to share in a few words with someone about something that might have taken me years of frustration to learn?

However, there's asking for clear and concise advice and then there's going overboard. Furthermore, there's something to be said for learning life's lessons oneself instead of having them just given to you when you might not be ready.

Win/win doesn't always work

I cannot recount the number of people that now want to take me for lunch, coffee, and bend my ear for advice on getting their book published. It's my pleasure to offer advice, but with an already hectic schedule, time is a resource that is difficult to share. I travel so much of the year that when I'm home, I have a list of over 100 friends, family, acquaintances, and potential business opportunities that I have ignored or didn't have time for while writing a book. Trust me, I'm not alone. Offering lunch or dinner doesn't cut it. I would estimate that over 90% of the time when I offer my time, advice, and resources to the person that wishes to write a book, they're wasted. When I share an hour of expertise that could save or make thousands of dollars and potentially cut a person's learning curve by ten years, why wouldn't I want to share that information and save someone the years of blood, sweat, tears, money and time that I expended? However, it's a huge annoyance when that information is mismanaged, unappreciated, or not used or followed up.

Intelligent asking

It's been said by many and bears repeating: You cannot and will not make it in business alone. You need others—their support, intellect, advice, and expertise. Sometimes you can call upon others to pick their brain and sometimes you need to be ready to pay for what you're asking. You're likely unwilling to work for free, so when you're asking for something, try putting yourself in the other person's shoes. Ask yourself if you'd do that for someone else.

Practice being a good giver too if you're going to hone your asking skills. There's something to be said about the notion of karma. You're not always going to be in the position to pay for someone's advice or be able to repay it. Be sure to find others who need help; when they solicit your advice offer your services. Sometimes you may even find someone that you know you can help even before they ask you.

I'm not talking about negotiating here. It's not asking in the sense of trying to get a hotel room upgrade or a discount or advanced sale price at a department store. In this sense of asking, I want you to consider your network: those people you know and the people they know. They can streamline and fast track your career, your love life, and more, however, you must ask intelligently. I've devised a list of do's and don'ts to follow along with some crazy asking I've experienced over the years.

Do

Ensure you're reaching the right person at the right time. If you want to get into the financial industry, for example, you wouldn't expect to call Warren Buffett for advice. You'd go to the place you currently bank and see if someone will spend a few minutes with you to point you in the right direction. Or, you could reach out to your network – does an acquaintance, friend, or co-worker have a friend, spouse, or relative in the financial industry? They might be able to help you connect with someone willing to offer you some advice that could save you years of effort, time, and money.

Research. I can't stress this enough! Know as much as you can about the subject that you're seeking counsel on and the person that you're calling upon.

First, your topic. Know as much as you possibly can before reaching out to the person who can take you to the next level. If you want to write a book, perform a Google search about writing and publishing, attend a workshop at your local college, and visit the library or bookstore and invest in all of the books you can. Then, when you have a solid understanding of the industry, you'll ask better questions and thus, likely received better answers.

Second, spend some time understanding the person you're seeking advice from or at the very least, put yourself in their shoes. Are they a busy executive who likely receives many such requests for their time? Offering to take them for lunch or dinner might seem like a fair exchange on your side, but for them, it's just another time sucker. When asking others for help, set the parameters for that person to assist you in the way that works best for them – i.e. would a brief phone meeting suffice? Do e-mail discussions work best? Will they be attending a networking or social event that you'll be at where you can chat? Do they have a blog and so could answer your question and provide advice to others as well?

The PVP:

Not everyone is as busy as they seem. We all make time for what's important in our lives. Many successful individuals genuinely enjoy talking about themselves and their business. They may not be asked often for their advice and will delight in your request. When doing your research on the person you're asking for help, for example, are they married with four kids and travel a great deal? You can imagine that their time is spread pretty thin. However, if they're single, in a phase in their life where they've slowed down, or are nearing retirement, they might absolutely enjoy the offer of being taken out for lunch or dinner to share their war stories, insights, and experiences. The bottom line is—do your best to know who it is you're asking a favour from.

Be specific. Don't expect someone else to find your purpose in life. Do your own homework first, then seek their advice. I receive query after query from individuals wanting to write a book. They contact me or seek me after a presentation and tell me they want to write a book and ask how should they go about it. In five questions or less, I can determine if they're not serious or have no intention of ever writing a book and have wasted my time. "What type of book would you like to write?" I'll ask. The answer usually is something like, "I don't know. I'd just like to write a book." "Are you thinking of fiction or non-fiction?" Too many times the answer to this question is, "What's the difference?" If someone specifically asked me, "So once my manuscript is finished, what's the best approach to finding a traditional publisher?" Ah, this I feel compelled to answer and help this person. Their question alone tells me how serious they are and the research and preparation they've done as opposed to somehow thinking someone else will hand them their dream on a silver platter.

Follow-up with a thank you. After asking anything of anyone, follow up with another thank you. Most people barely thank those they seek advice from at the time, perhaps not even realizing how much the other's time is worth. If someone takes the time to spend a few minutes with you in person, on the phone, or via e-mail offering you advice that you've asked for, always send a follow-up. Either a quick e-mail or, even better, a thank you note in the mail. This will reinforce the fact that the person's time was not wasted and the advice appreciated even if not used. If you need to go back to this person again in the future, you'll likely receive a warm reception from someone willing to assist you again.

Be honest about what it is you want. An old friend called me up a few years ago out of the blue. We used to be extremely close and for many reasons, lost contact with each other. When I received his call, I was absolutely delighted. He wanted to get together for lunch and catch up. I was thrilled, cleared my calendar, and moved him to the front of my appointment line. After a long lunch of catching up on the years gone by, just as we were heading out of the restaurant door, my friend wanted to tell me about the amazing business opportunity he had discovered. He wanted to discuss how it changed his life financially and in other ways and how it could do the same for mine. It was an MLM (multi-level-marketing) company selling health and cleaning products. I was shocked and speechless. Is that why he wanted to get together with me and connect after all these years? Was it simply that he wanted to sell me and sign me up as another on his down line or did he really miss me and wish to genuinely get in touch? Unfortunately, it wasn't the latter. He hounded me with a number of calls after that lunch insisting that I should give him my client list (as if that would ever happen) so he could offer this amazing opportunity to them too. Needless to say, after his outlandish request, misleading lunch and boorish behaviour, by the third call I wasn't so polite and told him to take a hike. Not only did he ensure that we would never be friends again, he'd certainly lost me for life as a resource. And who knows, if he had prefaced the reason for our lunch honestly from the beginning, I might at least have heard his sales pitch for his MLM adventure. If he had called me out of the blue, and stated that he was working on a new marketing initiative that he'd like my feedback on, it would have been fine, plus it would have been great to catch up on old times. I'd at least have been in the position to decide if I'd like to hear about his venture, wouldn't have felt hurt and misled after our lunch, and would likely still be friends with him. Be overtly upfront and honest about exactly what you're asking from others. You may get a meeting with someone by pulling the wool over their eyes, but I assure you, you'll not get what you're looking for in the end.

The gold is in the details

I'm often fascinated at how few people make an attempt to stand out in business today. Certainly much lip service is paid to the importance of follow-up and simple yet profound gestures, yet it's shocking how often it doesn't happen. However, when it does, watch out! That person and effort will stand out. Not everyone will lavish praise, but in today's fast-paced, narcissistic world when someone genuinely provides terrific service, they eventually will be rewarded.

In your book, write down all of the unique and consistent ways you work to stand out. In today's corporate culture, it's surprising that pleasantness, showing up for work on time, and doing what you said you would is actually considered excellence as opposed to expected. It's easier than ever to stand out and takes but a few moments more of your time, energy, resources, and creative power. Here are a few ides for standing out from the crowd:

- Use your calendar and set reminders
- Remember people's birthdays and send an e-card or card in the mail
- Send cards in the mail—thank you and otherwise. So few people today receive anything handwritten anymore, and most have a mailbox full of bills and unsolicited junk mail. Send handwritten thank you and anniversary cards.
- Collect business cards and enter the information in a database. If you don't have a database program, simply add the name and contact info in to a Word document and create labels for each contact. It's not as effective as a database, however, it's better than having them sit in your drawer. Be sure to write on the back of the card how you know the person, where you met, the date, and any other specific information about the individual. Do not leave this to memory.

- Send Christmas and other holiday cards to those on your database. Handwrite these. Do not just sign your name on a generic card—might as well not send it out at all. Include some personal information so that the recipient knows that you wrote it.
- Have a personalized, friendly, and specific voicemail. Always announce when you're not in the office, on vacation, or experiencing an unusually busy time that is making it difficult for you to return calls in a prompt fashion.
- Gift-wrap items. Can you attach your card to a sample of some sort? Perhaps two chocolates in a decorative Cellophane bag with your card attached with ribbon? What small thing could you do to not only stand out, but also make people feel special? After I had given a writer an interview for a piece she was writing, I was not only pleasantly surprised to receive a copy of the magazine in the mail a few months later but also felt remembered and extremely special when the writer had wrapped the magazine in pink ribbons and attached a thank-you card. It only took a few extra minutes of her time and pennies worth of ribbon, but it affected me immensely and I remember it to this day. Should she ever call needing my assistance again, how willing will I be to support her efforts in return?
- Give gifts commensurate with the situation. Did someone refer you a client that will make you a tidy commission or help you get a job? This definitely isn't the time to cheap out. Send them a gift to show your appreciation and ensure you're top of their mind for that next referral.

Sidebar:

I heard Oprah once talk about her first meeting with Dr. Phil who, I'm sure you know, has his own talk show produced by Oprah's company. She told the story of Dr. Phil coming on her show as a one-time guest, as an expert and author. By appearing on her show guests become successful and authors become instant best-sellers. She's said that she's never expected anything from a guest, and so few people ever really thank her, but Dr. Phil was one of those rare individuals who did and stood out as a result. He thanked her with small tokens of appreciation, kept in touch with Oprah's staff, not just to get on the show again, but to genuinely help them with their issues, and continued to supporting their efforts "just because." Did Dr. Phil simply get his show by thanking Oprah, keeping in touch, and selflessly support their efforts? Of course not. He got the show because they knew he was an expert in his field, was a good guest, and had what it takes for a new show. However, there are likely hundreds if not thousands of equally qualified experts as good or better than Dr. Phil. Did he stand out due to his heartfelt thanks to Oprah? Quite likely. Can you imagine going on the Oprah show? How excited and nervous you'd be? How focused and concerned you'd be about doing a good job? Would you stop to think about Oprah and her team or would your attention just be on yourself? It's a lesson I remind myself of often—that a heartfelt, authentic thank you, even when and especially when we're feeling a little self absorbed, goes a very long way.

- Use an e-mail signature—don't require people to hunt for your contact info. If they have to, they might not contact you at all.
- Use an e-mail auto responder when you're away from the office or unable to promptly return missives. Don't assume that not returning an e-mail for a week is acceptable if the addressee didn't even know you were gone from the office.

The PVP:

Regarding some details such as sending thank you cards for example: you might not do this forever. I must admit that I rarely send cards any longer. With thousands on my list, it is impossible, cost prohibitive, and unfriendly to the environment. However, if I were starting out in business again today, I would absolutely make this practice part of my personal marketing plan as I did fifteen years ago.

- Always follow up when you promised and even when it's unexpected. So few people really get this. Have you ever found yourself waiting for information from someone? Perhaps it was a realtor who was to get back to you on the offer you put in for a home. Or, you've been sitting on pins and needles waiting for your banker to call to let you know if you've been approved or declined for a loan. They promised to let you know by midweek and it's Friday, four thirty in the afternoon and still no call. Finally, the following week, they call to let you know the answer. As they do, they mildly apologize for the delay in getting back to you but they too were waiting on some information.

- Be proactive in calling people, especially when you don't know the answer or have all the necessary information. If you promised to call someone by midweek and you're still waiting on some detail, contact them and let them know just that. You have no idea if they're waiting on that information and how very important it might be to them. It's a small yet profound detail that so many neglect. Simply touching base and following up on a promise by informing that the situation is still unresolved, then setting a new date and time for your follow-up will always set you above the crowd.
- Be specific. Listening to others make appointments, schedule follow up, and so on often makes me cringe. I'll hear someone say, "I'll touch base with you next week." The person saying that might think Thursday or Friday is just fine as it falls within the parameters of "next week." However, the other person might think anything later than Tuesday by noon is pushing the "next week" window. I've seen business lost and deals fall apart with such vague and careless follow-up. Be specific. If you'll call them next week, let them know it will be later in the week, or by the close of Tuesday, the latest. Your expectations and someone else's are likely to clash at times. State your follow through and if a different date or time is needed, renegotiate with the other party on a new time frame then and there as opposed to potentially blowing your opportunity.

Don't fear failure

There isn't a mistake in the proverbial book that I haven't made. Whether it was with my finances, credit, marketing, writing, or business, I've made most of them and continue to do so to this day. I'm glad to report though, most of my failures and mistakes are new ones. I used to fear failure. I don't anymore. It still scares me, but it doesn't immobilize me. I won't tolerate, however, making the same mistake more than once. When and if that happens, I turn my world upside-down to ensure that it never occurs again.

As a reminder, I hope you've now purchased your blank paged book and have created the suggested "feedback" folder I recommended earlier. Ideally, your blank book should be small enough to fit in your purse and be sturdy enough to endure banging around in there for months or years. Record every thought—positive, negative, or indiffent—in your book's blank pages. These recordings will serve you later in life and in defining the policies and rules of You Inc. Your feedback file should serve as an objective location for recording your upsets, disappointments, and those events and life episodes that you classify as defeat or failure.

You truly make so-called failure your friend by understanding its value and importance, and by understanding that it's valuable feedback. You no longer fear trying anything again because of the terror that you might not success. I'm not the first or the last author that will emphasis this fact. I can tell you personally, that when I reflect upon anything in my life that I would classify as successful, it is a direct result of the mistakes and failures I've endured. My successes have the common denominator that I learned from those errors and corrected the behaviour the next time.

I further believe that were it not for those many mistakes, I would not have the solid corporate policies that I have today that have served me so well.

When I decided to enter the world of professional speaking, I had some experience from my financial career; however, it was never as a professional because I wasn't paid. There's a new level of energy, expectation, and, of course, fear, when you're paid to do something as opposed to doing something for free. In the past, I consoled myself if I bombed a presentation with self-talk such as, "Well, what do they expect for free?" I was interested in improving my skills and abilities as a speaker, but it wasn't overly important to me. It was a small element of my life in the financial industry.

When I sold my firm and sat down to design the offering of my new company, The Prosperity Factor, I knew very quickly that unless you are famous, you can't earn a living from selling books. I knew that I needed to add professional, not amateur, speaking to my company's services and tried to figure out what my other offerings (either products or services) could be.

With little experience in any of the ventures of my new company, my corporate policies were slim. When you're a new author, you're so thrilled to be picked up by a publisher that you have few to no corporate policies or demands. As a newly paid speaker at the time, if someone paid any amount, it was thrilling. My demands, expectations, and checklists were minimal.

It was only through trial and error and my careful recording of those lessons that I was able to, in a short period of time, create a working manual of corporate policies and personal rules that have fast-tracked my career as both an author, speaker, and now media personality. My work is not done and it never will be. With each trip, talk, book, and media interview, I pull out the notebook that I too have in my purse and add to what I've learned from each experience. Today, those additions to my book might be a word or line or two. When I first started, I wrote dozens and dozens of pages.

Your next corporate steps

I hope you've taken the time to at least start to define your corporation: What you value, who you will hold yourself out to be, and who you won't. It's a work in progress so be sure to document along the way. You've already defined the assets you have and looked at how to increase your cash flow.

In the next chapter, we'll explore how building a personal brand will take your corporation to the next level of excellence. In the chapter following that, we will look at the many ways to support your new VIP employee—You!

Chapter 3

Brand You

A natural extension of your corporate policies will lead you into thinking about what "brand" your personal corporation (you) will hold out to the world. Within some time, your brand will help further define many of your corporate policies, and will help to alert you when things and happenings don't fit your set rules or ideal brand.

Personal branding is a process that helps individuals to easily identify the policies of a person or their career. It has been noted that while previous self-help management techniques were about self-improvement, the personal branding concept suggests instead that success comes from self-packaging. The term is thought to have been first used and discussed in a 1997 article, "The Brand Called You," by Tom Peters.

Peters defines a brand as, "a promise of the value you'll receive."

Think about the last time you ordered a pizza. Was it from the hundreds of mom and pop stores near by? Chances are, it was from one of the big chains. Why? Likely because you know exactly what you will get from the large chain pizzerias. Thin crust, thick and gooey, cheap and plentiful, whatever your preference, you likely know the big guys that cater to your wants. The little store around the corner that dropped the black and white flyer in your mailbox might have the best pizza in town, but they're lacking a brand. As Peters says, a brand is the value promised. An unknown doesn't have a defined value to the public, so, many will go with what they know.

I just entered the words "pizza" with the location of "Edmonton" on the canada411 website and the results showed 605. No wonder most people would choose a chain!

Think about how this applies to your life and the potential benefit as well. People, likely you too, are busier than ever before. As a society, individuals in North America are bombarded with more informaiton and choice than ever in history. We're spoon-fed and hypnotized at times into believing what's best for our lives through adverstising. As fast-paced as life is, people don't have a great deal of time to analyze options.

Advertisements are on the street, all over TV, and pretty much everywhere you look, whether it's the back of a receipt from the grocery store telling you who does the best and fastest oil change in your city or even the blurb on Facebook selling you on what movie to see this weekend. If they tell us enough and their message aligns with our wants, we'll buy it without question. And as long as they keep telling us what to buy, we'll generally remain loyal.

This is valuable information for your own life, both corporately and personal. Once you've defined what you and your company stand for, your brand is simply a natural extension of how you hold yourself out to others and the value they can expect to receive from you. As a personal brand, it's not always as simple as holding yourself out as Starbucks, Pepsi, or Toyota. Sometimes it will be more nebulous, such as the brand you display to your spouse, friends, and family. In your corporate life, it's easier to create something concrete.

If you were to truly open up a company today, apart from the perspective shift of You Inc., you would need to think about the foundation and look of your company. What are the demographic and psychographic characteristics of your ideal customer? What company colours, logo, and look do you wish to present? And of course, what you stand for as a company must be reflected in your brand. Is it value, exclusiveness, quality, or effectivness that you're selling to the public? Within a second of hearing the name or seeing your logo, your brand should convey these attributes.

What do *you* stand for? What do you want someone to think about your value the second they meet you and in every interaction with you? Think about the brands you currently have in your life now. When you buy a cup of coffee, what store do you choose? And how loyal are you to that brand? If you're an avid Starbucks fan, and there isn't one near by, would Tim Hortons do or would that be mutiny? How about the coffee in your home? The yogourt you eat, the pop you drink, the brands of dairy you consume or the grocery store you shop at. What brands are you absolutely loyal to and which ones are you willing to substitute when they are difficult to obtain? Will you drive out of your way to shop at a grocery store that's less expensive? Look at the car you drive, the washer, dryer, or fridge you purchased recently. How about your computer, electronics, and even your watch. Examine with new eyes the advertising and marketing campaign that has made you loyal to your favourite products and services in addition to their value. Remember, there's an array of products and services on the market that might offer the same value at a lower price. Why do you choose to stick with the ones you do? And what made you try them in the first place? See advertising in a new way and understand how the large marketers use the message to define their brand.

Think of these brands for a moment: Häagen-Dazs, Mercedes-Benz, the Fairmont chain of hotels, Ruth's Chris Steak House, and Tiffany's jewellery. I assume that you equated those I listed as oppulent, luxurious, possibly dependable and expensive. (In relative terms—Häagen-Dazs ice cream is really just a few dollars more than its cheapest competitor, whereas with Mercedes-Benz the spread is obviously much larger.) What comes to mind when you think of these brands: H&R Block, Best Western hotels, President's Choice food, IHOP or Denny's, and Kia cars? You likely thought of value for the dollar, inexpensive, or convenience. Even if you've never purchased a Mercedes-Benz or driven a Kia, you're likely aware of their brand, the value they hold out to the public, and what they stand for. Keep in mind though, a brand says as much about the product or service as the person purchasing it. A Mercedes-Benz may be expensive, exclusive, and luxurious and that's exactly what the person purchasing it is looking for. They're hardly likely to ever even consider a Kia and vice versa. They might entertain the notion of a BMW, Lexus, or another luxury vehicle, but the chance they'd look at a Hyundai, Lada, or the like, no matter what the matching features were, would be slim. Conversely, no logic in the world or amount of advertising would convert the inexpensive car seeker to entertain the notion of spending twice or even four times as much on a luxury vehicle. They're totally different markets.

Does brand guarantee value? Absolutely not. Not always, anyway. Consider again a Mercedes-Benz, which I happen to drive. Most would agree that even though they are expensive, they are well engineered cars. Do they ever produce a dud? I would vote yes since I've had mine in for servicing much more than the domestic brands I had before. If you've never dealt with them, one might assume that a luxury car dealer's service must be impeccable. I too believed that, but only received excellent service the first year and would now, years later rate their overall service as very poor. So Mercedes' adverstising and brand convinced me to purchase a car from them once by aligning themselves with the type of car purchaser I am. Due to the fact that I didn't experience a superior product or service for the expense, I would not, no matter how much their brand tells me to, purchase their vehicle again. (This is my experience only—I do have a number of friends who are quite happy with their Mercedes'.)

I've always been a fan of the Dell computers. I've purchased more than six computers from them, and other than my first laptop, I'm absolutely thrilled with the company. Many individuals I've met over the years have tried to convince me to switch to a Mac, by telling me about the features they have over their PC counterpart. Despite the "cool" person I'll turn into based on the Mac commercials, I'm not convinced.

Analyzing Dell's advertising and direct flyer marketing, they provide excellent value. They're generally much less expensive than Apple computers since they sell to a large number of computer buyers. One might deduce that to keep costs down, they have buyers purchase online as much as possible, and therefore their services must be limited.

One thing that has kept me buying Dell and will likely have me doing so forever more is their absolutely impeccable service. I have called on Dell to fix problems that I knew were a result of my software, not hardware (most computer companies will only provide support on their hardware). Even though my warranty had expired a couple of years ago, they're always willing to support. On the last two occasions that I called Dell it took several hours for my computer to be diagnosed and fixed. They actually called me back later that day and on another occasion, that night (plus it was a Sunday evening), to ensure that the problem was resolved. It is revolutionary for a company these days to proactively follow up to ensure the job was done right. They even go so far as to send out an electronic survey the next day to solicit your feedback about what they could have done better.

Dell's brand to me is about providing affordable computers to the average person. In my experience, their brand also equates to true excellence in customer service. Most business people would agree that not only would their office shut down if their computers were to fail, but they'll personally shut down as well. It's a techie's world out there and we're at their mercy. With such trust being invested in the company an individual purchases from, it would take a great deal more than a desire to be cool or have a better tool for me to switch to a Mac. But then again, I'm likely not their market. My point is, a company can provide a low cost product followed by luxury service. We all might wish to aspire personally to that brand value.

This week, I want you to purchase three cups of coffee outside of your home, to-go, and save the cups. If you don't drink coffee, order tea. If you do neither, get a friend to save their cups for you.

I want you to visit a Starbucks, a Tim Hortons, and a generic coffee shop around town (a mom and pop type shop). Bring these three cups together and examine them extremely carefully. What does each cup represent? What does their brand mean to *you*? Are you even their target market? Think about who is and why they chose the colours, logo, and type of cup they did. Examine the cup's sleeve (if provided) and size, thickness, etc.

With Starbucks, you'll notice their clean white cup with green logo and writing. I find it brilliant to read the quotation on the back and the invitation to the drinker to visit the Web site and submit their own quotation to possibly be chosen. Notice their sleeve as well and, I suppose, the fact that they provide one at all. Who is their main target market? Perhaps yuppies who are willing to pay over $5 for the average coffee? People who are willing to pay more for the value that Starbucks provides them? Although they might be very busy, they're still willing to wait for their coffee to be custom brewed.

Notice the difference in colours between the Tim Hortons cup and that of

Starbucks. The last time I visited a Tim's, they didn't have any cup sleeves and if you asked because the coffee in one cup is just too hot, they'd put your drink into a double cup. I wonder if Starbucks customers would think of this as an environmental sin? Tim's also has the enticement of rolling up a rim and winning a car, a bike, coffee, or doughnut. Tim Hortons has very different food choioces from a Starbucks and always has the coffee brewing when you walk in, reducing the wait. There are a fewer choices at Tim's, but mostly it's like the original Ford—you can have any colour so long as it's black. Notice, too, the staff at both stores. Did you find one has employees with a bit of an attitude? After all, they're not coffee servers—they're baristas. Do you find the same level of enthusiasm for your double long caramel Americano?

Patrons are not just paying for what goes into the cup. They're also aligning themselves with the values they've come to know from either Starbucks or Tim's.

What about that third cup from the corner coffee shop? It's likely a plain, Styrofoam cup with a plastic lid. No sleeve and the contents can vary. What does that cup say about the business' brand, their value, the cup's contents, and the commuinity you've become a part of (in the coffee wars world anyway)? Absolutely nothing.

Recently, while in Vancouver, I found an Italian café on Robson that has some of the best food I've had in Canada. It was a tiny place, locally owned. I ordered their quesadilla to go and took it back to my hotel. I'm sort of like Billy Crystal's character in the movie, *Forget Paris* where he orders veal Parmesan in every restaurant in every city he visits. My vice is a quesadilla. I can say, without a doubt, across Canada and the US, this was the best one I had ever had. I ordered and took back one for dinner every night I could. Each night I stopped in, the fellows made me feel more and more at home. It was usually around eight that I made it in and they even offered to let me phone in advance so I wouldn't have to wait. One night, extremely hungry, my plan was to get another quesadilla and also walk to Capers (a local upscale grocery store), which was a few blocks down from the Italian restaurant. I thought I'd go to Capers first since it was about a quarter after seven and then hit the Italian café so that my dish would be warm. I was walking on the oppossite side of the street and noticed the café looked dark. Odd, I thought, for a quarter after seven in the middle of the week when I was usually there later. I crossed over and sure enough, they were closed. There wasn't even a sign on the door saying what their hours of operation were. I guess it was up to the customer to guess.

I was starving and thankful I had checked on my way to Capers or I wouldn't have bought enough for dinner. Although not tragic in the least, it was amazingly disappointing and irritating. I was looking forward to this dish. If I had known their hours of operation in advance, I would have ensured I arrived earlier.

Do your customers know your theoretical hours of operation? Are you driving away customers when you don't need to? These fellows that ran the business deserved a break indeed with an early night home and I guess they closed up shop prematurely as it was likely a slow night. This is where the small and big guys differ. You'll rarely see a large chain or franchise close up because it's slow or not have a sign with their hours. They know their brand implies consistency at the very least.

The very last night during that trip to Vancouver, I was able to savour my last and best quesadilla. The take home box was a simple white pizza box and as I took my last bite, I realized there wasn't anything on the box to remind me of the café's name, address, or phone number. I did pick up a card earlier in the week, but lost it. The next time I'm in Vancouver seeking my new favourite dish, I can only hope that they haven't moved and I can remember where they are located.

Don't be the blank Styrofoam cup or plain pizza box. Are you waiting for others to define you, leaving them with a less than memorable last impression? Your brand needs to be about substance—what makes you unique and defines your style. Ensure you've taken time to define yourself and then align with your market. You can't and won't be all things to all people. But don't let others label and brand you because you haven't done so.

To paraphrase Jay Abraham's sage advice from his audio program, *Your Secret Wealth*, never, ever, ever, ever stop educating others on what it is you do and what makes you unique.

Think of a few brands now that would most align themselves with what You Inc. stands for. Define what values and benefits they hold out to the public that you do as well. Are you solid, reasonable, reliable, and a little country like a John Deere tractor? Would Nike's slogan of "just do it" resonate more with your way of approaching life? Are you dependable and loyal, relating to State Farm's slogan—"Like a good neighbour, State Farm is there"? Or are you cool, hip, on the cutting edge of technology? Could you compare yourself and You Inc. with the iPod or the Mac campaign?

Now list all of the companies you can think of whose brand and/or slogan aligns with who you are right now:

____

____

____

____

____

____

____

List now all of the companies you can think of whose brand and/or slogan aligns with where you'd like You Inc. to be in the future:

List why; the values of those companies (as close as you can estimate); what markets they serve; what makes them unique; what is it about their substance, style, and message that keeps their competitive edge; and what you will adopt from all of this.

Now list what value *your* brand stands for in as many words as you can:

Any successful company knows the importance of market research and when possible, captures the feedback of their customers and market through a survey. Is it likely that what you think of your brand and the value you hold out to the world is not perceived similarly by others? I'd like you to consider developing a survey and contacting your friends, co-workers, and anyone you can think of and ask them the following questions. Explain in your note why you want their feedback—that you respect their opinion and want their honest thoughts. Ensure that you thank your participants promply for their time and let them know how much you appreciate their suggestions (whether you'll use their information or not). Here are some sample questions. Feel free to add more to the list:

- If you thought of me as a company, given what you know about me and how I hold myself out to the world, what would you say is my over all brand?
- If you thought of some major market brands (car companies, products, services, hotels, etc.), what companies or slogans would you say are most like me?
- If you could describe the value that I consistenly hold out to the world, what would you describe that to be?
- What do you think of my overall appearance? How would you rate my look, personally and professionally from 1-10 (ten being highest).
- If there were one or more things that I could change to make success in various areas of my life easier, what would they be?

What do you think about this notion of surveying those in your life? Do the questions make you nervous? Would you dare send this out? I highly encourage you to do so. First, it's not easy to hear the feedback of others, especially if criticism (constructive or not) is offered. Plus, those close to you may or may not answer honestly depending on how sensitive they know you to be. Encourage them to be honest. If you try this and receive the surveys back, take a deep breath and read them as the CEO and President of You Inc., remembering that this feedback is extremely valuable. Also keep in mind that you do not have to agree or act on any of the comments forwarded. What I want you to look for are patterns. If many of your respondents echo the fact that you're dependable but also rigid at times and to a potential fault, perhaps you should examine that. If some don't understand your corporate uniform but you know that it mirrors and respects your market, toss those comments aside. The idea is that the honest feedback about what others consider your brand to be is vitally important. If you think you're holding yourself out as Starbucks and many others see you as a Tim Hortons cup of java, or worse, the blank, unidentifed brew in the white Styrofoam cup, you have some work to do!

I travel all over North America on business, and I'm often shocked by how few hotels survey their business guests. As women, we have different travelling needs than men and are a highly growing market. Last year, I stayed at a hotel in Washington, DC, that was directly marketed as a woman friendly hotel. I was thrilled and couldn't wait for my stay. Upon arrival, nothing was further from the truth.

As a small boutique hotel, they were thin on the front end staff. Travelling with two suitcases, my laptop case, and my purse, my hands were full indeed. They lacked a bellhop or there wasn't one around. A few steps in from the front door were two large sets of stairs on the way to the elevator. Are you kidding me? Who has two huge sets of stairs to lug one's luggage up on the way to the elevator? Up in my room, I quickly noticed as I unpacked that this wasn't the female friendly hotel I was promised. The bathroom vanities were rediculously small. There were some benefits, such as an amazingly comfy bed and a few more upscale toiletries, however, there wasn't a makeup mirror or hair dryer, which is usually pretty standard in most hotels. Anyone familiar with the female business traveller knows that many women do not enjoy eating dinner alone in a restaurant in a strange city. When I got back to my hotel the first night after a very, very long day, I was a little surprised that the hotel didn't even have a restaurant. They did have a grill with four greasy options which were only available till 10 p.m. Before I retire for bed in a hotel, I lock every latch I can along with the usual hotel interior lock to reassure me of some security from hotel staff or others that may have access to the room. At least if they were to unlock the door (say the cleaning person in the morning and so on), with that interior latch locked, it would stop them from opening the door. This hotel did not have any of these security features. It simply had one lock and didn't even come equipped with a "do not disturb" sign.

Upon returning home, I received an electronic survey from the hotel and rated them poorly in every category, which I think was fair. I'm quite sure that when I'm in DC again or in a city where this hotel chain has a location, I definitely won't stay with them again. After the survey, I didn't receive any follow-up or what I felt was care or attention for my concerns during my stay, or even a thank you for taking the time to give them my very valuable feedback. After travelling all over North America in the past three years, I can shed some light on the little things that make a hotel great, but that hotel missed their opportunity.

The lesson learned from this hotel for me, and hopefully for you as well, is that just because a brand, marketing, or advertising campaign tells the public something (their style), it still needs to be backed up with substance. You can tell your market over and over again what you do best, your specialty, and benefits, but if you don't deliver, the damage can be potentially worse than remaining generic without conveying a message. At least with the latter, the expectation remains low.

Who is your customer *really*?

In your corporate life, who is your customer? If you're employed, you might suggest that your boss and the customers of that business make up your customer base. If you're self-employed, you might see your clients as your customers. As you examine your new business, You Inc., who is *your* customer now? Who do you serve? Who could be a customer? Where are your obvious and less obvious markets? Might I suggest to you that it could be almost anyone? Yes, anyone. True, you have a current market and that may or may not change, expand or contract ever. But thinking on a larger scale as you do now by being the CEO of You Inc. you really don't know the possibilities that lie before you—what new businesses you might own, work for or with, or who really will be your customer one day.

When I worked for the bank, individuals with large amounts of money were my customers. To some degree, because I relied on them to identify and refer me these high net worth individuals, the employees of the dozen or so branches I oversaw were my customers too. When I opened my firm, my clients were individuals who were also very wealthy. One might extract that the only individuals I needed to treat well, serve as VIPs, and pay attention to were the wealthy. That couldn't be further from the truth.

Were those really my only customers? Actually, when I published my first book, the UPS guy who delivered my mail purchased one of the very first copies. The point is, you have no idea who might be a potential customer, boss, partner, or resource one day. As the CEO of your corporation, you understand this, have the foresight and vision, and treat everyone as if they might be your customer one day.

When I was at the bank and had my firm, if I hadn't treated everyone I met along the way with respect independent of wealth or status, I can assure you that I would not be doing what I am today. Selling investments to the ultra wealthy didn't require me to make time for the postal delivery people, but I did. Today, one of the many offerings of my corporation are books that cost about $20. Who's my customer now? Just about anyone.

So, I ask you again to think of the many customers (one-time transactions) or clients (ongoing releationships) that you serve. Not only is your boss not your boss anymore, he, his wife, his friends, and more are now your customers too. What about your mail delivery person? Do you even know their name? The receptionist at your doctor's office, not just your co-workers, but their friends, family, and those in their network as well. Obviously, I could go on and on.

Your advertising and marketing campaign

I know you don't have an actual budget and even if you did, you're unlikely to take out a billboard advertisement or buy a series of television commercials telling the world why you and your personal corporation are special. However, you still need a strategy for telling the people in your world over and over again why and how you benefit their lives.

Why do you think Pepsi and Coke continue to spend the dollars that they do annually to keep their brands top of mind? If you've bought a cola recently, you'll know that there aren't really many choices. There are some no-name brands, the odd specialty cola, and Pepsi and Coke. So with such a small market of choice and worldwide brand recognition, why do these two companies continue to tell their market that they're the best, innovate constantly, rebrand, and more?

You too must become as shrewd in telling your world about your accomplishments, benefits, value, and uniqueness. This is not an easy thing for most, and many women especially, fight against it. Generally speaking, I think men are better at boasting about themselves. We're raised as children not to brag and as women we have more on our plates than the average man. According to the 2005 General Social Survey, which examined developments in time spent on paid work and unpaid household chores between 1986 and 2005, women still do most of the housework and tend to feel more time-stressed than men do. Men's contribution to the total household chores rose from 54% to 69%, but women still remained steady at 90%. Not only do they have chores at home, but women also generally have a high participation rate with their children's extra curricular activities and ever increasing work pressures. Women have more to tell the world about.

Consider first who makes up your world. Your spouse, kids, friends, family, co-workers, boss, clients, volunteer organizations, and more. They are the customers and market of You Inc. They can bring you happiness, joy, opportunities, peace, satisfaction, or quite the opposite. They can bring you up or tear you down. You need to educate them—advertise to them constantly about what it is you do, have done, have done for them, your value, and your uniqueness. Do not expect them, on a regular or even ad hoc basis to tell you why you're special, valued, important, and loved.

Many women are exceedingly successful at the role of martyr. They take care of everyone, sacrificing their own needs and putting the needs of others above their own. They hide or belittle their accomplishments when complimented and rarely point out their strengths and merits. They hope others will notice, remember, and make their efforts worthwhile. So often this is not the case. Think back to the work you've done for others this week or month alone. The many things at home and at work that went unnoticed. Now, think of how many times this month you were upset with your boss, client, someone at work, your kids, spouse, or others. Did they not notice when you dressed up and got your hair done for that important meeting? What about the entire weekend you spring cleaned your home and your family barely said thank you? How about the lavish dinner you put on for friends and family? The hours of preparation and cleanup time that came down to the 30 minutes it took them to shovel down the food without much thanks and minimal praise? Have you felt like the Little Red Hen this month, waiting and hoping for the praise and help you so justly deserve?

If so, I have two words for you. Stop It! Do not wait to point out your value now to everyone you meet. Is it boasting? Not necessarily. Sometimes, I suppose it could be construed by some as such, however, if you wait for praise and acknowledgement, you may never, or as readily, receive it.

Think how busy you are. Wouldn't you appreciate someone you love, care about, or respect taking the time to point out something that you've done and didn't receive acknowledgement for? It's not easy for many and if it's downright difficult for you, start small. Look to your spouse, parents, kids, or friends as a beginning point. Ask them if they enjoyed the meal you cooked or point out the great job you did painting the fence, cleaning the house, or knitting the sweater you just made for them. Remember, too, in asking for acknowledgement, you're also at times risking criticism. Your family may hate the dinner you prepared, but at the least your effort needs to be praised. Your family may really not like your choice of paint colour for the new family room. Again, your effort needs to be pointed out. Perhaps only you know that it took 30 hours to redecorate the room, seven hours for dinner and cleanup. Advertise and let your market know your value and never, ever, ever stop!

You might be thinking that you don't have anything new to tell others about, that they *should* recognize your efforts, and it's somehow diminished if you have to tell them. Like asking a spouse to pay more attention to you or to tell or show you they love you—many women will argue that it's not worth it or less meaningful if you have to ask. We do this in our personal lives and oftentimes, to our detriment, in our perfessional ones as well. We must tell the world about our value every opportunity that we have.

I saw two billboards this year that really caught my attention. They were each advertising products that are fairly well known to many and I thought didn't really have a new "offering" to sell. I was wrong. The first billboard I noticed a few months ago was for Shreddies cereal. I laughed so hard when I saw it and pondered its brilliance for some time afterwards. I'm sure you're familiar with Shreddies cereal even if you don't eat it. They're square bits of whole-wheat. The billboard exclaimed, "New and improved Shreddies. Now, diamond-shaped." It was hilarious and totally caught my attention. It reminded me of a cereal that I hadn't thought about since I was a child. They simply turned the square on its side and jokingly advertised that they weren't mere squares anymore—now they were diamond-shaped.

The second campaign that caught my eye was one organized over this past summer for Baileys. I personally have never had a Baileys drink, but even I can guess at how it might taste. Baileys is fairly well known to anyone who has ever had a liqueur or specialty coffee on a cold winter evening. However, this summer, they re-educated their market about the "new" Baileys Shiver. Simply add ice to Baileys and you too can have a refreshing summer drink! It's the simplest thing in the world and anyone could have thought of it, but the question is, would they? Would the winter Baileys customer think to add ice in the summer? They weren't chancing that their customer would think of it.

The next time you're in the market for a cocktail and visit a liquor store, look around at all of the specialty products and notice how many of them have a little recipe book around the bottle neck educating the consumer as the the many recipes and options for that product. And when you visit your grocery store in the future, see if they have a magazine featuring their products along with tantalizing recipes that sell more of their products. My all time favourite example is the Kraft *What's Cooking* magazine. It's an absolutely beautifully shot, well put together magazine featuring simple, time saving recipes that's not only free, but delivered to my home each month.

How often do you tell others about how they can better use you, your talents, your strengths, and your abilities? Are you educating your market, customer, spouse, friends, and more? In today's environment, you can't wait for your customers, whoever they might be, to best figure out your strengths and benefits. You need to tell them and do so often and creatively.

When do I need a brand?

I think every individual, company, city, province, and country needs a brand and then needs to communicate that message.

Let's take a stay-at-home mom, for example. She may not think she needs to define her own corporation or brand. After all, her intention might be to raise the kids until they leave home. She will interact with many during her career as a mother—teachers, other parents, spectators at the soccer games and piano recitals, and more. Perhaps one day, when the kids are all in middle school, she starts to get restless and wants to open a business from home or work part-time. The network and individuals she's met over the years through her children now become valuable resources. Although she didn't consciously develop her image, her network has formed opinions about her over the years. When she goes to them to sell what her new company is offering, to ask for help getting a job, or even request a reference, will they assist?

I don't care if someone is starting from scratch, is at the bottom of their industry and wanting to climb high, or is a student or unemployed. The time to define You Inc. and your brand is now, before others do. Not knowing with absolute certainty what your career or industry will look like next month or next year, how your company, market, or sector will change, and if you'll be calling upon someone that you never thought you would, it's vital to open and keep open ever door now and in the future.

During a recent trip to Vancouver, I was thinking a great deal about the notion of one's brand and debating if everyone should have one. I picked up a magazine that was supplied in my hotel room—*The Vancouver Review*. In the Spring 2008 issue there was an intriguing article titled, "Celebrity Cashier." The story was about Carmen Louie, a cashier at a local market. What was Carmen's claim to fame that won her a feature article in this magazine? Her success in learning over 4,000 names of customers who shopped at the market over the four years of her employment. Her inspiration? First, she wanted to genuinely make patrons feel good by remembering and saying the most important word to them—their name. Second, she admired the owner of a little grocery story near by. She noticed the owner knew everyone who came in by name. Carmen took the time to record the names, details, and unique features of customers in a little book by her till to allow her to personalize her service. In Carmen's small yet significant way, she improves the lives of others by treating them as friends instead of simply customers. Can you imagine what Carmen has also done to improve and grow the bottom line of that market? And should she wish to seek another employer one day or open a grocery store of her own, Carmen's larger vision of what her role is (not just a cashier, but a purveyor of old-fashioned service), she'd likely succeed at many career paths.

As your corporate policies change to suit your current personal and corporate lifestyle, so too should your brand. After you've read this chapter, go back to the policies and rules you drafted in chapter two. Do they align? Do they complement each other? Is some refining in order?

Looking after your largest investment

Your ability to earn income is the largest investment in your life. You might think it's your house (or future home), your pension at work if you have one, or your stock portfolio if you've built one, but you're wrong. None of them come close to the power and breadth of your ability to earn income as an employee or by becoming self-employed.

As it's the most valuable asset in your corporation, it would behoove you to take care and perform preventative actions to protect your investment—you! I learned at 33 that not taking small steps to take care of my teeth can lead to a great deal of pain, some damage that cannot be fixed, and a huge bill at the dentist since I don't have a health plan. If I had visited my dentist regularly, I wouldn't have had the excruciating pain of two teeth becoming abscessed while I was on the road. The tooth (thank goodness, a wisdom) that couldn't be saved had to be pulled. The other will likely need a root canal and hopefully not an implant.

It goes without saying that you must look after you, but it's much easier said than done. I truly believe it's within most women's DNA to look after others first. We take care of so many, rarely are good at saying no, and more often than not, don't ask for support, recognition, or acknowledgment when we should. We can wind up feeling worn out, unhappy, bitter, or worse. No one is going to take care of you better than you. Since you've been given this opportunity, this investment called you, you must treat it respectfully and with the care and attention that you would an heirloom or massive investment.

The branded vs. the authentic you

Recently, I had the opportunity to audition for a new show with the theme of branding. The producer kept structuring the idea of how to brand someone yet peel back the layers, like an onion, to uncover their true and authentic self. Take after take, I couldn't please the producer and it's no wonder they passed on me for the position of host.

I didn't say it during the shoot day since TV land is often different from real life, but your brand and your authentic or real self can be as varied as night and day. Your brand reflects what your corporate image should convey. It's about respect for your market and stands as a badge of consistent value. Your authentic you cannot be in total conflict with your brand. People can see if you're uncomfortable with the message and meaning that you're projecting. Starbucks coffee in a Tim Hortons cup and vice versa would soon be found out by their market and would likely take down each company. It's about style *and* substance. But it's also a grey area with many fine lines. I'm not even going to state a PVP here as your brand and the real you are paradoxical by nature. Your brand is an extension of parts of you, but it is not you. You must first seek what makes you authentic and then refine your brand incrementally.

Part of my brand and the value that I portray is that of extreme professionalism, exclusiveness, and specific expertise. Even though I'm no longer a practicing financial professional, people often see me as a fiduciary, or a person to trust for financial advice. Since I've invested for the ultra wealthy during a good portion of my career and am now a trusted media personality, I've carefully crafted and refined my brand over the years. Visually, I must present myself as I just described and in a way that my audiences would expect me to be. Even though I wear the hat of a writer many days a year, it would not be appropriate to show up to a media interview or presentation in jeans. I'm somewhat branded by my audience as a financial focused person even though I sold my firm and don't practice. If I were solely a writer, it might then be acceptable to show up in jeans, for example.

Many who know me can pick me out of a crowd or see my Louis Vuitton coming before they see me. It's a brand that works for my brand. Plus, I despise shopping (although I love buying) and will not succumb to the latest fads in accessories each season. In my early twenties after a boyfriend purchased my first LV bag, I was hooked. The practical side of me could justify the costs of future purchases. For instance, I used to spend at least $200 per year on a purse that would wear out or go out of style by the end of the season. Add that up over a ten-year period and that's $2,000 in just a decade. Most LV purses can be purchased for less than that. They never go out of style, are absolutely indestructible, and I still use all of mine, even the ones that are over ten years old. As my brand must portray many things, exclusiveness tops the list. Therefore, I've chosen to drive a Mercedes, write with a Montblanc pen, and carry a LV valise. Although my true self isn't concerned with the brands I use, using them doesn't take me outside of my comfort zone. My brands would not work for someone who's always been more practical and purchased a no name, less visual brand or for those that perhaps seek a more unique and one of a kind accessory. Your brand and those you choose to bring into your life must reflect you, but remember they're *not* you.

The PVP:

Simply because someone purchases a Mercedes-Benz and Louis Vuitton purse, it doesn't mean every purchase or service they seek is luxurious. They may have a car that cost $80,000 and a purse that cost $2K, but still buy the no-name ice cream. The individual driving the base car without power windows and dressed down, who dickers about prices, might actually be in the market for a $20,000 home entertainment system. Be cautious when judging a person by their appearance, toys, and assets. Do not make assumptions.

I'm a genuine, kind, loving, and mostly, non-judgmental individual. I know first-hand that a person's toys and things do not define them. But again, we're talking about brand. My look is classic and, although I do purchase some expensive clothes and things, they're still practically assessed. I might have a suit on that costs less than $200 that will not go out of style. Yes, my accessories might cost twenty times my suit, but don't think that because I spend on some things I spend the same on others. Keep that in mind about your market. They might be lavish with a car purchase, but the same individual might cheap out on ice cream.

In my time off, I do still wear my Louis Vuitton belt with my jeans. I like it and it's a practical belt that will still look great years from now when a regular one would have worn out. At the end of the day, when I'm able to be myself, my brand is relaxed, but not abandoned. That's why it must, absolutely must, be an extension of you, but not define you. If I were to trade in my uniform for a leisure suit and my Benz for a Smart Car, I can assure you I would feel out of sorts and eventually would crash and burn, or in the least, I would portray a phony exterior to my many markets.

Do be sure to try on as many options as possible before absolutely defining your brand and determining how it extends from the true you. When you do peel back your own layers and explore what makes you happy, remember your brand, your uniform, and the value you're portraying to your market must reflect you, but won't necessarily assist you in finding who that truly authentic you is. Be patient and willing to experiment. But also listen to those gut feelings and follow what feels right. That, above all, will help you define you and your brand. It can't be forced and won't reveal itself overnight. Think as the big corporations do and remember the person within yours—you!

Chapter 4

The CEO called You

As the CEO and president of You Inc., you are in charge. You set the rules, seek the counsel of outside experts when necessary (and have the self-esteem to do so), and work hard at building upon your strengths and reducing your weaknesses. Get ready to know what you know and of course, what you don't. These are two essential traits in a successful and long-lasting CEO. You needn't be strong in every aspect of your corporation, but you need to know what you do well and why, and to nurture it often. It's also essential that you understand not just your weaknesses, but what doesn't inspire you. The self-assured female CEO is confidently vulnerable at times, but always resourceful (especially when she doesn't feel it at all).

This chapter is about empowering you not with a tool chest of theoretical notions, but a jewellery box of diamonds in the rough waiting for you to polish: They are time-tested concepts executed in my own life and that of many others; they are the result of years of personal mistakes that you can now avoid, and they are ready for you to cut and polish to the exact finish you desire.

Become an investigative journalist

Trusting the wrong person or source could cost you much more than potential embarrassment; it could cost you a great deal of time, money, your health, and possibly even your life. I'm not suggesting that you question every bit of information offered to you by the media, your friends, or those you trust, but I do caution that when you're acting on any information, you must be aware of the correctness of the advice or material in question. The more you trust the individual or source offering this data, the more vigilant you must be about its accuracy.

A few years ago when my mom had a rental property, my brother, in passing during a card game, told her she could sell her rental whenever she wished with no tax consequence. During a casual conversation with my mom, she mentioned this seemingly small nugget offered by my brother. When I told her the opposite was actually true, she questioned my authority on the subject.

Sidebar:

In Canada, you can sell your principle residence without paying tax on the increase in the value of your home from the time you purchased it (assuming it did increase) until the time you sell it. Your principle residence is a property that you primarily live in. If you have two homes you lived in equally, for example, you can only deem one your "principle" residence. You cannot write off the interest on the mortgage of your principle residence unless that mortgage is specifically attributed to an income-earning project. For example, if your home were fully paid off and you then took a mortgage on it to fund the purchase of a rental property, invested it in a selected investment portfolio or business venture, your mortgage interest could then be tax deductible. However, the average individual's mortgage is structured so that they cannot deduct their interest, although if their home increased in the value over time, they would benefit from the tax free growth when they sold it.

The reverse is true with a piece of real estate that is not a principle residence (one that you do not live in). With this type of real estate, you would pay capital gains taxes if the property increased in value from the time you purchased it to the time you sold it. There is a calculation that factors in many other considerations such as cost for buying and selling the property, etc. If the real estate is rented out, that income is also taxable. As a benefit, any debt or mortgage on the property would receive a tax deduction on interest paid and other expenses for maintaining the property (i.e. if you had a manager look after it). Always seek the advice of a qualified tax accountant, lawyer, financial advisor, and realtor if you're considering real estate as an investment.

It's funny that sometimes family won't trust you even though you might be an expert in a subject. I reasoned with my mom that during my twelve-year career as a financial professional I spent a great deal of time specializing in the needs of clients that owned real estate. She still didn't believe I was right. I asked, didn't she remember that I was a board member on the Apartment Association of my city? I even further tried to convince her by telling her about the many estate planning presentations I had done in the past.

She still didn't fully buy in that I was correct, but at least called her accountant who confirmed that I was in fact right. During a casual conversation with her son, a very successful businessman, but with limited financial expertise, my mother was more open to believing his advice over my professional counsel. I would have the same frustrating experiences with many clients over the years who chose to trust some neighbour's advice over mine or that of a mutual fund manager with decades of experience and years of schooling. Time and time again, I've witnessed friends, family, and clients that heeded the unfounded advice of others to their financial detriment. Should my mother have acted upon my brother's advice, and sold her home at an unfavourable time, she would have been shocked with a tax bill that might have been higher than it had to be. It would certainly have been unexpected and would likely be unbudgeted for.

I too have fallen prey to accepting wholeheartedly the advice of those that I admire, respect, trust, and feel are dependable sources of credible information. I suppose since I've become a writer delivering information that will be trusted by hundreds or thousands, I have a new fiduciary duty of doing my best to ensure that the information I disseminate has been verified and is as accurate as possible.

While writing *The Woman's Guide to Money*, I was reading an article in a magazine that I've been a fan of for years and trust immensely. It's an alternative, healthy living publication and I faithfully pick it up every month. This issue was focused on the many prescription medications that Canadians are taking and their adverse health effects. The particular article that caught my eye was about how the big pharmaceutical companies are trying to patent placebos. Placebos are used in many medical studies. When given by a doctor and told it's medication, it has been found that a patient can benefit as much or more from a placebo than from the pill itself. The article was projecting that the drug companies could make billions of dollars by capitalizing on this simple pill.

I was infuriated and thought it was about time an article was written exposing the manipulation of those made vulnerable due to their poor health. I was thrilled that the writer discussed the many benefits of belief and why a placebo works in the first place. The fact that the pharmaceutical companies were capitalizing on this human miracle of belief and healing, to cash in was upsetting. How appalling, I thought, and wanted to include a reference to the article in my book to support the case I was presenting to readers about placebos and nocebos.

During the editing phase, my godsend of an editor Dan questioned this article. He went above and beyond what his role on the project required by doing some research as to the merit of this information. With some digging, he found a number of Web sites debunking the notion that drug companies were getting into the patenting of placebos.

I was embarrassed and horrified to say the least. I was going to pass this incorrect information on to my readers based on two things: one, my total belief in this very trusted and credible magazine, and two, my disbelief that the public health provided by the drug companies could be anything altruistic. I, of course, acknowledge the many, many life-saving and beneficial medications on the market, however, it seems these days, there are more on the market trying to fix what we as humans need to address on our own instead of taking the easy way out and turning to medication.

Common sense should have prevailed, but those two beliefs overshadowed my normal reasoning. If I were actually thinking for myself instead of believing this writer and magazine, I would have questioned the fact that drug companies were patenting sugar. A drug company can't do that. They can't own, a naturally occurring substance. They'd have to develop their own unique formula to register a patent.

I suppose no one would have died at the end of the day, or lost money, sleep, or time if Dan hadn't caught my mistake. However, it would have caused me considerable embarrassment, humiliation, and I would have deemed it a personal failure to my readers. It was simple laziness on my part or a lack of understanding and appreciation for truly checking my own source, independent of my belief that the magazine and writer checked theirs.

I could share with you countless more examples from the past few years since I've been writing where I've deliberately or casually sought the knowledge of others and trusted what they said. Then, once I investigated further, I found them to be incorrect. The point here is not to seek revenge or use fact checking to point out that the person was wrong. It's to ensure that *your* belief is valid.

What if a doctor told your loved one they had cancer and it turned out to be a misdiagnosis or a mistake with a file? There is a belief that because doctors are extremely well trained and educated they don't make mistakes. The same logic can be extended when a teacher might categorize your child as being slow, having ADD, or worse. What about your financial future? Whose facts are you trusting and at what cost?

Fact checking can't be limited to acquiring information and advice from others. You must be careful when of encouragement, criticism, and anything that affects your self esteem, what you believe to be true or your capability to do anything. Don't fall prey to my billboard example, the boyfriend that tells you that you'll never "make that much money in your life," the friend that tells you you'll never be a good mother, or the boss who informs you you're just not talented enough. Distance yourself from all information you've collected and see the world of knowledge and advice as a journalist would. Practice impartiality.

The PVP:

No one can make it in this world based solely on what they know. We all need what others know and can teach us. Knowing when to call on those in your network for their advice and expertise can greatly decrease the time it would take you to find out the same information. We also need to employ experts in our lives—doctors, lawyers, financial professionals, and the like. The caveat, though, is that it's still your responsibility to check your sources and ensure that information is correct. Remembering, too, that the more you trust the individual and purveyor of that information, the less likely you are to doubt it or their accuracy. Don't fall prey to this. Always check your sources!

Be very careful who you hang around with

I've always prided myself on being independent and fairly self-assured. But how can one not help but be defined by those we surround ourselves with, for better or worse? And who influences you more than those intimately close to you? These are the people that can potentially bring us up in life or do us the most harm.

If we admire them in any fashion, it can open up the possibility of exploring new aspects of life and ourselves. I don't care how set we are in our ways. If we decided tomorrow to surround ourselves with health fanatics, those behaviours, attitudes, and lifestyles would be bound to rub off on us. Conversely, if we were to replace the people in our lives and chose those that lived for the moment, partied every night, and abused substances, sooner or later our inner judgment would be tainted. Basically, those that we surround ourselves with eventually assist in defining our rules, and what's acceptable and justifiable in our world.

It's essential that you carefully examine those that you spend the most time with. Do they build you up or bring you down? Certainly it's not always that simple and clear-cut. You may have several people in your life that can provide both comfort and frustration—sometimes within the same day. I'm not suggesting you dump those that challenge you, otherwise you might not have a soul to communicate with.

Take an inventory of those you spend the most time with, those with whom you are most intimate, and examine what you'd like more of in your life. Are they in conflict? Do they align? Would you like to be more of a go-getter, but all of your friends are unambitious and your spouse sleeps until noon on Sundays? Instead of wiping the slate clean of those in your life, perhaps you could join a running group and start introducing yourself to people who are already succeeding at what you'd like more of one day. Those people will give you permission to consider new rules and possibilities for your life.

After my relationship ended with my first real boyfriend when I was 21, I thought the way to get ahead in the man's world that I chose to work in was being tough and more masculine. Growing up with two older brothers, I could easily be one of the guys. The problem is that a woman who tries to act more male misses what makes women unique and special. Women can bring many benefits to the table, and these get left behind when she tries to be just one of the guys.

It took my next major relationship to open my feminine side. The man (yes, much older again) that I spent my early to mid-twenties with treated me like a queen. He was close to the knight in shining armour the fairy tales had promised. He thought I was brilliant and the fact that I was so much younger than he made him appreciate my maturity that much more. He gave me permission to "be a lady" and explore my ultra feminine side as he always insisted on taking care of me in a number of ways. After feeling intellectually inferior and having to prove myself tough and able to take care of myself in my previous relationship, this situation was absolutely refreshing. It felt great to be thought of as an equal. (I had a great, high paying job at a bank at the time, although I didn't make as much as him.) Many of my friends commented over those years about the change they had seen in me, how I softened and seemed to embrace my feminine side. It took this man's constant yet gentle encouragement to help me understand that I could be accepted and appreciated while not having to prove to anyone that I was one of the boys.

As I refined my micro rules for my personal corporation, this man in my life liked to dress up as much as I did. On a casual Sunday afternoon, instead of wearing jeans and a shirt as most people do, our uniform was black pants and dress shirts or some business casual attire. During the week, we both wore suits to work and almost never, as a couple, wore jeans. We were very similar in many ways and it was easy for both of us.

Fast forward to my thirties and the relationship I've had with Wyatt the past several years. We couldn't be more different from each other in almost every way. I was attracted to Wyatt for many reasons, but the initial one was his unusually high intellect (compared to those in my circle of friends at the time). He had and has a superb vocabulary, is well versed on a variety of subjects, and is educated and informed on topics I had never even thought of. He was very different from the man in my previous relationship, and although he immediately treated me as an equal and with respect, he didn't revere me and put me on the pedestal that my last love did. Curiously enough, I was finally ready for someone in my life that would challenge me, wasn't a yes man, or abusive like my first guy. However, Wyatt was and still is very, very different from me. It's taken me most of our relationship to appreciate these differences. I wanted to give up a number of times and once in a while, still do. In the past, I chose men that I could learn and grow from, but who at their core, were still somewhat or very similar to me. They were overambitious, type-A personalities like myself. Again, to paint you a picture, Wyatt is totally, in almost every way, with the exception of our core values, different from me. It creates many challenges for us both to be together. But true growth comes from those who think, act, and do things differently than us. I must preface, though, by stressing the importance of having the same core values as your partner to be able to make it through those challenging growth times. Your core values must be agreed upon, voiced, and aligned for your relationship to last.

Wyatt has given me a new level of permission that I needed in my life. For years he encouraged me to find my authentic self. Through our many adversities and differences, he accepted me unconditionally and taught me to care less about what others thought of me and tune more into what I thought of myself. He was the first person I had met and spent time with who was truly non-judgmental of me and my actions. He didn't care what others thought, which was something I was battling personally at the time.

My first boyfriend challenged me by thinking of me and my life as insignificant. I used that disrespect to get tougher. My second relationship softened me and assisted me in getting to know my feminine side. My current relationship, the most important, encourages both the tough and female me, but more importantly, the real me.

I'm not suggesting that the only way to find change in your life and bring out new and empowering beliefs and behaviours is simply to change the love in your life, but when you wake each day and spend numerous hours with someone, their views on life will make an impact on yours. They can improve your environment or sully it. We play a part in every moment and are absolutely responsible and in control of our lives at the end of the day. It is easier though when our life partner, friends, family, and social circles work to build us up. And it's imperative that we use the times when we allow ourselves to be broken down as lessons to use as armour for the future, not build up scar tissue.

Although my relationship with guy #2 was generally much easier, with fewer arguments and disagreements since we were so similar, I didn't grow as a person. Had I stayed with him, I would have been blissfully ignorant as to the opportunities I would have never known. I would have been happy with what I had—likely.

Today, I am unequivocally doing, working, and serving others in ways I had never dreamed could exist for me. Service has always been top on my career value list. In the financial industry, working with a majority of clients who were wealthy, helping them to make more money, was rewarding most of the time, but not truly fulfilling. I always volunteered as much as I could to fill up the hole of service, but I selected organizations that challenged me corporately and could benefit my networks and résumé instead of choosing groups that I was passionate about, which only made that hole grow larger over the years. Hindsight is an amazing thing.

Today, I am an author, speaker, and regular media personality only because of Wyatt. Case shut. To be sure, I had to be the one to take risks, run with opportunities, work the long and arduous hours to finish these projects, and feel the fear each time I walked on stage or faced the cameras, however, the personal growth, those opportunities, and my career path never, I can say confidently, in a million years, would have crossed my mind if not for him. It was only with his continual planting of seeds, working with me to see a brighter future, and introducing me to material that I've spent so many years researching, that I am typing these words for you to read. I'm living a life more rewarding, enriching, and fulfilling than I could ever have dreamed.

Be very careful of whom you share your time with. Should you have disagreements with others and find them frustrating because they're so different, be careful not to toss aside and judge those individuals too hastily. It's about creating a balance in your life network. Assess all of your relationships and ensure that you have a healthy mix of individuals who are like you, easy to be around, inspire, and positively support you. But be sure to include those that call you on your crap, will never be "yes" people, and will think differently to you and challenge you to strive to reach new heights. Do not be afraid of or intimidated by them. Watch, listen, and learn if you can. Make a conscious decision to spend time with each person in your life and when needed, add new resources to your network.

Sidebar:

The relationships I'm referring to in this section deal with generally healthy yet possibly undesirable partnerships. I'm not referring to abusive relationships, which need to be addressed quite differently. If you are in an abusive relationship of any kind or know someone who is, seek help immediately. Look in your Yellow Pages for resources. Visit a library to make safe phone calls or gather information on organizations that can help to end the abuse you or someone you know is suffering. If the abuser lives with you, please be courageous but also very careful when seeking help. Don't make calls from your home if possible or search for help on the Internet, as searches can be found later and may anger and set off the abuser. Find solace with a friend, at a police station, or in library resources. If you work with an abuser, please take the same careful steps. Meet with authorities or lodge your complain with executives, but make those calls off-site and out of your office.

When taking stock of those in your life, take a corporate stance: Remember that no successful company seeking to innovate and grow will continue to hire the same type of people; they'll have an appreciation for those who think, act, and see things differently. As the president and CEO of your corporation, ensure you're not bringing more people on board who duplicate others already there. You're not going to tolerate those who bring the corporation down with their negative attitudes and destructive, mismatching styles, but you're also not going to fire or not hire someone simply because you don't get them or they're too different. Be objective at all times. Look for complementary as well as challenging styles to your own.

I'm reminded of a friend of mine who worked for one of our major arts not-for-profit organizations in the city. She was frustrated with the continuous deficit of nearly a million dollars annually. The donors were generous, gifting several million a year, not to mention the actual performance sales, which were solid. As we discussed what was going on with the structure and staff, she lamented that not only were employees impulsive and flippant with budgets because of the frequent lack of accountability, but also, they hired all the same type of people. She cited that the new head of marketing was a creative artist types who was actually a retired performer with no specific marketing education or experience. My friend had exceptional skills and expertise, but was passed up for the position because she was from "outside" the arts community. Left brain, linear companies need creative individuals. Creative companies hoping to be innovative need type A individuals to do the books. We must embrace each other's differences. I encourage you to welcome different types of people into your new life. Your new corporation's future is dependent upon the diversity of your network.

The 1% solution

My business coach and sweetie, Wyatt, offers this creative thought. There are a few books on the market touting the 10% solution. The notion is to do just 10% more for a life of improvement. Wyatt offered the 1% solution to me during one of our coaching sessions and I've found it to be easy, practical, and genius in its simplicity. I know from my advising days that if everyone simply saved 10% of their income during their lifetime, most would be financially set in retirement or at least, have a solid financial foundation. Unfortunately, very few ever do. Have you practiced this prudent financial strategy? Statistically speaking, likely not. What about 1% of your income? How simple and painless would that be? Apparently, Scotiabank has figured out this notion of simple savings with their Bank the Rest program. It is a brilliant and, I think, revolutionary concept of disguising the pain of saving by blending it with spending. The concept is that by rounding up your purchases to the next $1 or $5 increment, by the end of the year, you will have an amount saved that seemed to come about effortlessly during your daily spending. Scotia gives the example that you would turn your everyday lunch purchase into $975 of savings at the end of the year, if you ate lunch out each day, five times a week, and you enrolled in the $5 round up program for an entire year. Assuming your lunch costs $6.25 per day your purchase would be rounded up to $10 and the difference would be $3.75, which Scotia would transfer at the end of the day into a high interest savings account with no fees. Nearly a thousand dollars at the end of the year is enough for you to take a vacation, buy new furniture, or make a significant RRSP contribution for your future. In five years, those effortless steps will grow your $975 to $4,928.47 (assuming a modest 2.75% rate of interest and that you continued the program with the same criteria for five years). That's a significant long-term benefit. Most of us wouldn't miss a few dollars from our account and Scotia has smartly marketed the Bank the Rest program by saying "you don't have to change your spending habits to become a saver."

This isn't an advertisement for Scotiabank and their products, however, I don't know of a another bank currently employing such a well-packaged system for simply, yet almost unnoticeably saving money. If you'd like more information about the program or to enroll, whether you're a Scotia customer or not, visit *www.scotiabank.com*.

I truly believe that in this new millennium of casualness, blurred lines, and overly relaxed gallantry, it's easier than ever to stand out in every area of your life. Never before have people dressed down more, demanded less formal restaurants, and shown up in their jeans to black tie events or the symphony. In Alberta, our government recently started and massively advertised a campaign called Create a Movement. One radio advertisement I remember in particular I heard as I was driving. It featured a young boy calling a life insurance company. He sounded as though he was around ten years old. The boy starts asking the insurance agent about all different types of coverage. The agent, perplexed, asks the child how old he is and why he's calling. The child replies that he needs to look after his estate early, since his generation is the first in history that will have a shorter life expectancy than their parents. I thought what has the world has come to that our provincial government has to educate parents and kids via the radio waves and Internet as to what should be common sense—we need to move, get fresh air, and eat healthy. It seems that common sense is not so common for the average individual any longer.

You need look no further than the lack of customer service you're likely to receive today in the retail sector. True, there are exceptions. I recently visited Montreal and shopped the stores of St. Catherine Street exhaustively. Almost, without exception, every store employee worked extremely hard to wait upon me, greet me upon arrival, search for alternative sizes and styles, and they even upsold me at the check-out counter by asking if I'd like sunglasses with that hat or a purse with those shoes. Having shopped thoroughly in every other major city in Canada and many in the US, I can report that the service is not as consistent as that which I found in Montreal. Far too often, I can browse a deserted shop for 20 minutes before a sales person acknowledges my presence, let alone assists with sizes and options. Some seem so bothered I've entered their store or interrupted their phone conversation with their friend that they haughtily ring my purchase through with a roll of their eyes. It's certainly not limited to retail. One can find the same poor attention to detail and service in the hospitality, car industry, and more.

This is fantastic news for both you and me. We can simply improve our world, our chances for success, love, happiness and much more by purely increasing our effort just one simple percent each and every day. Choose what you wish. One day it might be to focus on your relationship. Instead of something big and effort-filled to let your spouse know how much you love them, you might simply leave an I Love You Post-it Note on the bathroom mirror. Two seconds, three words of writing, and rip the note off and adhere to the bathroom mirror. Today, you may wish to be a better friend. In the dozens of e-mails one of your acquaintances has to fish through and reply to in a day, how pleasantly surprised might they be seeing your e-card? With Apple's free e-cards, you don't need an account or even user name and password to remember. Pick a card, write a "thinking about you and hoping you have a great day" kind of message. In two minutes or less, with minimal effort and no cost to you, you've made someone feel very special and thought of. And who knows, they just might have needed that more than you could know. For work tomorrow or that client meeting, you might just straighten your hair today or get up just five, not thirty or sixty minutes earlier this morning and yes, forget the workout, but do five minutes of tummy crunches. Is your house a disaster and the yard full of weeds? Do you have hours of work and nowhere to find them? What about two minutes to a cleaner life? Not an hour or day of labour and devotion. Just two minutes. Clean out the cutlery holder in your draw. Wipe down one shelf in the fridge. Pull six weeds.

I recently had a summer barbeque at my home. Having a tremendous number of friends and a very large family, my menu had to be carefully planned. I always analyze not just the cost of the food but the ease in preparing it, grilling it, and presentation. For this gathering, a few huge and superbly priced salmon fillets from Costco were on the menu in addition to other things. Salmon is the easiest dish in the world to barbeque since it requires little preparation and not even a turn or much monitoring. I wrapped it up in foil, cut a few onion pieces for flavour, and sliced a few lemons and arranged them on the fish for taste and presentation. During my grilling, a fellow from my gathering came over to see how the food was coming along. We checked the salmon together and he seemed amazed at the presentation of it even before it was in the dish. I felt like a gourmet chef as he declared, "wow, I guess that's what people without kids have time to do." I took it as a compliment, but was taken aback as well. He and his wife have three kids and, true, I don't have any. However, how much time and effort does it really take to cut up a few garnishes of lemon, find a nice plate to serve it on (mine was a trendy, new, oversized square plate that I picked up a Superstore for under $10), and drizzle pre-made store-bought dill dip? Since salmon, unlike burgers, meat, or other grilling options takes almost no effort to cook, was it really such a big deal to spend less than 1% extra effort to impress my guests and make them and myself feel special?

Think now what 1% increments you're willing to try in your life this week. Pick one area of your life each day and have fun—it's just 1% of your energy. Put on some mascara when you normally wouldn't without a special occasion. Or, take 1% of your monthly income and start an investment account or buy something fun and rewarding for yourself. What about just 1% more effort in calls made or research conducted—how might that propel your career? Just one more page written with the goal to finishing your book or a few extra minutes of studying?

Now, declare today, I will commit to improving my life and those around me by simply 1% this week in the following areas with the written specific tasks of:

Work:

____
____
____

Personal development:

____
____
____

My appearance:

____
____
____

My friendships:

____
____
____

My family/children:

____
____
____

My spouse or seeking a new love:

____
____
____

Hobbies or finding one:

____
____
____

Contribution to others:

____

____

____

My environment (your home, office, car, etc):

____

____

____

Cleaning up my clutter (e-mail, cupboards, drawers, closets, filing at work, etc.)

____

____

____

These are amazingly small steps that, I promise, will add up over a week, month, year or lifetime. Don't discount that planting even the smallest seeds will multiply before you know it. If you choose to work toward improving your life incrementally up to 10% above your current energy levels, you'll see those seeds bearing fruit quicker and more abundantly.

Goal setting vs. do setting

In my first two books, I detailed sections outlining the importance of goals and how to achieve them. I also had detailed formulas for analyzing your goals and testing them according to your life values (what I called the acid test).

Setting goals is a great way to focus. As I received feedback over the years from others, I've heard from so many that they know they "should" sit down and list their goals, but rarely do.

I must admit that at times I haven't taken my own advice. As eager enthusiasts who read my book approached me after talks, the first thing they would ask is about my one, five, and ten-year goals. They assumed that I would have some extreme clarity and be able to spout out, with detail, exactly what my life was to bring as if I were a fortune teller.

What I found in these instances is that I would fumble and give vague answers with a bunch of qualifying statements and sometimes wishy-washy remarks. It was time for me to stand back and understand why specific goal setting wasn't working for me either, even though in theory it's a valid process.

Most individuals don't have a clear idea of what they want from life if they have any idea at all. Many of us know what we don't want, and sometimes that's an excellent start, but if our future is fuzzy, then the act of sitting down to set goals becomes an unclear extension of that.

There are times to set specific and times to set vague goals. You may want a new living room sofa, so you start saving for it and get it. You may have a goal of going on a family vacation next year, plan for it, and then do it. Specificity in part is the key. You know what you want, you know or find out what's needed, and you go after it and likely get it.

The danger, excitement, and I believe, opportunity, lies in the unknown. It is one of the great paradoxes of You Inc.—you set goals to focus on, but you also must consider that if you're too focused in one direction, you might just miss an opportunity of a lifetime.

As stated previously, I never in a million years thought, or had a goal, of writing a book. I was quite happy running my financial planning firm and it was simply out of necessity and at the suggestion by my business coach that I wrote my first book. I also never intended ever to be in front of a camera for media interviews or speaking professionally. I sat in my office, advising clients, and was content and quite focused on acquiring other smaller financial firms to fuel my growth. If I had concentrated on my goals of buying other businesses and staying within the financial industry in the same capacity, I would never have been open to the possibilities in the world of writing, publishing, and speaking. However, it was not "goal setting" that opened the world of authorship to me. So, if goal setting helps some of the time but does not guarantee that you'll achieve what you desire and could hinder you from actually seeing an opportunity that's better for you, what is the missing element?

Do setting

I have spent a great deal of time examining what the missing element is and in one word, it's *doing*. "Do setting" is a less formal mode of goal setting. It's structured in smaller chunks such as daily to-do lists. When you are uncertain of what you want, where you want to be tomorrow, next month, year or decade, you might find those time frames fuzzy. Do not despair, but do! Do something, do anything! Even if you think what you do has absolutely nothing to do with your desired goal, you never know what side benefit it might produce, what nugget of knowledge or insight you may learn, or the people you might meet along the way who will change you life.

I write these pages only because of "do setting" that had absolutely nothing to do with this book. Last spring, I returned home from being on a number of speaking, media, and book tours. I was absolutely burned out. I had never been truly burned out before and wasn't sure how to handle it. I couldn't think another minute. After a few days of deciding what to do with my summer and my new career, I found inspiration in a wheelbarrow that had never before been touched, in my yard.

As a financial geek most of my career and a staunch suit-wearing, French manicured, don't-get-the-hair-wet-or-break-a-sweat kind of girl, I must admit, yard work and gardening has never been on my list of hobbies or goals. Ten years in my current home and I don't think I had ever mowed a lawn or shovelled a walk in the winter. I'm far from a diva, but getting dirty and sweaty just wasn't my thing.

That all changed thanks to the inspiration of my wheel barrow starring at me one summer day as I sat on my patio gazing out into space, looking for the universe to provide some life clarity. Within a few months, I had absolutely re-landscaped my backyard. I traded in my suit and pearls for gardening gloves and shovels. I dug, planted, sweated, and had the summer of my life. I had no clue what I was doing most of the time, since I had no experience with the simplest of backyard challenges. I dumped over too-full loads of dirt with my wheel barrow, used oil paint when I should have used latex, and spent as much time fixing my errors as making headway.

During this new physical phase of my life, a side that I didn't know existed within me, many things happened. I gained appreciation for that which I never paid attention to or realized existed like the multitude of unique bug life, migratory birds, plants, shrubs, and flowers. But more importantly, this phase shattered my limited belief in what it was that I could do. I'm not sure when or where along the way in life I bought into the belief that getting dirty and doing what my neighbours told me was "man's" work was outside of my ability. I'm not saying I'm gifted, talented, or even slightly skilled in the green thumb area, but I do love it. It's a love I never would have discovered if not for being burned out and having a wheelbarrow for inspiration.

Something curious also started to happen. As I started to "do" things in my yard, my mind became exceedingly clear and creative, which has also never come naturally to me. Ideas flowed with more ease than ever in my existence. I would paint for an hour and write down thoughts for my book for two hours afterwards. As I focused on doing something else, the doing of a goal I hadn't even set yet was starting to occur.

You too will find countless times in your life when you are bored, restless, uncomfortable, despondent, miserable, burned out, and more. Embrace these times. They could be the start of a new career, life love, hobby, or the realization of a dream you didn't know you even had. The key to remember though is to "do" something when you don't have a clue "what" to do. You must arrive at that doing with trust. Trust that although you have no idea what the connection is or will be towards what you truly desire, it will become apparent in time. Try it for yourself. Ensure you give the process enough time before you pass judgment. It might take a week, year, or even a decade to see the full circle of your efforts and how do setting sometimes trumps the highly touted goal setting.

The PVP:

We do need goal setting. It goes hand in hand with doing. However, when the absence of clarity exists, that's when you must use do-setting. When you do know or have an idea of what you'd like in life, that's when goal setting is effective and most enjoyable. You'll find some goal setting strategies in the following pages and I encourage you to pick up a book or audio program specifically designed to assist you in setting, defining, and assessing your goals.

Determining what you want from life

Starting with your core values is certainly a beginning in identifying what you want to do in life and extract from it. As far as examining the type of career or business that's best suited to you, even ones you've never considered before, you must first find one or more traits that define, drive, and move you. What thing do you need to do? Once you've identified that, and are open to a world of possibilities, you'll find that there is no one industry, career path, or position that exclusively fits. Hopefully, over time as you understand and seek this common denominator, you'll find not only clarity, but also more options.

Consider all that you take pleasure in. Think of the jobs and positions you've held in the past. List all of the things you enjoyed most from them, even if you didn't necessarily like the industry or specific job you held. For example, if you were a server in your teens, did you love interacting with people? If you've had a job in manufacturing, did you love creating something that others would use? Or, seeing a product that you helped build? If you were a social worker or in the health care field, did serving others and improving their quality of life drive you? List as many details as you can think of and try to be as specific as possible. Each time you list something you liked from a job, volunteer position, or another activity, next to that, ask, why did you like that? It will help you drill down to your common denominator.

Identifying your common denominator

Please list your current and past likes from jobs, volunteer work, hobbies, and friendships.

____

And why? ____

____

And why? ____

____

And why? ____

____

And why? ____

____

And why? ____

____

And why? ____

____

And why? ____

____

And why? ____

____

And why? ____

____

It may take you some time to complete this list and if you have more than ten items, do pull out a separate sheet and keep going. See if you can locate a common theme in your job satisfaction, friendships, and hobbies.

Using myself as an example, I found my common denominator to be "of service," but specifically giving advice. There were a number of secondary common themes, but that one was the most prevalent in each of the positions I've held. However, it wasn't until I become a writer, speaker, and media personality, in addition to my career in the financial industry, that I could see the common denominator. In examining my new career a while back, I asked myself, how can I be so happy and fulfilled in this new career, which is very creative and so different in every way imaginable from my life at the bank or when I had my firm, but yet I loved those positions and felt totally fulfilled at the time? I too completed the above exercise. What stood out was that in each position I've had in my career, I was able to serve, which is very important to me, and was able to achieve it through giving advice and solving problems. In my financial firm, I solved financial problems and gave my clients investment and other planning advice. Now, in a new world entirely, I still achieve those same goals by giving advice through books, columns, media interviews, and lectures. I'm serving through very different media. My current career path supports my common denominator and, as a result, I still feel fulfilled, even more than I could ever imagine.

However, if my new career had been creative, as it is, but my end result were say a painting, or some art that was a personal expression but didn't potentially solve a problem for someone, it would have left me feeling totally unsatisfied. Your situation might be exactly the opposite.

Consider your common denominator with friendships and hobbies. In my above example, in my hobbies in order to feel fulfilled during my down and personal time, my common denominator is to create things that can be seen, felt, and are complete, such as planting a tree or flowers, painting the house, or renovating a room. My hobbies solve no problems at all (assuming the house and yard weren't falling apart in the first place).

Take time to explore this concept, whether it comes easily to you or takes a while to extract. When you know what truly inspires, motivates, and drives you personally, and corporately, when you are with family and friends, you'll find you have clarity as to why you're doing it. You'll also find that opportunities open up as you discover what else exists out there for you that could still provide the same level of satisfaction.

You might need further assistance with this exercise. The purpose again is to figure out what else in the world exists for you. Perhaps you can make a new career of it once you've identified it, or could serve your community in some capacity by knowing this strength. Identifying what you're good at and what you enjoy can open up your mind to opportunities that might crop up at some magical time unbeknownst to you—sort of similar to my billboard story. Opportunities may be staring you right in the face in the most unusual of locations.

List every minute detail of things you enjoy or areas you feel you have some strength in. Do not negate the importance of something as seemingly effortless as watching TV, being an avid sports fan, watching the business network, a fan of fashion TV, a knitter, gardener, painter, house cleaner, cook, and so on. List as many as you can.

____

Now ask yourself, what can I do with that? Where could I serve my community with these talents and interests? What industries or specific positions would benefit immensely from my knowledge, enjoyment, and abilities? If you can't spot anything immediately, enlist the support of your friends or a mastermind group to assist you in identifying like patterns and opportunities.

Our self image, strongly held,
essentially determines what we become.
-Maxwell Maltz

Achieving your goals

We all have the same 24 hours in a day—it's the only thing in life that *is* equal for all. So how are you spending your 24 hours?

Successful people have just as many challenges and problems as everyone else; they've just learned to solve them better. You're never going to get rid of problems. What's your definition of success? Are you setting yourself up for success or for failure?

Success is the progressive
realization of a worthy goal.
-Earl Nightingale

How do you define success?

I personally love the Earl Nightingale definition above. What does it matter if you were successful last year but are not now on the road to a new and worthier goal this year? Each night when you go to bed and each morning when you arise, you have only yourself to answer to. Are you defining success on your own terms or according to the terms of your peer group, friends, family, or colleagues?

What do you personally define as success? Do financial achievements, emotional and spiritual growth, friends and hobbies form part of your definition of success? As you consider what success means to you, ponder the words of Ralph Waldo Emerson and his wisdom from over a century ago:

To laugh often and much; to win the respect of intelligent people and the affection of children; to earn the appreciation of honest critics and endure the betrayal of false friends; to appreciate beauty, to find the best in others; to leave the world a little better, whether by a healthy child, a garden patch or a redeemed social condition; to know even one life has breathed easier because you have lived. This is to have succeeded.

Many of life's failures are people who did not realize
how close they were to success when they gave up.
- Thomas Edison

Life's a cookie

Life and our universe are magically and wonderfully mathematical in nature. If you suffer from innumeracy, not to worry. It's really as simple as a cookie recipe.

Let's assume for a moment that we'd like to make a batch of traditional chocolate chip cookies. There are certain ingredients that we must have on hand. We know we need sugar, butter, chocolate chips, and flour. The other ingredients are important too, but the four ingredients I just mentioned are the basics of our recipe. If we take the flour, for example, and want to make our cookies a bit healthier than the norm, we can replace the less nutritious white flour with whole wheat, rice, or even Kamut flour. However, we do need some type of binding agent. Should we stray too far from the norm and mistake the ingredient of flour for applesauce, we will likely end up with a mess for the garbage – it certainly wouldn't result in chocolate chip cookies.

Life as a recipe

Life isn't much different. There's always a methodical and logical recipe for anything we'd like to achieve in life. Sure, we can personalize the recipe and deviate from the norm with secret ingredients, but just as with math, 5 + 6 + 4 will always equal 15. Change the sequence of the numbers, move them around, or even break the six down to two threes, you'll still end up with 15. This is the way of our universe. So why are we perplexed when we change the numbers and don't end up with the correct end results?

Many years ago I listened to a conversation my cousin was having with his mom. She was complaining about her weight and that she just couldn't shed any of her excess pounds, which were many. Her ten-year-old son piped up with the magic solution—it was so easy for him. He said, "Mom, if you want to lose weight, just eat less, and exercise more." Simple, right? Eat less or healthier and exercise more or more efficiently. Yet why do so many North Americans remain obese and overweight? It's actually become an epidemic in our country. Imagine, people in other countries are dying from malnutrition and a lack of the basics, while we're dying from a lack of understanding of a simple formula that would stop many of the diseases caused by inactivity and obesity.

No matter what your definition of success or the result you're looking for, there's a logical, mathematical formula, that when followed will produce success for you. The important elements within the formula will not only ensure achievement over time or increase the likelihood of achievement, but, also and more importantly, they ensure that the journey is enjoyed along the way.

I've created a simple formula that even the most terrified of mathematics can follow.

Your Daily Success Formula

Appreciation + Focus + Strategies + Action = Success

Appreciation: One can look no further than the example of quickly famous movie stars. Why do so many people turn to drugs and alcohol when they have it all? Money, fame, friends, and everything one could desire, yet all too often we read about these stars turning to deadly substances to find "more" or that something that's missing.

Appreciating everything that shows up in your life and being grateful for what doesn't or hasn't shown up yet is essential. Do you know someone who is lucky? If you interview the "lucky" person, they almost always tend to be extremely grateful for what they have in life, even when they don't have much. The result? They usually attract more of it into their life.

Focus: Our second ingredient requires us to become experts at deletion. Once we've set our goals, focusing on what we want is critical. We must further keep our attention on our desired goal and let go and avoid all that puts our attention on what we don't want.

Turn off the news. Change the subject with those around you who refuse to stop talking about all that is wrong with the world, especially if they're not willing to do anything to change it. Fill your mind and life with events, activities, people, and stimuli that assist you on your mission in life.

An investment in knowledge
always pays the best interest.
- Benjamin Franklin

Strategies: Whether it's losing weight, cleaning up your finances, or starting a new business, you need strategies and the knowledge of *how* to accomplish what you desire, in addition to the other elements of focus, appreciation, and action. Strategies and knowledge alone, however, are not enough to achieve success. Which takes us to the next step—action!

Action: Take any simple step towards achieving that which you desire. Eat a salad tonight, Google "financial management" during your morning coffee to empower yourself financially, attend a free business planning workshop, or go to the library this weekend and check out a book or audio program that will move you closer to your desired goal. Although you might feel some of these actions are insignificant, they, like planted seeds, will eventually spring to life.

I don't know what your definition of success is, but I know that using the success equation will exponentially propel you towards your goal with greater ease, happiness, and enjoyment.

But what if it could be better? I love Deepak Chopra's explanation of why we settle for a life that's less than it could be. He sums it up by saying that we choose a life of "known hells" over "unknown heavens." It's much easier for most of us to live in a self-imposed "hell" because of its familiarity. Heaven is possible, but it's unknown and scary, so we don't even dare dream of the possibilities that are available to us. We pity ourselves, view those who achieve their dreams as "lucky," and go about our daily routines.

Now and then I go about pitying myself and
all the while my soul is being
blown by great winds across the sky.
- Ojibwa saying

There is greatness within you that needs only to be directed for you to achieve a life that is greater than you could ever imagine. You were born an original and there is a great purpose for you, and only *for you.* Comfort is your greatest enemy.

Les Brown tells this great story in his audio program, *The Power of Purpose*.

There is a man sitting with his dog on a porch. Another man is walking by and hears the dog moaning quite loudly. He asks the owner why the dog is moaning and in such pain. The owner casually responds, "Oh, he's sitting on a nail." Perplexed, the passerby asks, "Well why doesn't he just get up off the nail?" The owner then replies, "Well, I guess it just doesn't hurt bad enough for him to get up off the nail. It just hurts bad enough for him to complain about it."

Haven't we all been there in our lives; perhaps you're there right now? You moan and complain about your relationship, your job, your friends and family, but you do nothing about it. You just moan and groan when you could just as easily get up off that proverbial nail and do something about your life.

Getting Motivated

Whenever I present a talk, I usually get a few people who come up to me afterwards asking how I'm so motivated. I'm sure you've heard of a type-A personality. I'm a self-professed Triple-A. At a recent lecture, one woman inquired how she as a B-minus can get motivated, perhaps not to my level, but at least increase to an A.

Countless experts proclaim that motivation comes from within. I suppose I agree with that. But how do you get motivated then when you're not? It's my theory and experience that when one is seeking inspiration, one first needs an external experience. Through the internal interpretation of that experience and how it interacts with your values, you can find motivation.

For example, if contribution is high on your list of core values, it might take seeing the suffering of others to inspire you to action. Sitting at home, watching TV and wondering what to do that day or with your life would be a difficult way to find some inner inspiration. Someone might ask you to volunteer with them at a soup kitchen, visit a retirement home, animal shelter, or the like. After that external experience, you might then be motivated to action that you wouldn't have identified internally.

Although I do come across as highly motivated, I do not, almost ever, start my day that way. I am often as lost, uninspired, tired, and at times lazy as the average person. I struggle with the purpose of my life and day as much as you or anyone else. However, I do have a system that works for me. I have a keen awareness of what drives me, as well as a daily recipe that I'll share with you shortly.

In identifying your core values, I highly encourage you to complete a values exercise. I highly recommend that you pick up a copy of Tony Robbins' book, *Unlimited Power*. There you will find what I believe to be a life changing exercise on exploring and identifying your values. It's true that if you are not aware and living by your own core values each day, happiness and true motivation will likely elude you.

I discovered my core values early in my adulthood and the discovery has severed me well. Values are also a critical element in many of the major decisions you'll make in your life. My top two values, tied in their importance, are passion and family. I also use the word "excitement" interchangeably with passion. Specifically regarding family, I refer to being in proximity to my immediate family. If a day or week is lacking in excitement, passion, or connection with my family, I am usually unhappy. My life goals and projects that I decide to take on must align with those values. At times I've ignored them and quickly found out that I could not be internally motivated for any period of time without them.

For me, I must have something each day that excites me, but also must be in alignment with my family.

I live in Edmonton, Alberta, and would have a much easier and likely more successful career if I lived in Toronto, Vancouver, or in any major US city. I'm quite sure that the external stimulation in those places would require less work on my part to stay focused. However, that would ignore my other top value, and so I have compromised with travelling a great deal, but still calling Edmonton home.

You must identify your core values as well. My strategies for motivation could be extremely different from yours, but my formula for external motivation will work independent of your core beliefs. What you need to work on is your interpretation of external factors and how you will make them work for you personally. If security is your main value, like mine of passion, we could be inspired by attending a financial planning workshop, for example. It's an external event and you might take away how comfortable your life could be if only you started planning now. You might start your next day feeling better about your situation already and could finally make that call to meet with a financial advisor. Someone like myself with passion as their top value, might be motivated by the lure of the more exciting and luxurious lifestyle that the seminar discussed and then make planning for my financial future a priority. Whatever your core values and inspirational drives, it's often an external event that motivates us internally.

If your house were on fire, you would certainly be immediately motivated to get out. Someone trying for years to lose that last ten pounds might do it in a month for a significant event such as their wedding. And a person who had an impossible time waking up early in the morning, especially during those cold winter months with late sunrises, might jump out of bed at 5 a.m. without an alarm if they were going skiing that weekend. Your motivation depends on what moves and drives you and your interpretation of such factors.

Earlier in this chapter, I talked about the 1% solution. You might need to have an overwhelmingly significant experience to get motivated. It might be an idea you heard, the encouragement of a friend to start a business based on that idea, and then going home to purchase a $10 Web site domain name as a start. It might be a lyric in a song that moves you to tears and connects you with an appreciation for the day you didn't start with. Be careful not to overlook the small elements of life that present themselves for you to extract your internal interpretation of drive.

My daily motivational recipe

Again, I'm not sure why people think happiness and joy, focus and dedication, and motivation and a positive outlook on life come naturally to me. I assure you, they don't. I start my day usually pretty early and have seven alarm clocks to help me get up, plus I subscribe to an Internet wake-up service that calls me once each morning with a snooze option. I start my day figuring out how I will be happy and what I will choose to inspire and drive me that day. It is something that I work at each and every day of my life. This is great if you also struggle with living your optimal day as well.

Waiting for an interview on a TV station in Vancouver, I met an interesting expert in the green room also waiting for his slot. He was a memory expert and was sharing some tips on how to remember a person's name—something I and so many others struggle with. When I asked him if he was gifted with a great memory or if remembering names came naturally, he answered, "no, not at all, and that's the great news for the average person." See, if he had some natural memory talent, it would be impossible for him to create a duplicable system. He shared with me that he forgets things all the time. That's why he relies on a formula and anyone could use it if they wanted to.

The same is true with motivation, a positive mental state, and the pursuit of daily happiness. It's a muscle: It needs work. No matter how close or far you are from your ideal life and day, there's always a reason to be either positive about it or wallow in self-pity. There are many successful (by some people's definition) individuals who are grumpy, struggle emotionally through life, and are unmotivated. I would question how "successful" they really are in a wholistic sense.

If motivation does not come naturally to me, and it doesn't, then my system just might work for you, too. Keep in mind though, this is my time-tested system. I can assure you, it will change your life. You must practice it every day and once it becomes part of your daily ritual, you must seek to customize it to your unique life. Think of it as a recipe. When you're first learning a new dish, for any chance of success at achieving the desired end result, you must follow that recipe's ingredients and measurements precisely. Once you've tried it a few times, you can play around and have some fun, switching to your personal tastes and adding more or less here or there. Despite your changes, you'll still have a recipe of sorts that you follow or will have memorized your own version.

Try my daily motivational recipe and adjust it as you wish. Think of it as a metaphor for a daily eating guide if this were a diet-based book. You may wish to switch out my "protein" for another, but don't confuse a carbohydrate for a protein or it throws off the entire regime.

Everyday must do's:

Fortify yourself with exercise.

I'm sure you're not surprised that this one took the top of the list. If you're like me and many others, exercise might not be a priority in your life. You might justify that you simply don't have the time or ignore the importance of it altogether. I suggest that movement can truly change your life, how you feel, how you hold yourself during the day, and your ability to handle what comes your way.

I have absolutely despised exercising in the past and have clung to every excuse and justification as to why I can't and won't do it. I now realize that I've done my best to set the rules up in advance so that I couldn't win. I've joined gyms that I didn't feel comfortable at, vowed to walk in the morning during the winter months (if you've ever been to Alberta in the winter, you'd know how unpleasant walking in the cold and dark can be), and with travelling, gave up on packing the runners that I never used.

Logically, I know the health and energy benefits of exercising. At times I have followed a regime and enjoyed it, but I've always quickly fallen back into my old habits. For the first time in my life, though, I think I have a plan that will stick and you might like to entertain giving it a try.

I must preface with the suggestion that you need to find what works for you. Do you enjoy a stroll outside and being in nature? Or are you like me, that you'll only walk with a purpose, where there must be an end goal in mind? Do you enjoy team sports and interacting with people while you move? Perhaps a buddy system would work best? Or do you need accountability and flexibility in your schedule? Maybe hiring a personal trainer once a month and joining a gym that's open long hours would work best for you?

For all of the above reasons and despite my many needs and excuses, the perfect workout I have found is amazingly inexpensive, easy, flexible, and most importantly, profoundly powerful. It's Tae Bo. A few months ago, my office received a call from Warner Bros. I had a brief chat with the past producer of the *Ellen DeGeneres Show* and the *Tyra Banks Show* who was interested in possibly using my expertise in some way for a new show they were developing. In my corporate world, that call was second only to if Oprah's office had rung. The producer wanted to fly me out to LA in a few weeks. After the initial excitement subsided, a huge bout of fear, insecurity, and second-guessing about my abilities overwhelmed me. To ease my mind and anxiety, I knew I needed to do something to make me strong in the few weeks before the meeting. I remembered that about a decade ago I had purchased the Tae Bo VHS series from a TV advertisement. I'm quite sure I hadn't tried the program more than once. I pulled the tapes out and blew off the inches of dust that had built up on them and the VCR. A small room in my basement was about to transform my body and life. If you were to meet me in person, you'd see that I'm tall and fairly thin. You might think from looking at me that I'm fit, but until a few months ago and for most of my life, that couldn't be further from the truth. I popped in the tape and attempted the basic workout with the host, Billy Blanks. I thought I would nearly die! I've never had much cardio ability and thus failed at most workouts in the past. I also bore easily, but after this session, something was different. I felt strong. I felt powerful. I felt centred. Sure, there was still nervousness about my upcoming meeting, but I was holding myself differently after those 30 minutes, even if I had to walk in one spot since I couldn't do most of the kicks and punches. By the end of three weeks, I had the tape memorized and could easily perform each of the routines. I really can't tell you how this simple program has truly changed my life. For the first time, not only is my body strong, but my mind and sprit seem stronger too. Yes, I have missed days of my scheduled Tae Bo. When travelling, it's impossible to find a VCR. But I was pleasantly surprised that for under $30, I could buy the DVDs, which now go everywhere with my laptop and me. And yes, each morning I drag and pep talk myself into the workout, but once completed, I'm renewed. I highly encourage you to try the system for yourself. I can absolutely guarantee, that after a few weeks of front kicks, jabs, and punches, you'll feel strong too. Once you see the transformation that you have physically and mentally gone through, you'll be hooked! I can further promise you that in a short time, whatever problems you have, you'll feel more in control of them. That jab might be focused (metaphorically, of course) at that bully at work, or the front kick directed at a bill collector. I don't care what condition you're in now—start today even if you have to walk in one spot for weeks. It gets easier. If not Tae Bo, find what works for you. Move as much as you can. During times of lethargy and unmotivation move, move any part of your body, but just move!

Get up 30 minutes earlier

I know you're likely not getting enough sleep as it is. So, then losing just 30 minutes of it won't make much of a difference. Plus, I can promise you that if you dedicate those extra minutes to exercise, you'll gain more energy than you can believe. Alternatively, try going to bed 30 minutes earlier to compensate.

You likely don't have enough time in your life either—time for you, your dreams, goals, hopes, your well-being, your body, mind, and spirit. When was the last time you picked up a book just for you? Or took the time to plan your life or simply had a quiet, leisurely cup of coffee before the kids woke up in the morning?

Not only is it more peaceful in your home and outside during the early morning, but there's also an energy I can't explain when one is up before the sun. There's serenity and quietness before the city awakes that allows one to think, plan, or just be.

You'll never find time for what's important in life like writing that book, exercising, or simply arriving at work calm and ready to handle the day instead of flying frazzled through the door. Try this simple notion. If you'd prefer the 1% solution, what about waking just a few minutes earlier this week, and maybe ten minutes more next week? Before you know it, you'll easily arise 30 or more minutes earlier. You could try this strategy at night, going to bed thirty minutes later, however, I would encourage you to try the morning strategy whether you're an early riser or not since most of us are too tired at the end of the day to use the time constructively and usually have too many evening distractions. Either way, consider that if you made available 30 extra minutes every day for a year, you'd have three and a half extra hours a week, 14 a month, and over 180 in a year, which is equivalent to 22.5 work days per year on your side. Can you imagine what you might accomplish in life, the time you could have for yourself and more if you simply woke up a bit earlier? I can assure you that at the end of the year, those few minutes of lost sleep won't be nearly as significant as how your life can change with that amount of time on your side.

Practice meditation

There are countless books, audio programs, and free information on the Internet on how to meditate. The effects are often immediate for both mind and body and can be long-lasting. Deepak Chopra tells us, we think 60,000 thoughts per day and 95% of those thoughts are the same ones we thought yesterday. It's no wonder many of us are feeling a little insane at times. Meditation is the practice of clearing and quieting the mind.

I have tried meditation over the years, in a traditional sense, and have not found much success. My thoughts, perhaps like yours, race and are at times, seemingly uncontrollable. I have a number of audio programs designed to guide the user to "quiet" their mind for relaxation and more, but I find that I'm either unable to become quiet, start to fidget, or, because I'm generally sleep deprived, end up falling asleep.

If you find my description of meditation similar to experiences you've had, don't give up. You, like me, might just need to practice a less traditional form of meditative being. I think to be creative, to relax mentally and physically, and to allow your mind to feed you back what you've taken "in" from life in the most effective form, you and I must get quiet.

You might find painting your home, cleaning old drawers, and other seemingly "mindless" or monotonous work just the meditative solution you need. If you work in a job with a great deal of mental pressure, you might try physical work as a meditative exercise since an overall change in perspective could induce a quiet mind and possibly even encourage long-term creativity in the process. If you're mostly physical at work and your job allows you to expend little mental energy, you might consider focusing your down time on learning something new, trying a puzzle, crossword puzzle, or figuring out something more mathematical or linear.

Whatever your choice of activity, try something meditative, either traditional (like taking a class) or physical (such as yoga, painting, or the above examples). Make it a priority to simply quiet your mind each day even if only for a few brief moments.

A prescription for daily focus

Following the vein of Chopra's theory about the number of thoughts we think, it's safe to assume that many of those are negative. How then does one take further control of those thoughts and use them for positive direction?

I might suggest reading as much as possible, but with the amount of reading required for most of us on the job and at our computer, many are forgoing books for other sources of information. Plus, the time constraints of our modern day make it more difficult to find the time to read.

However, consider carrying one book with you at all times. You may not have the time or energy at the end of the day to read for pleasure or profit, but I can assure you that keeping a book with you at all times and reading a page here or there could add up to as many as twelve books read at the end of the year that you wouldn't otherwise have read. What about when you're waiting at the doctor's office, for your kids to get out of a late soccer practice, in the meeting at work that's starting 30 minutes late, a long unexpected line up for concert tickets, or grocery shopping. Just two to five minutes here and there can add up to hours a month. Keep a book handy in your car, office, home, and, better yet, your purse at all times.

No net time learning

The best solution I've found for filling your mind with positive reinforcement and setting a powerful tone for the day is to listen to an audio program. For simple inspiration, motivation, learning a second language or a skill that could help your career or relationship will affect your day in ways that are far-reaching and long-lasting. You might only have a few minutes while doing your hair and make up, or during your drive to work. You could try wearing an iPod if you ride the bus or at any time during the day when your full concentration is not needed and when thoughts can run rampant and create worry and stress. Audio programs can be bought directly; you could start a swap with other like-minded friends; purchase them from iTunes at a reasonable cost; or borrow them from the library for free.

Another time for runaway thoughts, generally negative and unproductive, is just before bed each night. Consider creating a nightly regimen of winding down with a relaxing audio program. As an example, I will often listen to something esoteric and thought provoking, not one that is particularly upbeat, but more of an "ah ha" type program from the likes of Dr. Wayne Dyer or Dr. Deepak Chopra. They both have soothing voices with a cadence that relaxes and makes me sleepy. I might listen to them for only a few minutes while washing my face and brushing my teeth, but I'll listen to dozens of programs a year simply while getting ready for bed. It sets a relaxed tone as it allows me to forget the litany of things that happened in the day and instead encourages me to concentrate on their messages and voices.

Experiment and find programs that work for you and try them at different times of the day. In the evening, for example, you might want minimal stimulation. In the morning, you might prefer someone exciting or a topic with energy that's thought provoking or allows you to learn a new language or skill. I enjoy the likes of Tony Robbins, Les Brown, and other high-energy authors in the morning, but would likely find them and their message too stimulating at night.

This one aspect of my life, this little ritual I perform every day listening to something to direct my thoughts each morning and evening absolutely keeps me focused and motivated. Give it a try!

Your theme songs

I don't think there's anything that can change a person's state of mind quicker than music. Think of a time that a song reminded you of something that made you weep, feel immense excitement, exhilaration, sadness, empathy, and more. Music moves us in so many ways. The lyrics are modern day poetry that touches our soul in a way that nothing else can. Each person's interpretation of the song, arrangement, and lyrics is different.

Today, I want you to find at least one theme song. Pull out your blank book (discussed in chapter two) and at the top of one page, write "Theme Songs." When you hear a song that makes you feel strong, powerful, appreciative, that puts things in perspective, I want you to write it down. Then, find a way to create a CD for yourself or arrange an album on your iPod where you can easily access those theme songs in one location.

I've listed a number of songs that are simply my suggestions to elicit different moods to set your morning or drive home to an upbeat tone. Of course, I have no idea what type of music you like or what words and compilations would resonate with you. So try mine out, or explore your CD library or ask others what songs motivate and move them. Try downloading songs, if you haven't already, from iTunes (*www.itunes.com*). On the iTunes Web site, you can purchase a song for 99 cents without having to buy the whole CD.

My songs are:

"Don't Worry, Be Happy" by Bobby McFerrin
"Are You Havin' Any Fun?" by Tony Bennett and Elvis Costello
"What a Wonderful World" by Louis Armstrong
"You Raise Me Up" by Josh Groban
"Man in the Mirror" by Michael Jackson
"Fighter" by Christina Aguilera
"Beautiful" by Christina Aguilera

____

____

____

____

____

Consider purchasing the last two of my suggestions, even if you're not a fan of Christina Aguilera. And if you do, watch the "Beautiful" music video on *youtube.com* if you haven't seen it before and read the lyrics for "Fighter" (just type "Christina Aguilera Fighter Lyrics" into Google and you'll easily find them). If you listen to "Fighter" on your way to work or home after a tough day, I can assure you that you will find strength from her words and the sheer energy and power of the song. Even my seventy-year-old mother relates to it.

The PVP:

Knowing when to flip your "light switch" of energy is essential. You can't and won't want to be motivated all the time. You need to practice being off as much as you might need to practice being on. While studying the ideas listed in your daily motivational recipe, determine now what day each week you're off emotionally, mentally, and physically. You might not be able to be "off" in every way on one given day, but if it's only an hour or two each week when you can turn the light switch off, you'll find turning it on easier too!

There are a number of old standbys that you may wish to include in your daily checklist along with adding any that you already do or used to do. Don't discount their simplicity in keeping you focused, motivated, and positive.

- Pray or give thanks every day. Even if only for a few seconds in your head.
- Marvel at nature—the setting sun, the full moon, how the trees know to drop their leaves at certain times of the year.
- Take lots of small breaks. Move around, stretch, and get outside when you can.
- Find a happy song that you can sing in your head or hum at any time of the day, or something that moves, inspires you.

- Learn to fight.
- Do something that scares you.
- Laugh often—watch and read funny things. Laugh at yourself often.
- Create a happy dance—it can simply be a few movements of your arms legs or a combination of them. You needn't perform this in front of others (unless you wish). But create some happy movement in a form of "your dance" that you can use as an anchor whenever you want to feel joy and lighthearted, especially when a moment in your life might be anything but.
- Read, do crosswords, paint, garden, plant and dig something, play with animals and kids, cook.
- Get enough sleep and water.
- Be cautious of what you ingest: food, drugs, water, vitamins and more. You can't feel motivated if your body isn't working properly. We'll explore nutrition later on in this chapter. Read magazines from the health food store, and online about health issues that you are facing or interest you. Your body must feel good for you to feel good, so become a health expert.

Sidebar:

Always read the side effects of any prescription drugs you take. Also, look up any over-the-counter medications' side effects on the Internet and their labels. You might find that with some medications it's physically difficult to feel your best. I've taken simple over-the-counter pain medication for most of my adulthood and during my teens. Over the past few years, I've been able to reduce the amount of medication I take by nearly 90% by drinking enough water, exercise, proper diet, and nutrition.

I've struggled with a life of high anxiety and emotions. I thought it was part of me and the side effect of being a highly passionate and excited person. I've also not been very aware of my body in the past and haven't always "listened" to it. One day, after not taking pain medications for several weeks, I had to take a couple for an abscessed tooth. Other than the tooth pain, I had been feeling physically and emotionally terrific. Within an hour, I started feeling anxious and worried. For no apparent reason at all, I started feeling a sense of fear and shakiness. For the first time in my adult life, after going weeks without daily pain medication, I could truly "listen" to my body and how it reacted to the drugs. Was my anxiety all these years caused by the constant use of ibuprofen and ASA? It's not a listed side effect, so it wasn't something I was aware could occur from use at all. Now, since reducing the amount of painkillers to almost nothing in a given month, I can report that my anxiety has almost completely disappeared. It's something that has followed me my entire life. It is an issue I've battled and worked on for a long time. I never realized that a simple, over-the-counter painkiller that I was used to taking almost daily caused my anxiety. Carefully examine all that you ingest and when you have emotions that seem irrational, are difficult to control, or you are simply not feeling your best, make a list of foods, activities, water levels, supplements, and medications and seek the counsel of your family doctor or a naturopath to assist you in identifying what triggers your optimal mental and physical well-being, and what might be hindering it.

It all starts with the 24 hours you have

The time is always right
to do what is right.
- Martin Luther King, Jr

"If only" and "one day" are the twin enemies that you will encounter on your path to what you desire. "If only" I had more time, more intellect, more money, more you-name-it, but the most popular excuse by far is the lack of time. Listen, the only thing that is equal for everyone in life, and possibly the only thing that we have in common with the billionaires and those whom we view as successful, is the fact that we share the same 24 hours in a day. No more, no less. It's what you do with those 24 hours that makes the difference. And how about our good friend "one day"? Today is the only day you really have. There is no guarantee that we're going to be here tomorrow. "One day" must become "today," so why not do today what you can? The only thing I can assure you of is that, if you're counting on "one day," that day has arrived and it's called today!

Always the more beautiful answer
who asks the more beautiful question.
- E.E. Cummings

Many people I talk to tell me that the most difficult part of writing down their goals is their own lack of clarity about what they actually want. You may know that you don't like your job, but may not know what else you'd like to do. Here are two exercises to get you started.

The first, offered by Jack Canfield and Mark Victor Hansen in *The Aladdin Factor,* consists of the "perfect day" exercise, which can help even the most uncreative person determine a wants list.

Life isn't about finding yourself.
Life is about creating yourself.
- George Bernard Shaw

Find a quiet place in your home and allow at least 15 minutes a day for dreaming. I'd strongly suggest that you put on some relaxing music and have a pen and paper handy for when you have finished the daydreaming. Just allow yourself to go through a 24-hour period in as much detail as you can. Imagine yourself waking up in the morning. What time would you wake up and to what? What kind of bed would you have slept in? Who and how many people would you wake up with? Would you have any children, more children, a different spouse from the one you have now, or no spouse at all? Would you have time to read the paper or write your book? What would you eat? Would you be waited on or have breakfast out with your friends? How would you get to work—would you drive or go as a passenger? Where would you go to work and what time would you arrive?

Basically, go through this in your mind with as much detail as you can and check your judgment at the door. Just act "as if" you lived a perfect 24 hours, and imagine what it would look and feel like. Once you have fully visualized your day, take your paper and pen and immediately write down every last detail. Don't skip this step thinking that you'll be able to remember everything. Writing it all down starts you on a path, or a track, towards the manifestation of some of the details you've just created. You are commanding your conscious and subconscious mind to go out and create what you've just imagined. If you don't have the time to do this as soon as you have finished your imagination session, use a tape recorder to record the details so that you can write them down later. If you don't believe that this process will work for you, hide what you have written in a drawer and pull it out in a year, two, or ten years from now. I assure you that you'll be amazed at how many of those things will have come true for you.

Being aware of what you truly desire is the first and most important step to its attainment. You'll be amazed at the magic or coincidences that start to happen in your life once you've focused on those desires. Suddenly, people who can help you achieve your goals will just show up or books on your bookshelf will grab your attention and provide the answer you are looking for. Once you've commanded your subconscious to go after something, watch it happen. It's been said that when the student is ready, the teacher will appear. The teacher may have been there all along, but until you, the student, are ready, you won't see the teachings being offered. Look closely at your life for the teachers and teachings right under your nose.

Another very simple exercise, which may help you identify what you want even before you spell out an actual goal, encourages you to look at the people you envy. Look at what they have, what their life is like, and what it is about them that you envy. As you do this, consider blessing them for what they have that you don't, but would like to have. If you were to curse them for what they have, it would remind you of what you lack and instill in you the belief that what they have is wrong and it won't manifest in your own life. If, for example, you're envious of your best friend's new 10,000-square-foot house, wouldn't it make more sense for you to value your friend's achievement and learn how she did it so that one day you could own such a home? How can you expect to manifest it in your own life if you think it's wrong for your friend to have this home? Either you'll never achieve a home like your friend's, even though you've told yourself you want it, or if you do actually get to the point of owning a home like that, you'll be unhappy with yourself and when showing it to your friends you'll remember how wrong you thought your friend was.

Chunking: Rome wasn't built in a day

Overwhelmed is an awful and uncomfortable place to be. It's inefficient and generally not an enjoyable state. When you find yourself stressing about the litany of things you need to do, think about the old riddle: "How do you eat an elephant?" Of course the answer is, "One bite at a time." Rome may not have been built in a day, but each day brings a fresh and full opportunity to start on your goal. If you've always wanted to write a book, you could spend a few minutes each day, not more than 10 or 15 minutes, writing about your passion. With just a few minutes each day, at the end of the year you would have a pretty significant book, likely over 300 pages. What are the steps you need to take to reach your goal? If your project seems overwhelming or impossible, you haven't taken the time to "chunk" it down. Once you start on what seems like the most insignificant steps towards that which you desire, magical occurrences will begin to reveal themselves to you. I don't know how they occur, but it's true that when your "why" is strong enough, the "how" takes care of itself. Just when you need someone at a particular time, they magically appear. Remember the great law discovered by Sir Isaac Newton—an object in motion tends to stay in motion. By tackling the details of your goals one by one, you'll build momentum, self-esteem, an improved self-image, and, over time, your causes will produce your desired effects.

Don't Get Your Hopes Up

In speaking with friends and clients who have set only vague goals or who might be planning for an event, I discovered that many have adopted a bizarre thought process when visualizing the outcome. When I ask about what's happening in their lives and they share with me something that could affect them positively in a wonderful way, they'll often add quickly, "Oh, but I don't want to get my hopes up." I've also been guilty of this, but I realized at an early age what a ridiculous notion this is. This idea seems to be that, if we don't get our hopes up, it won't hurt as badly when the event doesn't occur, or the disappointment will somehow be lessened because we have convinced ourselves that things will not go as planned. Or perhaps it's for social justification, so that when a friend asks us about a goal that failed to work out, we can gracefully accept defeat because we hadn't gotten our hopes up.

I remember thinking logically about this absurd behaviour of my own and actually documented two events that I wanted very much to happen. In one instance I "got my hopes up" and mentally committed to the event. With the other, I was much less involved and lied to myself that it didn't matter whether the event took place or not. What happened with respect to these two occurrences and my informal experiment? Much to my own surprise, I was equally disappointed in both case—the one where I was fully engaged emotionally and the one where I wasn't. I decided that if I was going to be disappointed anyway, wouldn't it make sense to be 100% engaged, especially if the disappointment wasn't going to be lessened by being 50% engaged? Furthermore, I had to question whether my lack of enthusiasm and visualization had led to the unsuccessful outcome. If I had poured my heart into it, could I have achieved my goal?

I'm sure you've had an opportunity or relationship or some other occurrence in your life where you have set yourself up to fail before even going after your goal. I know we're crushed if something doesn't work out. This is the danger when we measure our merit in terms of the goal, as opposed to the person we have become on the journey towards our goals. That's why I subscribe to Earl Nightingale's definition of success and a worthy goal: it's the pursuit, not the end result.

Cheerleaders, reality checkers, and dream killers

[Friends] cherish each other's hopes.
They are kind to each other's dreams
- Henry David Thoreau

Sharing your dreams

Be careful who you share your goals and dreams with. Remember, first and foremost, your dreams are YOURS! They weren't created by or for the person you're sharing them with, so before you decide to make them public, keep that in mind. Don't expect another person to see your vision—it's yours.

Sharing opens up the opportunity for the person with whom you're sharing your dream to pass judgment. You might not even be fully convinced of your dream and could be quickly swayed by the opinion of this person. Why are you sharing with this person? Are you looking for their approval, praise?

There are some decisions in life
that only you can make.
- Merle Shain

Be aware of the "tribe" mentality. You probably belong to a tribe of some sort, either formally or informally. Generally, tribes have expectations for their members and set a certain ceiling for what can or cannot be accomplished. Tribes like to keep their members in line. When you share your goals with your fellow tribe members, you run the risk of finding that your aspiration is above their ceiling.

Be careful when following the tribe.
You just might step in what they leave behind.
- Wayne Dyer

Who are you sharing your goals with? Is it someone who knows more about the topic than you? Are you seeking another's advice and opinion in preference to your own? Is the person qualified to lead you? Are you just looking for someone who will listen to you? Perhaps you should seek the counsel of a support group. If your goal is to become a writer, for example, and your best friend is a very analytical dentist who hasn't read a book since university, what is your friend going to offer you in the way of advice? What does he know about being a writer? You would be better off joining a literary group or attending a workshop at the local Writers' Guild to learn about the challenges and benefits of becoming a writer.

Risk more than others think is safe.
Care more than others think is wise.
Dream more than others think is practical.
Expect more than others think is possible.
- Cadet maxim

Listen to everyone but proceed with your heart. Everyone does have something valuable to say and contribute. Listen to everyone, but distance yourself from that advice and then follow your heart. It's better to lose pursuing your dream than to succeed doing what's not in your heart!

Whether you think you can
or whether you think you can't,
you're right.
- Henry Ford

Cheerleaders versus Reality checkers

I have both of these types of individuals in my life. My mother has always been an obvious cheerleader. No matter what crazy idea I dream up or how far out of reach it seems, my mom always cheers me on without the slightest hesitation or hint of doubt. My brother Dave, on the other hand, is a natural analytical thinker and "reality checker." His mind is so full of statistics that he can sometimes appear negative. Until just recently, I never really understood how both of these personality types could help me achieve my goals. I would often go to my mother when I needed an independent opinion about the validity of my goal and she would cheer me on even when I knew I wasn't ready to proceed. If I used my brother as a sounding board when I was starting off on a goal or brainstorming an idea, he would scare me so badly with "doom and gloom" scenarios and the number of things that might go wrong that I wouldn't even start on the task for fear of a massive failure. Now, both my mom and brother are capable of reacting in very different ways from this normal pattern. My mom will often comment on some critical flaw she has observed before I set out toward a goal, and my brother does show cheerleading traits when he sees that my goal has the potential to become a reality. But, for the most part, my mom is my cheerleader and my brother Dave is my reality checker. So why not use them to my advantage? Generally speaking, I always brainstorm my dreams and goals with my mom. She puts me up on such a high pedestal that no obstacle seems insurmountable after five minutes with her. Then, when I'm ready to go after my goal, I enlist the opinion of Dave, as I know he will point out plans B to Z and provide protection strategies that will allow me to plan in advance for possible obstacles. Identify these different support people in your own life, and use their natural strategies for greater support just when you need it. The cheerleaders and the reality checkers see and evaluate goals and dreams differently. Keep that in mind when you decide to share your visions.

Dreams come true.
Without that possibility, nature would not incite us to have them.
- John Updike

Become a student of life

So often, after we've finished school, we give up being a student. I remember reading somewhere that a large percentage of people never read another book after high school or college. We may take a course or two, attend lectures and possibly upgrade our degrees, but few people are true students in life. Why reinvent the wheel when you can model yourself after the success and achievements of others and learn their secrets in a fraction of the time?

Learning is not attained by chance,
it must be sought for with ardor and attended to with diligence.
- Abigail Adams

When I first started my career in the financial planning industry, I was an 18-year-old girl in a world of grey-haired men with decades of experience. I didn't have the first clue of what success meant to my current or future clients or me. We had a branch meeting one day and one of the investment companies that our firm dealt with sent an energetic lad from England to impart some marketing wisdom. My seasoned associates attended but turned a deaf ear to this fellow's outrageous and passionate ides. I was totally enthralled with the notions presented and acted upon one immediately. This man gave the suggestion of contacting all of the powerful business people in our city with a letter. The letter was to request a brief meeting to discover what specifically made them successful. It was to be a fact finding meeting only and not one intended on selling any product or service.

After our workshop, I immediately headed back to my office, dug out my Chamber of Commerce directory and quickly highlighted the companies and owners that I knew were successful in my city. I drafted a letter and sent it out to over fifty of these prominent presidents and company owners. I decided to follow-up with phone calls since I didn't hear from a single person nearly two weeks after sending my letters. This was an extremely uncomfortable process for me, but I figured that the worst thing that could happen when I called and requested a meeting was for them to say no. I recall that I received an invitation to meet with seven business owners at their offices. I had my interview questions ready and interviewed all the owners with delight and enthusiastic wonder.

My first question for each interview was, "what has made you successful?" To my surprise, each and every person stammered and paused a little and assured me that they were not all that successful. How could this be? I knew they were successful. They were written about and interviewed regularly by the press and had the recognition of almost everyone in the city. How could they not think of themselves as successful?

My litany of questioning provided me with some useful models of success, was enlightening, and by the end of each interview, I learned many of the secret ingredients to a successful life, as defined differently by each person. I also know that each interviewee felt a little more successful after they had verbalized their achievements to someone truly wanting to learn about their accomplishments and who actively listened. I took away a number of valuable insights, made contact with some of the most affluent in my city, and left them feeling edified as a result of our meeting: A classic win-win situation.

Learning is not compulsory...neither is survival.
- W. Edwards Deming

Become a student of life, as I did, and do so for a lifetime. Start by observing your friends, family, and associates. What do they do very well that you could learn from? Do you have a friend who is an outstanding mother multi-tasking with ease and efficiency? Perhaps you also have a friend who is a money management master? Why reinvent the wheel when you can model the successes of others and have fun in the process. You might be surprised that a long-time friend or family member that you thought you really knew has even more to share—it's just a few questions away. The key to a successful interview is great listening skills. Remember that you're not there to share or relate anything about yourself. The purpose of your interview is to use a Socratic approach to identify the equation or recipe for success in that person's life. Furthermore, you'll benefit the interviewee by allowing them to acknowledge what they've done well in life and affirm their achievements.

Surround yourself with people who believe you can.
- Dan Zadra

State management: Use your brain for a change

For imagination sets the goal picture
which our automatic mechanism works on.
We act, or fail to act, not because of will, as is so commonly believed,
but because of imagination.
- Maxwell Maltz

Personal state management is perhaps one of the most important tools I would like to share with you. People who can focus on what they want and then take the appropriate and necessary actions certainly have a much better chance at achieving their goals and dreams. But how about those days that you just don't feel like going after anything? Those days when just getting out of bed seems like a colossal chore. How can you hope to master life if getting out of bed is a monumental task?

Understanding what controls your state and then improving upon those conditions will make life, getting up in the morning, and all of life's challenges, more exciting and empowering.

Countless studies have been conducted on individuals who suffer chronic depression. Think of someone you know who's depressed or a time when you've experienced feelings of intense malaise. Look at that person's posture, their stance, their shallow breathing, where their eyes focus. Physiology is the first key in state management. If a person is slumped over, speaks slowly, with little to no life or passion, and stares at the floor, how could they not feel lethargic and depressed? Experience that composition for just a moment and couple that with depressing thoughts.

Now, stand up, clap your hands loudly, speak forcefully, or jump around for a minute. Take a few moments to appreciate what you have in life, who you love, what you love to do, and all of the opportunities that await you in the future.

Does this second exercise feel (a little) better than the first? Does your body feel stronger and your mind a bit more focused?

State management consists of a number of areas of focus and application. What you put into your body, how and how much you move your body, what you put your attention on, and a number of environmental factors can put you on top of the world or in the doldrums of despair.

You are what you eat

Tell me what you eat, and I will tell you what you are.
- Anthelme Brillat-Savarin

How you think, act, and even learn is affected greatly by what types of food you eat. A variety of foods are reputed to affect our moods and brain chemistry. Many individuals on low fat, carbohydrate-restricted diets can attest to increased feelings of depression, grumpiness, frustration, and malaise.

Conversely, when we head to Mom's for a big Sunday dinner or opt for a steaming plate of pasta or mashed potatoes, we usually consider such food as "comfort food." Can food really change our brain chemistry and our moods? Current research is telling us just that.

Does reaching for your favourite chocolate treat send you into an immediate state of satisfaction and bliss? There's a reason that chocolate is almost universally desired. There are a host of substances found in chocolate that have mood altering and lifting effects. Researchers believe that chocolate alters mood primarily by causing the release of endorphins, the brain's opiates.

Know your aminos

We are indeed much more than we eat,
but what we eat nevertheless helps us to be much more than what we are.
- Adelle Davis

There are two important amino acids contained in proteins that greatly affect your brain chemistry and can result in positive or negative moods. Tryptophan is an essential amino acid. The body does not make it, so it must be consumed within our diet. Tyrosine is the opposite as it's a non-essential amino acid and the body will produce it if it's not found in our diet. These two amino acids influence the top four neurotransmitters (brain chemicals). Serotonin, which is made from the amino acid tryptophan, and dopamine, epinephrine, and norepinephrine, which are made from the amino acid tyrosine.

Serotonin is the neurotransmitter that relaxes the brain. The other three, collectively known as catecholamines, are neurotransmitters that rev up the brain. Turkey and chicken contain tryptophan and when converted to serotonin, it gives us that "good" feeling. Carbohydrate cravings may be a subconscious attempt to raise serotonin levels, responsible for mood, sleep, and appetite control. (Source: Dr. Bill Sears, "Best Brain Foods: 11 Ways Food Can Help You Think. *www.askdrsears.com*)

Researchers at Brookhaven National Laboratory have shown that looking at our favourite, fat laden foods makes the brain release dopamine, the chemical associated with reward and craving. Physiologist, Mary Dallman at the University of California, San Francisco says that fat and sugar calm the brain, lowering levels of stress hormones. "That's why we call them comfort foods," she says.

Vitamins such as vitamin B6, vitamin C, folic acid, and zinc are also essential good mood nutrients. They're further needed to support the production of serotonin in making the feel-good brain chemistry.

For more information on foods that rev up and slow down our brains, visit *www.kelleykeehn.com* for a complete list and other valuable facts.

The more severe the pain or illness,
the more severe will be the necessary changes.
These may involve breaking bad habits,
acquiring some new and better ones.
- Peter McWilliams

Your environment has power

What would you prefer as an ideal workday? Option A involves taking your laptop and a briefcase full of files to the beach or spending your work day outside in nature on a warm breezy day with your iPod playing Pachelbel or your favourite calming music. Option B involves working in a tower full of electromagnetic disturbances, recycled air, fluorescent lights, and a barrage of humming and other annoying noises. Likely your choice is obviously A or some similar version. Why? We know that a peaceful and relaxing environment is the optimal atmosphere to induce creativity. Understanding your unique sensitivities to sounds, sights, and feelings will increase your chances for exemplary brainpower and physical states.

Music, whether at work or home, can produce an instant change of state. If you have teenagers or young nieces and nephews, you can relate to the instant state change that can occur when their sometimes nerve wracking music is too loud or has a pounding bass. Conversely, when dining at an elegant restaurant or indulging in a service at your favourite spa, it's no secret that they use specific music to enhance the relaxation response. Music is also an inexpensive and effortless means of diffusing disturbing background noises and focuses our auditory attention on the pleasant sounds.

Your environments at work and home are special places and a reflection of you, your brand, and what You Inc. stands for. What can you do today to add just that little extra that makes all the difference for yourself and others who might enter your home or office? What about some flowers? It doesn't need to be an expensive arrangement—it could be a single rose or a Gerbera daisy that might cost less than $2. Something alive, with colour and fragrance, can totally change a room. What about diffusing citrus or another stimulating essential oil? And lastly, how clean is your environment? Clutter weighs down our energy and spirit, even if we can't see it. When you need a change, aren't motivated, feel down or you simply need more prosperity—clean your environment. Clean your desk, your file cabinet, making room for new clients, and closets, making room for new clothes. Do you have any of those junk drawers with a bunch of clutter that's hidden away but you still know about it? Organize it or get rid of it. And those bits of food in your fridge and cupboards? You know the stuff I'm referring to—the teaspoon of ketchup in the fridge, the bits of spices in the cupboard, or the nasty freezer-burned items in your freezer. Get rid of them! You'll find as you clean that your environment isn't just lighter and brighter—so too will be your spirit, thoughts, and outlook!

Overcoming worry and handling fear

Fear and worry are conditions that can be downright debilitating. While state management and the above techniques will support the brain function and physiology for handling fear and anxiety, more attention is required to overcome these abrasive, grinding emotions. The following is a simple seven-step process for handling and controlling fear, worry, and anxiety.

Of all the liars in the world, sometimes
the worst are your own fears.
- Rudyard Kipling

More people die on Monday morning between 8 and 9 a.m. than at any other time; people are literally dying to go to work. But what holds you and me back from living a life of joy come Monday morning? Fear of "unknown hells versus unknown heavens," as Deepak Chopra so eloquently puts it. This worry and fear of the unknown has become so widespread that job dissatisfaction is now considered to be the number one source of heart disease! It's not what you're eating that will kill you; it's what's eating into you!

So what's stopping us as a society from doing the brave thing and pursuing our dream jobs? Bravery presupposes an overcoming of fear and doubt. Does this all sound too esoteric for your Monday morning?

I love the serenity prayer of Reinhold Niebuhr where he states so simply and eloquently the rightful place for worry:

God grant me the serenity
to accept the things I cannot change;
courage to change the things I can;
and wisdom to know the difference.

Really, there are only two types of worries. Those that you can't do anything about, so why worry about them? And those that you do have control over and can change. And if you can change them, change them. It still makes no sense to worry about them.

Fact:
More people are killed by donkeys annually than are killed in plane crashes.

Fact:
The odds of being killed by lightning are 1 in 2,000,000. The odds of being killed in a car crash are 1 in 5,000.

Fact:
The odds of being killed in a tornado are 1 in 2,000,000. The odds of being killed in a plane crash are 1 in 25,000,000.

The above facts, while interesting, certainly represent silly comparisons. But take a look at the second fact. Many more people are killed in car crashes than by lightning, yet if you ask around you'll likely discover that most people are far more concerned for their safety in an electrical lightning storm than they are when they drive their kids out of town for a hockey tournament. When was the last time you, or someone you know, worried about flying? It's absolutely useless to look at the odds as so few people, statistically, will ever die in a plane crash. These facts suggest that we often worry about things that, statistically, are unlikely to happen to us, so why would we spend one minute concerning ourselves about them?

Schedule Worry

Why not? We seem to schedule everything else these days. We schedule soccer practice for the kids, a meeting with the designer who will help us with our furniture purchase, or with the travel agent so we can plan our next vacation. Why wouldn't we schedule something that so many of us spend countless hours doing? At least if it's booked, we can focus on it fully.

We all know that most of what we worry about rarely comes true and will result in a negative frame of mind, so why on earth would we book it in to our lives—and on a regular basis, no less? I'm proposing that you try this little exercise for just 15 to 20 minutes each week. I guarantee that's less time than you would spend on the worries that seep into your consciousness throughout the day in a normal week. As worry thoughts creep up on you, pull out a sticky note or a receipt slip from your wallet or purse, and write down your worry. Then forget it! Just let it go until your scheduled time to resume your worrying.

The first benefit, of course, is distance. By the time your "worry" appointment arrives, the intensity of your worry will have lessened, even if only by an infinitesimal amount. Secondly, in a nation where most of us list procrastination as a major fault, this should be as simple as pie—put it off until later.

Do not anticipate trouble,
or worry about what may never happen.
Keep in the sunlight.
- Benjamin Franklin

Steps for overcoming worry

Take a blank sheet of paper and list all of the problems that cause you worry, anxiety or fear. Identify your top three concerns and on a second sheet of paper, write out all possible solutions for solving your problems. This is not an easy task and may take a few days, or even weeks, to complete. Add to your "worries" list if new ones arise, but keep tackling them as you go. The exercise of writing out your worries takes them out of your head and allows you to look at them and check their validity.

As you work through your concerns, and possible solutions to them, here are a few strategies that may assist you in the process:

First, **check your physical and mental states**. In order to develop your solutions list, it's imperative that you be at your best both mentally and physically. If you're slumped over on the sofa, staring at the floor and wondering how you're ever going to get that raise to help pay the cost of Mary's university education, you are not in any sort of position to solve your problem. Stand or sit up, take some deep and empowering breaths, run a few laps around the house, smile stupidly at yourself in the mirror, or read a few funnies in your local newspaper. Basically, do anything it takes to shake off a less-than-ideal mood before you can expect your creative juices to flow. If you're still not sure about what to do, act as if you are sure and ask yourself the following question: "If I was a (insert the adjective of your choice here: creative, confident, passionate, etc.) person, how would I sit, stand, breathe, and tackle this problem?"

Second, **try solving someone else's problem**. Have you ever found that it's amazingly easy to discover solutions when friends confide in you about problems they have? If you're like me, you will likely find many creative solutions for another person's problems because you're not emotionally attached to the issues. Try picturing your challenge and putting it far in front of you mentally. Now, pretend it's a friend's issue. This is a great time to bring out your imaginary friend from childhood, if you were blessed enough to have one. Pretend it's someone else's problem and distance yourself from it emotionally and see what solutions arise.

Lastly, ask yourself, **"What's the worst that can happen?"** This is an empowering question. Many times we worry about some event that may or may not happen, or anxiety builds in us about a project or some other obsession. What if your project doesn't turn out to be perfect? What if that relationship is over? What if you do lose your job? What's the worst thing that can happen? Will you die? Probably not. Will you starve and be thrown out on the streets? Again, most unlikely. If you can handle the worst that could happen and take a quick moment to picture the thing that you fear, you may find that it's not that bad, and that knowledge will bring a sense of ease to the current tasks at hand.

Step #1: Go big or go home

In the same way that you schedule worry, schedule other emotions too. Sometimes it's just not possible to do so in advance. Sometimes the emotion needs to be fully felt and everything else must stop. We fool ourselves into thinking that we'll just ignore an intense emotion, keep going through our day, and deal with it later. Just stop and take a 30-minute break. Trust me, you're going to waste much more time if you hold on, all day long, to an emotion that isn't serving you. Feel it fully—but put a limit on it. If you're feeling angry, look up that word, and every similar word, and then go for a walk and mumble all of those words to yourself. Work yourself up for a time, maybe 20 to 30 minutes, and get out all of that anger. Then, when you walk back into your house or office, it's done. You have experienced it fully and you don't need it to linger any longer. It may take a few times to get the hang of this method, but I promise that you'll feel more satisfied as a result. After a while, you won't need 20 minutes either; you'll find that you can fully experience the negative feeling and emotion in a few minutes and then move on, with the lesson learned.

It's like eating those low-fat cookies. You're craving sugar and chocolate and somehow you convince yourself that eating low-fat cookies with half the fat, but often as many calories as the full-fat versions, will satisfy your cravings. What usually happens? If you're like me, after you've eaten the entire bag and are still craving more, you realize that just a couple of the full-fat versions would have satisfied you. Don't be fooled into suppressing emotions or letting them linger all day like those low-fat cookies you nibbled at until you had eaten the entire bag. Have a few fatties, experience a full-out temper tantrum if necessary—alone and in a respectful manner—and feel more satisfied at the end of the day.

We live in what I like to call a "suppression society." Emotionally, physically, and spiritually we fall into the trap where society forces its "get over it" attitude upon us. We fill up with emotional toxins, and are shocked when they manifest into disease, mental illness, or mid-life crises.

William Blake, a British poet, painter, and visionary eloquently reminds us that suppression can be lethal in his poem entitled, "A Poison Tree":

I was angry with my friend;
I told my wrath, my wrath did end.
I was angry with my foe:
I told it not, my wrath did grow.

And I water'd it in fears,
Night & morning with my tears:
And I sunned it with my smiles,
And with soft deceitful wiles.

And it grew both day and night.
Till it bore an apple bright.
And my foe beheld it shine,
And he knew that it was mine,

And into my garden stole,
When the night had veil'd the pole;
In the morning glad I see;
My foe outstretch'd beneath the tree.

Centuries later, the words of William Blake still ring true and carry the same relevance in regards to our true feelings. In this suppression society, people with colds, flus, and emotional and physical aches and pains drag themselves to work instead of healing themselves first and worrying about work second. When someone dies in your family, you're lucky if you get a couple of days off work and then you'd better be ready to hit the ground running the day you're back because you've got to make up for lost time, right? Break up with the love of your life—better get over that one really quickly. It is not in the company manual and it certainly doesn't qualify for a day off. You're lucky if you get a drink out with a friend as you talk about your heartbreak. You can start now, with yourself, and demand that your work and world support the normal processes of living and dealing with physical, emotional, and spiritual challenges. Continuing to work as you try to deal with the issues will only lengthen the time it takes to recover. If your boss can't appreciate that when you are a healthy and whole person you are a more efficient worker, maybe it's time to find a new job. If you are your own boss, then it's time to have a chat with yourself. You will have time when you retire, lose your job, take an extended vacation, but who will you be then? As Wayne Dyer so eloquently states: "If you are what you do, then what are you when you don't?"

Courage is the art of being the only one
that knows you're scared to death.
- Harold Wilson

Step #2: Feel the fear and do it anyway

Susan Jeffers, in her book *Feel the Fear and Do It Anyway*, answered a question that had plagued me for many years. She states that everyone is fearful so our goal shouldn't be to eliminate fear, but to be aware of it, feel it, and "do it anyway." I regret that I didn't read this book when I was fresh out of school, as it would have made my angst about my fear more palatable and, by doing that, would have presented me with more choices.

In the financial world, which I have chosen to work in for the past decade plus, public speaking comes as part of the job. This simple task of speaking in front of others happens to be close to the number one fear for many North Americans and I was, and still am, no exception. Early in my career, anxiety would haunt me for weeks ahead of a talk, regardless of the size of the audience. However, speaking in public was necessary for my advancement and to procure further business for my firm, so opting out wasn't an option. Furthermore, I felt fantastic after each lecture as I had *faced* my fear, but as soon as my next talk was booked, I knew I hadn't *conquered* my fear. When nervous before a talk, and often one step away from a full-blown anxiety attack, I blamed lack of experience for my inability to control my nerves. Over time, I have become a tiny bit more comfortable in front of an audience, and it certainly helps to know my material. If several talks are booked close together, I get "used" to the pressure. Nearly 15 years later in my career, the nerves are still there and if I haven't spoken for some time, the anxiety is nearly as great as it was when I gave my first talk. I couldn't understand how hundreds of talks later given to thousands of people, and with the knowledge from their feedback that my message was important and well-received, my fear could follow me. Why, after years of public speaking courses and personal coaching couldn't I just get up on stage naturally with a successful end in mind?

Be kind, for everyone you meet
is fighting a hard battle.
- Plato

I think a job interview can be an intimidating and fearful experience for most interviewees. I certainly have had my share over the years and, just as with my lectures, it didn't matter how many I had, the nerves always followed me to each interview. It always felt daunting to be on the opposite side of the table from someone so confident and calm, who asked question after question in an effort to determine if I was worthy of that company. Finally, a year after I opened my own company, it was my turn to be the interviewer. And to my surprise, I was as nervous as I used to be when I was the interviewee. I was shocked! All of those years I had focused on my own fear and insecurity going into the interview process, and never once did I stop to think that the person on the other side of the table, who seemed so intimidating, may have been just as nervous as I was. Now that my turn had come to put question after question to potential staff, I wondered how I came across as an employer, whether my queries were the norm, and on and on.

After I read Susan Jeffers' book, it all became so clear. The fear may never disappear, but that shouldn't be our focus. The challenge is to feel our fear but to do the task anyway. It's so simple and calming to know that we all have fears. Take the time to share your fears with others and they'll likely share theirs with you. Also take the time to read or watch on TV the biographies of those individuals you respect. You may find out that, no matter how mighty that person seems, he or she probably has a list of fears as long as yours.

Don't waste yourself in rejection, nor bark against
the bad, but chant the beauty of the good.
- Ralph Waldo Emerson

Step #3: Do the opposite and focus on what you want

It's been said that if drivers who lose control of their cars and are facing an imminent crash would keep their eyes on the road in the direction they want to go, rather than on the collision path, they'd have a much better chance of avoiding an accident. Face in the direction you'd like to head, and not towards that collision course. And be very cautious about the words you speak and those that others say to you. Words can be as sweet as honey, or like thought viruses that seep deep into your subconscious. Society is full of thought viruses that we've conditioned our nervous system to accept. A mother lovingly cautions her child, "Don't spill the milk" or "Don't fall" as little Johnny is running.

What she doesn't realize is she's giving little Johnny's subconscious a command. The subconscious doesn't understand negatives, so when a person says, "don't fall," the mind has to picture falling and the focus therefore is on falling. Is that the reason Johnny has been falling lately? Remember the example in chapter three where I asked you to "not think of the colour blue"? How difficult was that? So it would be far better for the loving and concerned mother to encourage the nervous system of her child with a positive and focusing statement like "Please be careful when running, Johnny." It's funny, but it works with us big kids too!

So when the time comes to worry about your bills, for example, why not think about all of the income-generating possibilities you have if you just use the gold mine between your ears? What if, instead of worrying about whether you'll ever get married or have children or start that family you've always wanted, you do something totally different, yet ridiculously simple? You grab your pen and a blank sheet of paper and begin to write down all of the possible ways you could meet the spouse of your dreams. Many of your ideas might not amount to anything, but even if you think of a few good ones or run it by a personal support group for further input, you're now availing yourself of solutions that likely would not have arisen out of your previous self-pity and worry.

Courage is knowing what not to fear.
- Plato

Try this mental exercise for a moment. Close your eyes and imagine going up in the tallest building you can imagine. You're riding the elevator all the way up many, many storeys to the roof of the building. Now walk over to the edge, stand with your toes slightly over the edge of the building and look down. Now, slowly back away from the edge—or crawl if you must. How did that little exercise make you feel? The first time I tried it I felt slightly light-headed and I'm not fearful of heights in the least. But consider this for a moment; it was all in your mind. You weren't actually on that building's roof looking over the edge. You were sitting in your office or home safe and sound. Generally speaking, unless someone has a weapon pulled on us and death is imminent, it's unlikely that our worry is going to kill us. So remember to step off the ledge in your mind and see worry for what it really is—all in our minds!

Step #4: Remember what you've overcome before

Courage is resistance to fear, mastery of fear—not absence of fear.
Mark Twain

When my brother returned from an extended trip to Egypt some time ago, I remember being fascinated by his stories of the missing pieces of Egypt's past. He indicated that Egyptian historians did not include any reports of massive failures or defeats. They just wouldn't write about it. I thought this was quite brilliant indeed—don't report it and it didn't happen! I would like you *not* to act as the Egyptians, but to actively work to remember your failures. Our failures help us in so many ways.

An accounting of failures will help you overcome challenges. When you take the time to recall what you've been through, you then have a list of "compared to what" items. Once you have prepared this account and compared some of your current worries against it, I'm quite confident that you will think: "This is silly! Why am I worrying about this? If I could overcome that (insert great challenge from the past here), why am I concerned with this? Compared to what I've overcome, I can certainly handle this." I'm not suggesting that you go to great lengths to recall the past or to live in it for any length of time. Just recall and record some major challenges—the ones that ended successfully and, unlike our Egyptian friends, those that didn't. More importantly, make a list of what you have learned, the sort of person you have become because of the experience, and the challenges you overcame.

Remember my New York story? It was one of missed opportunity, but certainly not one of regret. In the middle of my teen years I was presented with a once-in-a-lifetime chance to work in New York City as a model. All of my friends and most of my family insisted that the decision warranted no debate or hesitation—it's New York City. I had to go because everyone was telling me I should. The story is long, but entailed all of the preparation that goes with a long-distance move, including closing bank accounts and countless sobbing sessions with my mom and other friends. What I didn't realize at the time, as I was only starting to work on the values and priorities in my life, was that family was more important, and always would be more important to me than a career opportunity or, better put, the pursuit of money. I didn't want to be a model and I loved my family, especially my best friend, my mother. Why was I leaving the most important part of my life behind for a job I loathed? So within 24 hours of my departure, and after thousands of tears shed later by my mom and me, I returned home to great relief and love.

You might be thinking, come on...New York? What's so tough about that?

Nothing, I suppose, but for me it meant leaving everything my life stood for at the time for something that meant nothing to me and in which my heart was not fully engaged. I learned a valuable lesson at an early age—measuring your decisions against your true values early on in the process will save you much pain and deliberation. Every time my mom and I live through a rough challenge together, we always say the same things (even though it's now many years later). I say, "At least we have each other and I'm not in New York," and then my mom gives a huge sigh of relief as she remembers that, for us, the ultimate gift is our time together.

Remembering our past challenges provides a wonderful gift that is full of surprises and lessons to hold on to. The lessons may be simple or profound, but I encourage you to take a few minutes each week to remember what you've been through. Answers to what you're going through now will magically reveal themselves.

Step #5: Come from a Spirit Of Gratitude, Appreciation, and Love

To want what I have,
to take what I'm given with grace.
For this I pray...
- Don Henley

Embrace a kind and giving spirit. This is one of the simplest and most effortless tasks you can perform. You can do it anywhere, any time, and in an instant! The world is a magical place, and I'm always amazed at how quickly life will snap its elastic band on me when I begin to pity myself.

I can't tell you how many times I've been driving or walking somewhere, totally absorbed in my own problems, with even perhaps a little "poor me" attitude, and then, almost in an instant, someone will cross my path and make me take a gasp—someone who's blind, homeless, or with a lot more problems than I have. It awakens me from my narcissism and brings out thoughts of love, gratefulness, and appreciation for all of life. These occurrences are as predictable for me as the sun rising —when I feel sorry for myself, which doesn't happen often any more, the world shows me how much I truly have to be grateful for.

The things you have to be grateful for could include the car you drive to make a journey that used to take people days or weeks to travel, the running water you've never thought twice about, or the medical advancements that have added significantly to our lives and that were unknown just a few short decades ago.

Do you know how many people in the world would give their lives to come to this country—to have freedom and to live anywhere in North America? To be free is such a wondrous gift that many around the world would gladly take our worst day. So the next time you're feeling down in the dumps and wish you had "that guy's life" or "that girl's life," remember the billions of people worldwide who would like to have *your* life!

Step #6: Develop a positive support group

Initially, this step might just involve you and your journal or a blank pad of paper. But I strongly suggest that you gather a group of like-minded individuals who have the common goal of getting together periodically to discuss solutions for each other's challenges. This need not be a formal or even a large gathering – two will do just fine.

Einstein, being the pretty smart guy that he was, basically tried to tell us that if we created a problem, how could we, by ourselves, see a way out of that problem? This group of your non-judgmental friends may decide to meet a few times a year to discuss issues that need additional introspection. So often we chat at a very superficial level with our friends. How are the kids? And work is still going fine, is it? And although deep issues might be troubling us, sometimes without our conscious mind even realizing it, we fail to reach out for some independent analysis.

If you're blessed enough to have some listeners in your life, and not just solution providers, this approach could prove most worthwhile. It allows you to set the stage to dissect and analyze each other's problems in a non-judgmental and non-solution-providing format. You don't want to risk following the advice of someone you shouldn't. The idea is to engage in dialogue about your problem and have the other person (or persons) help you to identify more creative solutions.

Now, I will caution you that sometimes you may not be able to find a group or even an individual to fill this role, and then your best friend may very well be a book or an audio program. Try befriending some excellent authors and use them as guides to self-discovery.

Look for a solution model. Do you know anyone who has had the same problem as you and solved it? Perhaps your answer is as close as a bookstore, the Internet, or a phone call to a good friend. Use the experiences of others to help solve your problems. You may find great comfort in sharing your experiences with a stranger in an Internet chat room or a local live support group. Learning how others solved the problems you're facing will bring encouragement and confidence that you too will be able to overcome your challenge.

Lastly, know when to seek outside help. Although friends and family members can be a wonderful resource in the search for solutions to many problems, there are times when your immediate peer group may have limited expertise, or be unable to provide what you are looking for. Sometimes you need to seek the counsel of a professional trained in psychology or psychiatry or even a local support group. You may also need the professional help of experts in other fields. Try taking a course in an area that could improve your qualifications and abilities and thus banish your feelings of incompetence.

In searching for a positive support group, you might realize that you already have one no matter how large or small. It may consist of just a spouse or a few friends and family members. As wonderful as these groups are and the support they lend to us throughout our lifetimes, the tribal consciousness as it were needs to be examined periodically.

Have you put much thought into what your peer group considers a social norm and what another group might consider as totally acceptable or unacceptable? For example, why do we tip at a restaurant? Gary Belsky and Thomas Gilovich in their *Why Smart People Make Big Money Mistakes* discuss a theory proposed by Russell Roberts, an economist at George Mason University. Roberts states that although no one knows for sure why most North Americans tip at a restaurant, he has some interesting conclusions on the matter. Roberts suggests that people frequently use social rules of thumb when interacting with each other, without conscious acknowledgement, as a way to make life a more pleasant experience. Another example is how we will wait in line at a grocery store or movie rather than pushing our way to the front of the line.

So how can the acceptance of these social norms affect our ability to attract wealth and abundance or simply lead a happier and more peaceful life? If we adopt the beliefs, behaviours and norms of our peer groups without conscious introspection, we could be in trouble.

Step #7: Compared to what?

People seem not to see that their
opinion of the world is also a
confession of their character.
- Ralph Waldo Emerson

So imagine this: you're scheduled to go on vacation for two weeks to some lovely resort or tropical island, and you're frantically working to get those long-standing odds and ends tidied up and off your desk before you leave. You receive a call just as you're in the middle of a procrastination breakthrough. It's your neighbour. There's something wrong at your house, and you must come home immediately.

You arrive home, having made your way through a crowd of neighbours and firemen who have gathered in front of your home. You see, with shock and amazement, that your roof has collapsed and a large part of your second floor has crashed into your ground floor living room. You're beside yourself. How could this happen? "What a tragedy," you start murmuring to yourself and then it hits you—"I'm supposed to leave on vacation tomorrow. Oh God, why do these things always happen to me?"

Although a roof collapse at your home is hardly a tragedy, you can probably relate to an event like this that seems devastating at first, but once put into perspective isn't so bad after all. I guess the question is: whose perspective?

So let's back up. Pretend that this incident did happen to you, but make a small change in the previous version of the story. You've just returned from the Middle East after reviewing your company's failing division there. You've had guns pointed at your head, faced check-points where the police shouted at your driver in a foreign language, and have narrowly avoided several car bombings. A week after your return, you come home to the same scenario. Your roof has collapsed and you realize that you're not going to make your vacation flight the following morning. What's your reaction? Think it's a bit different? After all, you're in a free country, no one has a gun to your head, you've never heard of a car bombing in your city, ever, and you've got house insurance. Not a very big deal. After all, no one was hurt, not even Fluffy the cat because you weren't able to get him back in the house that morning before you left for work.

And if that doesn't do the trick of putting the incident into perspective, let's take the collapsing roof example one more time, minus the trip to the Middle East. This time you get a call on your cell phone from your spouse five minutes after you arrive at your home, which is in shambles. Your child has just been in a major accident and you have no idea how serious the situation is. The house suddenly is the least of your concerns and is not very important at all, is it? It's the same event each time, yet I'm sure you'll agree that it becomes far less significant after a return from a troubling place in the world, or when faced with the death of a loved one. It's all about perspective.

In terms of perspective, there's an old saying, "wherever you go, there you are." I have, as wonderful friends, two couples who, coincidentally, both moved from their respective cities one weekend and both called me on a Sunday evening to let me know how the move had gone. The first couple I spoke with had moved from Calgary to Edmonton. The wife told me she couldn't wait to get out of Calgary. The city had become too big, too fast, and people were always in a hurry, rude, and too pushy for her liking. So, after living over 20 years in that city, she had left for the seemingly quieter location of Edmonton. The husband of the second couple I spoke with told me of a huge and unexpected snowstorm that had blown into Calgary that Sunday morning. This couple had moved to Calgary from Vancouver, and he reported that he was overwhelmed and shocked by the friendliness and courtesies extended to them by his new home city, Calgary. He also commented on how slow-paced the city seemed. To this day he loves every minute in his new city.

How could the first couple have such a different take on the same city? How could Calgary be warm and friendly to one couple and cold and fast-paced to another? Perspective makes all the difference. And, by the way, the couple who moved from Calgary to Edmonton now find, just two short years later, that their new home city is just as cold and unfriendly as their last. Could they, and not their surroundings, be the main contributing factor that leads to their opinion of the city? I'm sure their next destination, whatever city it is, will produce the same results unless they themselves become warmer and friendlier.

Embrace your critics

Great spirits have always encountered
violent opposition from mediocre minds.
The mediocre mind is
incapable of understanding the man who
refuses to bow blindly to conventional
prejudices and chooses instead to express
his opinions courageously and honestly.
- Albert Einstein

It seems that nothing is ever good enough for the critics. As I pondered on this subject, I thought about chefs and restaurateurs and how absurd it would be for them to serve only one item on their menu. There's a reason a restaurant's menu usually lists over a dozen items. Not everyone wants or likes the same thing. Can you imagine a situation where a chef puts on an event for hundreds of individuals, is told to serve the same dish to all of these people, and then becomes upset if some of them complain about or criticize their meals? We'd probably tell the chef not to worry about it as it's almost impossible to cater to the wants of hundreds of different palates. So why then, are we upset when we start on the journey of our dreams and encounter opposition or criticism?

The taller the tree, the more the wind blows.
- Wayne Dyer

Marilyn vos Savant, one of the most brilliant women of our times, was listed in the *Guinness World Records* as having the highest IQ for five years. She has an interesting take on critics in her book, *Ask Marilyn*. She points to the invention of the light bulb. Although significant and a truly life-changing invention, the light bulb still has its limitations. It can light a room, but it won't light your entire house. It's also very fragile and will break if dropped. She sums up the critic thus: "the critic remains silent in the darkness, but curses the light bulb as soon as someone invents it. In science, those who can do and those who can't criticize."

After all, what's easier? Building an office tower or burning it down?

As you focus your energies on your goals and dreams, you may find that the more you focus and the more imminent success becomes, the more likely you are to face criticism. You can't please everyone. Most of us know this at a logical level, yet we take it personally when a negative comment comes our way.

At the same time as you learn to free yourself from the opinions of your critics, I encourage you to embrace your critics, even though this may seem to be paradoxical. Those critics can also be teachers. Although we love nothing more than to receive praise and encouragement for everything we do, the critic may offer clues for improvements that we've never thought of.

I remember at a young age hearing a quote that I have held near to my heart ever since. It states, "The best revenge is to live well." Often we know we would enjoy taking out our revenge on those who have criticized us in the past, but to live well is truly to embrace the critics in our lives and to use their sometimes cruel assessments to our own advantage.

Any fool can criticize, condemn, and complain—and most fools do.
- Benjamin Franklin

Do we ever really grow up?

I think we're all still four year olds on a larger playground. We're all grown up, but that little kid filled with fear, just wanting to fit in and be part of the group, in large part, still lives in each of us.

To be nobody but yourself in a world
which is doing its best day and night to make you everybody else means
to fight the hardest battle any human being can fight;
and never stop fighting.
- E.E. Cummings

E.E. Cummings was born in 1894 and died in 1962. I'm not sure what year the above quote was documented, but he hit it right on the nail. Can you imagine what he'd think living in today's society? With the advent of credit, keeping up with the Joneses takes on a whole new meaning. The average North

American can have much more now in today's environment than ever before. It's tough to be the real you.

During my financial career, I specialized in retirement planning. That's when an individual or couple is faced with a major life change. The person is moving from working their entire life, saving and often scrimping to finally, one day, reach the glorious moment of retirement. Ironically, almost every time I asked a client what they'd like for a retirement income now that they're quitting or have quit working full-time, almost every individual would say, "Well, what's everyone else taking as an income?" How absurd and irrelevant, but a natural question. Of course, my reply was to clarify their wants. Did this person wish to spend their retirement modestly, did they wish to travel and golf and enjoy other hobbies. I suppose the questions, what did you do, have, and how did you live when you were working are the most important. I suppose if people compare themselves to others during their career years, they're bound to in their retirement years as well.

The point? Comparing never accomplishes clarity. We're often looking to justify our lives. We might think we're successful at a certain age if others in our peer group seem less successful at the same stage in life. Conversely, we may also berate ourselves if at 40 our friends are all married with children and we're still single and, seemingly, carefree. I have a few friends in just such a situation envying the choices of their married friends. However, I'm curious about how many of those busy families would love to have a day or week spent free of commitments, living a single life again. Or, given the opportunity to switch tomorrow, would we gladly take our own life back? Is the grass really greener? Or have we been taught, or better yet, bought into the notion that no matter what choice we've made in life, we should always be comparing to someone else to justify those choices?

Be kind to yourself and those you encounter in life. Spend less time criticizing yourself and those you meet and remember that we're all just little ones playing on the same playground, seeking to fit in, fear less, and be loved.

Chapter 5

Money doesn't buy happiness. Really?

Money is better than poverty, if only for financial reasons.
- Woody Allen

What great guru of past or present espoused the colossal myth that money does not equal happiness? And why have we bought into this falsehood that presupposes all of those with money are miserable and those poor, well, at least they're happy? That simply isn't true.

I know many wealthy people. I've counselled thousands of them in my financial career. True, not all of them are happy. Many are far from it. But most, not all, of the unhappy are usually unhappy for reasons that affect the rest of society. Their children are a concern, their health is failing, they worry about their future, and so on.

I have also counselled many clients as well as friends and family who were financially poor or even in severe debt. What I can tell you is that not one of them was truly happy. They all sought to improve their financial situation. Money might not directly purchase a life of happinesses, which is a very personal definition, but it absolutely improves the chances for happiness and a life of fulfillment.

Locate one mother who cannot afford to feed her babies, yet is "happy" with life. Find me an adult child whose parents' health is failing and they cannot purchase the best health care, dentures, or quality of life that this elder deserves. Identify a couple who has yet to fight as the bill collectors call and the repo guy is ready to tow the car. Or the retiree who's lost her life savings on a bad investment and has to declare bankruptcy with no working years left to replenish her portfolio. Is *she* happy?

The MasterCard commercials remind us that with the use of credit, you too can "now enjoy what money can't buy." Swinging one's grandchild around an immaculately manicured yard, enjoying the beach with your loved one, or seeing your child graduate are all priceless occasions that take, yes you guessed it, money to provide. Whether we enjoy, appreciate, and grasp those moments is up to each individual and it is up to them to decide whether happiness will result or not. But let's not buy in to the delusion that you can live in today's society without seeking material wealth. It's a matter of how you define it.

Perhaps you're one of those individuals I meet so often who would like to tell me that it's not about pursuing more, you're not in it for "the money," and so forth. Before you look up my e-mail address to condemn this notion, I would like to remind you that it's the way the world works today and you might as well play along instead of resisting the facts.

I absolutely love painting the outside of my house. It brings me peace and serenity that I've rarely experienced. Something about the monotony of it, being outdoors, complete with a humble waterfall and birds singing, makes me really happy. I reflected upon this the other day. I'm really happy when I paint. Not every homeowner shares the same view. To be clear, it's money that allows me to be happy. Note that I didn't say it makes me happy—that's up to me—but the money did *allow* me to buy my home in the first place and make mortgage payments, pay utilities, taxes, and so on. It's money that allows me to purchase the paint, a waterfall, and afford the day off to do so. It's money that provides bird feed for my chirpy friends. It doesn't guarantee happiness in and of itself, but it does provide the tools necessary for my bliss, should I choose to accept it.

I cannot think of happiness (short or long-term) in my life or any other's that can be achieved without money being at the core of it. What makes *you* truly happy? Think about it for a few minutes. Are they things, situations, moments that money can't buy? Perhaps it's spending time with your parents, the smile of your baby, really being there for a friend. What is it for you? Now, ponder how the financial support, the abundance and yes, money all makes it happen.

Let's stop, especially as women, holding on to this myth that money does not in fact buy happiness. It does, to a great extent, allow happiness into our lives. At the very least, the lack of money certainly doesn't support one's happiness, but generally leads to misery. When we're clear about that, the shift we should embrace is that it's alright and okay to consciously understand that money can make life better. We still need to extract our pleasure from the opportunities presented, however, without money, happiness will likely elude us in the long-term.

I've been rich and I've been poor. Believe me, rich is better.
- Sophie Tucker

Cheaping Out

As an author of several financial books and a lecturer on the same topics, women generally expect me, with regards to spending money either: to be a parental authority of sorts castigating them for their needless spending; or, make them feel guilty about spending money.

I can assure you, I do neither. First, my mission in life and purpose of my other financial books, which deal with the psychology of money, is to create a healthy attitude towards wealth. To be sure there are many that overspend. However, spending is a necessity: One cannot stop spending. Conversely, guilt is a useless emotion. Money doesn't care what it's spent on, if it's saved, or given to charity. It's the holder of said money that personifies its intention. When one feels guilt towards money or when spending, one is in a danger zone. Feeling bad each time money is spent will only create a feeling of deprivation in one's life causing further failures with money management.

Sidebar:

For the sake of brevity and considering those who have read my other books, for a full explanation of subconscious issues with money and a comprehensive guide to changing those core beliefs and issues along with a plethora of fun exercises, check out *The Woman's Guide to Money*. If this is a major issue for you, you might consider checking out my book along with a number of others I've listed in the references/resources at the end of the book.

The antithesis of the "spender" is the "non-spender/saver." I will address this personality trait in the coming pages.

First, I'd like you to identify what type of spending personality you currently have. In my experience there are four types of individuals:

The spender. This person loves spending or is often compelled to do so. Generally, the spending is not for essentials and little forethought goes into such purchases, which are usually on impulse and often are to fulfill some other subconscious desire (to obtain pleasure, an act of boredom, to obtain a positive state change, etc.).

The non-spender. This individual takes great pleasure in "not" spending or at least, not spending on themselves. They are often frugal and carefully think out purchases in advance. They do not necessarily derive any pleasure from spending on themselves but are sometimes quicker to spend on others or for the sake of a charity or worthy cause.

The saver/spender. I've purposely called this category the save/spender, since when someone "saves" money, he or she is still spending money, however, they are spending it on themselves for a future time. Whether the funds are invested in a home, retirement, or savings account, the money is still being spent, but is being spent on an investment or in some similar vein. The saver can be a hoarder, fearful of spending money in the current moment and can be "lack" driven. The saver/spender can also be simply responsible, logical, and prudent in allocating their cash flow: some for current enjoyment and some for the future.

The hoarder. This person hangs on to money and things for the fear of losing them.

The four personality types I have listed are oversimplified, vague, and stereotypical and every individual likely exudes several or all of the traits listed. For the sake of this section, I've kept the descriptions simple enough to use to examine these styles.

With my above categories, take a moment and write down the one that stands out most and aligns with your general personality type as #1, then your second choice, third, and fourth.

I'm most like the: ____

I'm somewhat like the: ____

I can be like the: ____

I'm least like the: ____

Now, list why you're most like the one you rated as #1. If you rated yourself most like the "non-spender," describe why. For example, "my parents were fairly poor and cautious of what they had. I know it was difficult raising us kids and so, I'm not sure if I'll ever have enough. Plus, my income is modest and I must be careful with what I have. I really don't need more stuff anyway and my kids and their hobbies take top priority." If you rated being a "spender" as your #1, an example of your reasoning might be, "I love spending. The impulse of it excites me and brings me pleasure. I often get home and regret what I buy or hide the purchases from my spouse. I'm in more debt than I'd like, but the rush of new things makes me happy."

Describe why you think you rated yourself as a spender, non-spender, spender/saver, or hoarder:

____

____

____

____

____

____

____

Now, describe what you're least like and why. For example, if you're most like a spender vs. a saver/spender, list the reasons, such as, "I never seem to find anything left over at the end of the month for me. Plus, I suppose I never really thought of 'saving' as spending on myself. I always thought of it more as saving for a day that might never come."

Consider doing the same exercise with your spouse. You may find some intriguing reasons why they're the way they are and why you are the way you are. You might be pleasantly surprised, from the dialogue that ensues, to learn things that you never realized about yourself or your spouse. Also, entertain the notion of doing the same with a few of your friends or workmates. Try to pick individuals who are different from you and elicit why they think and act tthe way they do with money. Deduce what lessons you can take away from them, and examine if the category you've been operating at consciously or subconsciously is still serving you. No guilt or criticism is necessary and you needn't share your style with them either if you aren't inclined to do so.

Spending traps

Personally, I've made every financial mistake in the book. Perhaps it was a needed lesson in humility, especially since I made many of those errors during my time as a financial professional. Knowledge does not necessarily equate to prudent execution or action.

Early in my adulthood, I read and listened to everything Tony Robbins had put out on the market, along with similar motivational authors. I adore Tony and still admire him to this day. However, there was a notion that I clung to which didn't serve me.

Tony, along with other authors I followed, prescribed the thought process to success of acting "as if." Oftentimes this strategy is brilliant. Consider the first time public speaker acting "as if" they are confident until they are. Or perhaps the young fellow wishing to ask someone out on a date. Mirroring the physiology of one who's confident and self-assured, especially when you aren't, will greatly increase your chance for success.

In addition, some of these authors have suggested, in a financial realm, that if one acted as if one were wealthy, already financially successful, and so on, eventually, the subconscious would believe this concept and the reality would eventually manifest.

As a naïve young woman, I took this concept to the extreme. Furthermore, working with clients who were extremely wealthy when I wasn't early in my career, the pressure, personally and professionally, to at least appear wealthy superseded my education and common sense. With each purchase I made during this time in my life, I affirmed that I would "act as if" I were already successful and wealthy and was actually doing the right thing for the future me. The pangs of guilt and discomfort were dismissed with the absolute pleasure I derived from spending. It didn't seem to matter if I was nearing my limit on my credit card or spending money that should have been allocated to paying debts or bills. Such thinking, I thought, was for the "lack consciousness." Those that didn't understand that there's more than enough in the universe and that when one acts and thinks prosperously, more will show up. Well, I do believe that's true to a degree, but it must be coupled with prudence and sound financial management.

Buying outside of one's means is not prudent. It gets people in trouble and is likely the reason Canadians are over $752 billion dollars in the hole with consumer debt alone (National Bank, 2004).

The PVP:

I know I said guilt is useless. Look at times when you've saved up for something for yourself and the money was set aside just for that purpose. During times of justified spending, like buying something self-indulgent, but necessary, like a massage or a new outfit, if you're feeling guilt because you think the money should be spent on the kids, paying down debt, or something else, then this emotion needs to be examined and corrected as discussed.

However, let's pretend it's Christmas. You're caught up in the spending frenzy the department stores and advertisers work so hard to build. You start over buying for the kids, your spouse, friends you don't even like, and family you rarely see. You get home, unpack your copious purchases, and with each item, you feel the dread set in. What have you done? You think forward to a month from now when the credit card bills come in and wonder how you got off budget yet again. This might be a good time for guilt and remorse to kick in if this has ever happened to you. You might even consider taking some of those items back.

The point of this PVP? There are times that guilt and feelings of discomfort are helpful. Examine when these feelings emerge and whether they're justified red flags or a buy-in of lack consciousness, that there isn't enough for you.

In my previous example of guilt, it was warranted. I knew that shrugging off reality and fooling myself into believing that I was aligning my subconscious with my future desired self was irresponsible. I spent most of my twenties examining and correcting this behaviour. I have learned, sometimes the hard way, that one must employ intelligent frugality, which I'll address shortly.

Behaviours of spending, to excess or reasonably, and behaviours of frugality aren't necessarily inherent in your being. One can switch to these behaviours within a day or even an hour.

A good friend of mine is quite successful and by most accounts, financially wealthy. He's not a billionaire or anything, but he does make a seven-figure salary consistently and has amassed an impressive investment portfolio over the years. All of his success has been self-made.

One day I had dinner with him and his family at a local restaurant. He was extremely proud of the new Porsche he had just purchased. He wasn't pompous about it – simply proud. I believe the car cost him about $100,000. Considering he earns around a million a year, that's just 10% of his average annual income. A $100,000 car might seem extravagant to most, but considering an annual family income of about $60,000 and a reasonable car purchase of say $30,000, that would actually be more extravagant at 50% of that family's annual income. Curiously, individuals with even less of an annual income are purchasing cars much more expensive than my friend's Porsche.

Back to my friend. He had purchased what most would consider (and even he did) a luxurious car that day. My friend had invited me for dinner and at the onset insisted on treating. When the bill came, he took a healthy pause to examine every item on the slip. He noticed that an extra coffee, which would have been less than $3, was charged on the cheque and hailed our server over. When it came time to add the tip, he asked the table what we thought of our service that night and what percentage he should add.

I found it interesting that my friend, although making a very pricey purchase earlier that day, still found it important to interrupt our conversation to call attention to the $3 coffee that had not arrived at our table. He also found it essential that the server receive a fair reward for service, but wasn't arrogant in simply flashing around his money.

My friend exudes behaviour that can change within a day or hour. Sometimes he is a flamboyant spender, an intelligent saver (which he always invests in himself each month), or he displays reasonable frugality along with the confidence to not care if someone thinks he is cheap.

I had another good friend and client in my life years ago. He displayed the polar opposite behaviour to my other friend. If you've read my other books, *The Woman's Guide to Money* or *The Prosperity Factor*, he's the fellow I refer to as Tim. He too earned nearly a million dollars each year for quite some time and also purchased vehicles over the $100,000 mark. However, Tim would never have checked over his bill and often handed servers his credit card even before they brought the bill. He tipped lavishly even when the service was dismal. And Tim never once spent money saving for his future. He was in fact, millions of dollars in debt. Tim was raised poor and was always trying to impress everyone else, including himself. He sought attention through being the big shot and proving he was rich. Tim was nearly 50 years old and shouldn't have needed to prove anything to anyone, but his lack of respect for money and his discomfort with it were keeping him poor. He didn't understand intelligent frugality or the inner game that's necessary to live a prosperous life independent of how much money flows into one's life.

My first friend felt good about himself and respected money—his and that of others. I remember when I first opened my investment firm years ago that he was one of the first clients to test my ability with a percentage of his investments. As a small business owner, he knew that resources in the early years are tight for most who set up shop. Whenever I met with a client, I presented all of their papers in a Keehn Financial folder. It wasn't much, but I thought it was more professional than simply putting them in a nondescript envelope.

After about six months of dealing with this client and friend, I received in the mail five of these folders back. My friend worked for an extremely successful company with enormous budgets and, remember, made seven figures himself. I couldn't believe that he would take the time to save these folders and send them back to me so I could reuse them with other clients.

Not only did he respect his own finances and cared about the budget of his company, but he also went to great lengths to revere the resources of others. If he was thought of as cheap sometimes, he couldn't have cared less. He knew that watching each dollar was important. I'm quite sure that is a major reason why he is successful and will be for the rest of his life.

The PVP:

There are times that pampering oneself is absolutely necessary. Yes, I said necessary. If you've never had a manicure, pedicure, facial, or massage, it's essential that you get one and soon. I don't care if you think you can't afford it or you're just not that kind of woman or it's not vital. It is. I'm always shocked by how long it's been when I ask a group of women when the last time was that they had any of these service performed. And what absolutely floors me is the number of women that will admit they have never had any of these professional services. Whether you work full-time inside or outside the home, a reward that's totally self-indulgent is absolutely essential periodically. And not just for women, for men as well. I can write pages justifying the health benefits of a massage, such as the increase in circulation and stimulation, the detoxifying effects, not to mention the healing and relaxation that's created. When you're lying there on the table with someone else making your body feel good and you're paying them with money from your efforts, it reinforces that money is not just something required for the many obligations in your life. At times, money should be used for absolute pleasure and enjoyment.

My mom had a neighbour who was sitting outside one day when I came over to visit. When I asked her how she was doing, before she answered, I could see she was glowing, which took me by surprise. She was in her late forties, and stressed because her husband worked out of town leaving her with all the responsibilities of the house, their three kids, and she was working at a paid job too. Generally, she was exhausted. That day, she looked like a million bucks. She answered and said she had a pedicure for the first time in her life. She reported, "It was the first time in a long time that I really felt like a woman." For under $60 this service made her feel like a queen and allowed her to indulge in some much needed personal time.

If getting a service performed at a spa is out of reach financially for you even if you were to save up, consider the beauty schools in your city. The services are usually performed at a fraction of the price of the salon, since the students need the practice. The environment and the end result might not quite be spa quality, but it's a viable alternative.

A final note on pampering—if you or a woman in your life has found herself alone as the result of a divorce, death, or has just been single for some time (children don't count), get yourself or her a massage. Women, I think even more than men, need to be touched. I know a great number of single friends that seem to get colds, flus, and just sick more often than those in a happy relationship. Now, that's not scientifically proven and is solely my observation. But think about how good it is to be touched. I think it is a basic human need. If you or someone you know isn't being touched (and laugh if you will, but, of course, I'm referring to being touched in a non-sexual way), consider the art of massage, a facial, or some other important indulgence.

Earlier, I had you classify which category you best fit into regarding spending. Now, I'd like you to think about what type of spender or non-spender you are in other areas of your life. For example, corporately, with others, with other people's money, are you the same type of spender?

My honey, Wyatt, is notoriously cheap with himself. He'd like to refer to it as intelligent frugality, but it's not. It's like pulling teeth to have him purchase anything for himself and he's aloof whenever I buy something for him even if it's an item he really wanted. However, when it comes to spending for me, for food or for my family, he's overwhelmingly generous. It's an important distinction to make. We all have areas where we spend less. It's a matter of context.

Take a few minutes to consider your habits and spending patterns in different areas of your life and again, list which type from the earlier categories most suits your current style (spender, non-spender, spender/saver, hoarder).

Your spending styles:

Corporately: ____________________
With family: ____________________
With friends: ____________________
For your children: ____________________
Donations/charity: ____________________
With volunteer organizations: ____________________
With other's money in general: ____________________
Other: ____________________

Notice too how these traits may have changed over the years for you. During my banking days, I had a fairly senior position with an expense account and above average marketing budget. As the bank was a huge corporation to me during those young career days with no limit in sight, I was quite lax in justifying the dollars used for marketing. I didn't really have anyone holding me accountable for those dollars used and in hindsight, was not as respectful as I could have been or would have been with my own funds. At that time, I would likely have classified myself as a lavish spender/over-spender corporately.

When I opened my own company, not only did I not have a salary or benefits any longer, I had the expensive task of branding and building a new company from scratch. In addition to the lack of salary and expense account I was used to at the bank, I then became an employer and had the extra burden of paying my own staff. I very quickly moved from a corporate spender to a corporate cheapskate. Every penny I could shave off and scrutinize, I did. Plus, years of volunteering made me realize that every dollar spent within a non-profit organization meant that it wasn't being used for the needs of that organization. I was taught the valuable lesson of frugality and respect for others' resources, plus, opened my eyes to creative alternatives.

The four personality types are within each of us. Sometimes we lean towards one more than the other, however, labelling yourself a spender or hoarder can be hazardous. In Neuro-linguistic Programming (NLP) they discuss the danger of using what they call universals. To recap, a universal is an inflexible statement that doesn't allow for an alternative behaviour, thought, and so on. For example, you always do this, or you never do that. Always and never are just two examples. If you've always been a hoarder with money, food, and general stuff, it doesn't open to the possibility and awareness of the times that you're also generous and giving. I've met many hoarders over the years and it's not a permeating behaviour of their life. It's usually in one or a number of areas of their live, but not *every* aspect of their life. An overspender isn't always generous and as free with their money, time, and resources, and they might be spending on themselves.

Making distinctions between how you act in different situations and circumstances in your life will allow you to examine and consciously decide if they suit you, if they were unknowingly adopted and adapted over time through others, and if you'd now like to continue with them.

My mom is one of the most generous individuals I know. Not only is she giving of her time, love, support, and money to her family and friends, but also to those she doesn't know. I've never seen her pass anyone on the street who has asked her for money without giving. I've witnessed her time and time again walking up to total strangers because in her words, "they seemed sad and needed someone to lift them up if even only for a second." Generosity is only one of my mother's many virtues.

However, a behaviour I wish she would consider changing, that I have adopted in some parts of my life in the past, is hoarding. Yes, a very giving and generous person can also partake in the lack consciousness of holding on to things. My mom, as early as I can remember, always had her good clothes, dishes, furniture, and so on that "should be saved for a special time." There's nothing wrong with that logic at all. One doesn't wear an evening gown to the grocery store. However, my mother has taken this conservation of things for a special occasion too far. She recently cleaned out her closets to give away some clothes to a woman in need and discovered brand new outfits (some with price tags still on them) from as far back as two decades ago. Growing up we didn't quite have plastic on the future, but to be sure, the furniture in the sitting room was just for that. If my brothers or I "moved too much" we were booted out. And the good dishes, well, you can imagine that those didn't come out too often.

I'm quite sure that you might identify with my mom's hoarding idiosyncrasy, as do I. The things my mom won't use, I, as an adult, have vowed to, for better or worse. I use my "good" dishes on a daily basis, and sure, many of them are now chipped, but I can always buy more dishes. And the cream sofas in my front room that I use, put my feet on, have naps on, and enjoy are now in need of replacement after the twelve years since I purchased them. And whenever I buy a new outfit, I do my best to wear it within three days of buying it. This behaviour could be a direct rebellion of growing up with my mom (she's a bit better now since I've nagged her over the years), but my reasoning, is, isn't "stuff" to be used? Otherwise, what's the purpose of getting more of it? For our use and enjoyment or to impress others on special occasions which may never come?

My aunt recently told me that instead of simply giving away all of her "good" clothes that she no longer uses, she would keep some for herself and wear them while gardening, which she does every day the weather allows. Her reasoning was, "why shouldn't I look and feel good for me even while gardening?" I concur.

So, generally speaking, I don't think of myself as a hoarder. Perhaps I work a little too hard to display the opposite behaviour in my life and just maybe there are times I should save a few things for special occasions.

How would you categorize yourself? Is your pantry full of food ready to expire, have you kept every bottle of wine given to you that's possibly passed its time, do you dust the candles around your house because you never burn them and instead keep them for show?

Take a few moments to complete the following. No matter how you classified yourself when I asked you, I'm sure there's times when you do the opposite. If you generally think you're cheap, and I want you to be clear with yourself that there might be times when you're cheap, circumstances where one should be frugal, but also that you are not cheap. There are times you're generous and giving with yourself and others. Then, you can choose to consciously exude whatever behaviour you wish in a given day as opposed to letting it take control of you.

I've given you some examples to start:

Spending Money

When it comes to spending money, I don't hesitate on the following:

(e.g. for food, on your kids, when buying a gift for someone, going out on the town, buying only good toilet paper)

____

____

____

____

Cheaping Out

When it comes to being frugal, the following are things I just can't or won't spend money on:

(e.g. brand labels, dining out, something for yourself, pampering, items for your house that aren't essential like fresh flowers, candles)

____

____

____

____

Hoarding

Currently, or in the past, I have hoarded:
(e.g. food, money, clothes)

____

____

____

____

Take a little time to think about your answers. They might take a few hours, days, months, or years to identify. The point is to decide if they still serve you, represent your conscious decisions in life, and if you'd like to continue with justifying why you do what you do.

Every dollar counts

A good friend of mine has a medium-sized company with a number of employees. Since they're required to drive a great deal, he supplies many of them with gas cards. One day my friend, shocked by the dishonesty of some people, shared the findings of an audit he did on the gas card statements that month. Not only did some employees fill up the vehicles of friends and family, some had even gone as far as to purchase their month's supply of cigarettes and lottery tickets on the dime of my friend's company.

There will be opportunities, corporately and in other instances, for you to feel that you are "owed" by your employer or some other institution or individual. I think the word to keep in mind is "transparency"! There will be opportunities to fudge or round up the hours you actually worked, the expenses you actually incurred, and so forth. Do not fall prey to the insidious notion that it will not be noticed. First, you'll notice and second, it's just not worth it. Always think transparency in every instance.

If you think you deserve more money for the hours you work because you did more in those hours for your employer or client than someone else did, have a frank discussion with them as opposed to billing for more and justifying to yourself that you deserve it. If you feel your boss or client doesn't fully appreciate you or isn't paying you what you're worth, don't risk your position or reputation by pulling the wool over anyone's eyes by taking more, hiding purchases, or possibly even stealing.

When I'm hired for speaking, I have a strict policy that my speaking fee includes all of my meals. It's a small thing, but it's important to me. Plus, I like to make my invoicing simple for my clients, so instead of nickel and diming them on food at the airport, a taxi ride here and there, breakfast at the hotel—I simply build my fee around those costs. My accountant and others in the speaking business tell me I shouldn't do that and should charge for each and every expense, no matter how minor.

When I check out of a hotel, almost every time the temptation is there to have all of my room charges taken care of by the company as most offer to do so. I take the extra steps to have the hotel separate my charges and pay for them myself. It's a very small thing (sometimes not so small depending on my attack on the minibar) but it is a corporate policy of mine. Most companies that hire me to speak are quite large and likely wouldn't care if I snuck through the personal calls I made during my stay, the movie and bottle of wine I ordered, or the dinner at the hotel with a friend. However, why risk my reputation or the possibility of not being hired again for thousands of dollars for a mere hundred dollars of room charges? If I were paying me as a speaker, I would only expect the same. Respecting someone's money, no matter what the context or circumstance, as if it were yours, I think, is an important policy for everyone to adopt. You'd be surprised how many act contrary to that logic.

But they're big; they won't notice

Don't fall prey to the opportunity to bill big companies extra or not perform at your best. If every employee acted this way, even the largest company would crumble. Many have.

Another corporate policy of mine is to fly only in economy when travelling domestically and someone else is picking up the tab. If a company offers to fly me first class, I suggest they still book an economy ticket and use the extra dollars (which are significant from economy to first class) as a donation to their company charity or as a reward to their employees. The reason? For the few hours it takes to get anywhere in Canada, it's a waste of money to pay double or triple the price for a better ticket. Although the company may be paying a speaker's fee to me that's quadruple the amount of a first class ticket, keeping my expenses low, I believe in great part, has earned me a reputation as a respectable speaker in the few years I've been doing it professionally.

What I've also come to notice in the hundreds of flights I've had in the past few years is how many senior executives and CEOs that I've met in economy have also employed the same corporate policy. When I first stared travelling professionally, I couldn't believe the senior level individuals that I met in economy who could certainly afford and justify sitting in first class. However, they remember and know that ever dollar counts and treat the company's money as if it were their own.

Before spending a dollar corporately or with the volunteer organization you belong to, examine each expenditure as if it were coming from your own pocket. Not only will you gain a greater appreciation for financial prudence, you'll gain a reputation of being shrewd and will likely expand your level of creativity!

The Pleasure Factor

At this point, I'd like you to make a detailed list of all of the things that do or could bring you pleasure, delight, or happiness and don't require you to lay out extra money. I think that people overeat, overspend, and overdo a great deal of unwanted behaviours and actions because they don't clearly know what does or could bring them pleasure. They're bored, lonely, scared, or simply comfortable. Someone I know who has had a weight problem for most of his life is a classic example. When I asked him to write down all of the things that brought him pleasure or happiness, his list took him some time to create and only included two things—food and TV. He forces himself to walk daily and eats fairly healthy, however, with a list of only two things that bring him joy it certainly doesn't inspire a life of fitness. No wonder he's consistently battling his weight and is supremely unhappy. However, he is very comfortable. What's the old saying? "The only difference between a rut and a grave is a few feet."

Since you've made it this far, I'm quite sure you're not interested in digging your rut deeper and are willing to get a little uncomfortable at times in exchange for a life of happiness and one that you truly deserve.

I want you to make a list of over 100 specific things that you can do at almost any time that could bring you joy, bliss, excitement, peace, and so on. Make this list as easy as possible. The key is to set the rules up to win and to create a checklist that you can pull out when you need a change, want to break an old habit, or just create a fuller life. If you have any difficulty with this challenge, take the exercise to your friends to elicit their ideas. You don't have to accept them, but be open to things that *could* bring you pleasure or happiness—especially if you've never tried them before or if they'd take you slightly out of your comfort zone.

Feel free to add any of your current standbys, even if you overspend and spending brings you pleasure, or if you're overweight and food makes you feel good or you know the health risks of smoking but choose to do it, be honest and write those things down. But please stretch yourself and write down the "coulds" as well. Another caveat is that this list should be action based. For example, if you take great delight in your child's smile or the twinkle in their eye, make this joy an action. If you're stressed out at work or bored on a Sunday afternoon, instead of reaching for a chocolate bar, heading out to the mall, or going for a smoke, what else could you do that would make you feel good? Could you take the kids to the park on the weekend? Could you take a break at work and flip through a family photo album that you keep in your desk drawer?

I've listed a few examples and highly encourage you to get to at least 100 even if it takes you some time and reflection.

Examples:

- Volunteering somewhere – serving food to the homeless on your lunch hour, driving seniors to appointments on the weekend, etc.
- Finding a new hobby – crafting, painting, knitting, crossword puzzles
- Spending more time with others – taking yourself out for coffee and people watching, calling an old friend out of the blue, sending a card in the mail to tell someone why they've made a difference in your life.
- Moving – taking a walk, working out, trying a new sport
- Cooking – trying a new recipe, searching the Internet for new ideas, making a homemade recipe book, taking a cooking class
- Learning – reading a book, listening to a new audio program, taking a class to learn a new language

You get the idea. List all of the actions that you could take with little effort, at work or while home, that could expand your life in addition to those you do now:

Reciprocity

In my last book, I examined the notion of fair exchange, and what Frederic Lehrman in his *Prosperity Consciousness* audio program describes as a clearing of accounts. The number of irate e-mails I receive to this day regarding the subject is curious to me. The concept is simple. In life, in relationships, people keep score of the good they do. Women, I think, keep better score. If you're married or in a relationship, think of the times you felt unappreciated for all that you do and in a moment of anger or hurt recounted many of those things to your spouse. Likely it ended with your spouse giving you a dumbfounded look wondering how you could remember that long list. And they may not even have any recollection of what they did.

Reciprocity is a reciprocation, a mutual exchange, or a give and take.

Lehrman's example of "clearing of accounts" goes like this. Let's say you have a friend. She calls you up and ask you to help her paint her fence this weekend. You happily oblige. Then, about two weeks later, she calls you up. Her car as died and she asks to use yours for a few days. You agree and willingly lend her your car. Then, about a month later, she needs help moving a few sofas and there you are again to assist. About a month later, you and your spouse have a very important awards ceremony to attend for your eldest child. You have two young ones at home that can't come. Moments before you're to head out the door, the babysitter calls and cancels at the last moment. You call up this friend of yours who you happen to know is free that night. You ask her to come and babysit for a few hours and she tells you no. She gives you some lame excuse about why she can't come, but you know for a fact that she is free.

If that were you, how would you feel in that instance? Would you say anything to that friend right then about how she didn't help bail you out? Or would you have a chat with her later? If you were like most and truly honest with the situation, you would likely have been hurt, possibly angry, or worse in that situation. Consider all you had done for her as the good friend that you are. You painted, lent your car with grace, and were there when she needed you. You simply asked for a small favour and it was not extended.

There are a few important points to this analysis. First, if that were you in the example, when you called your friend and she said no, would you have remembered what you did for her in the past? Be honest. Think of some friends or family in your own life. Does anyone come to mind that you feel "owed" by? Someone you've spent countless hours counselling through a divorce or breakup, someone you're always there for? Really think about it if one doesn't come to mind immediately. Notice the "list" that you've kept. I don't think we try to keep lists, but it's human nature.

Second, notice if you feel unappreciated in any way by anyone, hurt or even angry. Think back to friends in the past who you no longer keep in touch with. Why do you no longer keep in contact with them? Did you simply drift apart or can you think of some examples where you felt used and unacknowledged by them?

Back to my example of the friend for a moment. Consider if the accounts of your friendship were "cleared" with each interaction. Perhaps you painted the fence and she sent you home with a bottle of wine, a home-cooked pie, or some other form of thanks. Then, after she borrowed and returned your car, she offered to take you for dinner that night. And after moving the furniture with her, she had a box of chocolates ready for you to take home. Now, when you called her asking for her assistance, even knowing she's free and she declines, do you then feel as bad or hurt? Think about it. After each transaction or event, your friend gave you something to "clear" the account. It needn't be equal to what it would cost to hire someone to paint the fence, the full cost of renting a car, or payment equal to what a mover would charge, but something was offered other than simply a thanks (and sometimes that might not even be extended). It might be a gift, a returned service, or even cash. How would you feel then? Would you still feel owed?

Now, if you're like the numerous women who write their hostile e-mails to me already or if in a workshop would be blatantly annoyed with me at this point, you might be thinking, "wait a minute—this is what friends do for each other. They help one another, support each other and don't ask or expect anything in return."

Are you thinking something along those lines? It is true. There are times in a friendship or relationship of a personal or business nature when you are honestly assisting someone knowing and expecting that they can never repay you in any way—financially or otherwise. We're taught that friends don't accept money or expect reciprocity for the friendship. Right? But what about those friends, spouses, acquaintances, and family members that take and take while we give and give? Think of times of hurt or frustration. If you can honestly say that you've never felt unappreciated, unacknowledged, hurt or other such feelings when someone didn't recognize what you had done for them, then you are one of very few women out there and by all means, skip past this section.

However, if you were really honest with yourself, I bet you can think of an example or two. If you're feeling any disagreement or annoyance with this notion, let me first further clarify. Yes, friendship in theory should be selfless. And women are terrific at carrying this badge. We've been fed this myth that the more we do for others and the less we expect in return, the better we are as women. And the one that stands up and asks for something in return—acknowledgment or reciprocity—is somehow unsuccessful as a spouse, friend, or mother.

I was recently hired by an organization in Calgary to present a full day workshop for a group of their women attendees. When I explained this concept of clearing of accounts the women were as taken aback as I expected. I had them break into groups and discuss the concept a little further. As they opened up and were honest with themselves, some of them dared to utter out loud that yes, at times it would be nice to be acknowledged or receive some reciprocity and that's just okay!

One woman told us that she always prepares the family holiday dinners. She expressed that they take a great deal of her energy. Not only did she have to clean the house, grocery shop, and prepare the food, but also the financial expense of doing all of this was sometimes a bit of a burden. In the same breath as she recounted her frustration, that she loved doing it. She stated that when other family members ask to bring a dish of food, she always insisted that they don't and just their attendance was enough. I asked her why she didn't let them help out when her description sounded a bit overwhelming and not really a great deal of fun for her. She said that she really likes to plan her menu out in advance and often, some guest's dishes wouldn't work or what if she relied on someone to bring a main dish and then they didn't show up? After a few quiet moments, she repeated that although she does love entertaining her large family, it could be a bit of a financial burden at times. She further came up with the thought that, "What if I just asked everyone to pitch in $20? It's really not much for them and would nearly pay for my grocery bill. That way I could still plan for the menu I want." She seemed so empowered and relieved when she thought of that idea. It won't pay for her time to prepare her home, the meal, the grocery shopping involved, and the clean up, but it would ease her financial pressure. When I asked her if it would still feel like it was a burden to hold the family dinner if everyone pitched in, she seemed light up and had a smile. "No, it would be fantastic! It would free me to have more fun and I think I'd offer to do it more often." She ended her sharing by saying, "I'm not sure why I haven't asked my family for that before."

Other participants jumped in describing friends, neighbours, and others that they have cut out of their life or see less due to resentment and ill feelings. They admitted that they had never confronted these individuals to let them know their situation and many felt pangs of guilt even thinking of doing so. But my question to you is, is it worth it to lose that person in your life or harbour negative, even if very low-lying, feelings of annoyance by not saying anything?

One participant shared that she always drove her neighbour's child to school with her child. She reported that it was no big deal as she was driving her own child anyway—it was no real extra effort. However, after months of doing this for her neighbour, she started to feel a little used and unrewarded. She commented that her neighbour could at least offer a little gas money or something because if the neighbour had to drive her own child every day, there would be a cost and effort involved.

I might add that the women who are not telling their friends and family about what they would like in exchange for their efforts are solely to blame for their unhappiness. How could the family truly know the financial trouble of making dinner that that one woman went through? They might be absolutely delighted to simply chip in $20. They could be thrilled since they'd get a chance to contribute and don't have to go to the effort of making a dish or stopping at the store to pick up something prepared. They might be delighted to feel that they too contributed to the dinner and the few dollars for them is easy.

The woman whose daughter is getting a ride to school might have no clue that her friend is starting to feel resentment. Little does she know that if she doesn't offer something to her friend, her friend is going to start making excuses as to why she can't drive her daughter anymore and their friendship will start to decline and feel strained. Meanwhile, if this woman just takes the time, a deep breath, and with some courage lets the other know that although it's not a big deal, taking both children to school everyday takes time and resources—perhaps they could work out a fair solution together? Perhaps both could take turns driving the kids to school. Or if that doesn't work, maybe she could babysit for her once in a while or simply pitch in for gas money if none of those are convenient.

Another woman in the workshop shared something that I hadn't really fully considered before. I've always been on the side that we need to not be afraid to ask for a clearing of accounts from others. She shared a few stories where someone had done something for her and she offered something in return. She said they always politely declined insisting they *wanted* to do it or that in the name of friendship it was their pleasure. For her, it was an annoyance. She said that when someone didn't let her repay them (for her this was very important) that it then left her in a vulnerable position of owing them. This is how she interpreted a clearing of accounts and I wonder how often when we don't let someone buy us lunch, treat us to a gift, or allow them to bring them a dish for dinner that we're actually not allowing them to extend their feelings of worth, usefulness, and fair exchange. She further pointed out, which I have always believed as well, that it applies to something as simple as a compliment. When someone tells us how great we look or how fantastic a new piece of clothing is and we don't accept it, push their compliment aside or downplay it, we actually offend that person. With those actions, we're saying, not intentionally, "You don't know what you're talking about. You think I look good and I don't trust your interpretation."

A recent e-mail I received was from a woman commenting how much she liked my book, but totally disagreed with this concept of clearing of accounts with friends. She found it absurd and was not going to try it at all. She then followed that sentence by saying that she did have friends she no longer spent time with who abused the balance of their relationship. Either this woman didn't read her own e-mail or found it better to simply toss aside valuable friendships when the balance was out of sorts instead of exploring the idea of fair exchange and vocalizing when she felt upset.

I truly believe long-term relationships of any sort require a great deal of self-esteem on our part to keep them healthy. We need to be secure enough to accept a compliment, gift or giving from others and at the same time, need to let others know when we ourselves need something from them.

I'm not suggesting for a moment that you intentionally keep accounts, always ask others for reciprocity, or the like. That's absurd and makes life difficult. I simply ask that you examine the concept and see if it applies in your own life. When you experience an uncomfortable feeling within any type of relationship, inspect why that is. Instead of reacting in a passive-aggressive manner by quietly suffering, not telling the other person what you truly want, harbouring resentment by thinking that they should know what you want, or simply distancing or cutting yourself off from that relationship entirely, you can now choose to see how considering the notion of clearing accounts, at times, and explaining the concept to others, can help keep the integrity of your relationships for the long haul.

The final point is that we all have a fine line that does get crossed sooner or later. We're martyrs to a fault, but also to a point. The list of things we can tolerate is different for each of us and is also based on the individual we're extending our efforts to. Your list might be endless with your children growing up, but reaches a breaking point once they're adults. It might be much shorter for a neighbour than for a long-time friend. But consider, unless you're one of the very few in the world or aren't in touch with your true feelings, you likely have a list, if not many.

How do you go about asking?

This is a tough one for me that I still need to practice. It's also the number one question I receive from women that do agree with me on the fair exchange or clearing of accounts notion.

I always wanted to open my own restaurant growing up but knew that I never would. I have so many friends and an enormous family and have always had a difficult time outright asking for money, as many do from those close to them. I knew my restaurant would never last, since I'd lose money every time someone I knew came in.

Many women in the workshop echoed the same frustration with their current businesses. A great number of women who were self-employed or had a side product or service found that their friends and family *expected* to receive their goods or services for free. I must personally agree and experienced that when my first book came out. Each person I ran into (clients, friends, family) who knew my first book was out expected that I would give them a copy. Not fully understanding how the publishing world worked and that I had a cost to pay for each and every book, it was actually my fault, not theirs, for not letting them know I lost money each time I gave them a book. I suppose many of them assumed they cost the author nothing to give away.

As the women and I discussed a workable solution in such situations, we came up with the idea of being up front with those close to you about your product or service before they even ask. Some women conceded that they don't even market their businesses to those in their personal network as they're afraid they'll just lose money. And as any successful business knows, your personal network can be your most lucrative.

We came up with the idea, although so very simple, that instead of the awkward interaction with someone close to you either charging them and their feeling that they should get some special treatment as a friend or family member, or your giving the farm away for free and feeling resentment about it, you would state at the beginning of the process what your "special family discount" is before even being asked. You might have a cleaning service and state, "By the way, just so you know, my fee is $30 an hour, but for friends and family, it's always 15% off." If you work in some entertainment industry, for example, and friends always expect free tickets, you could offer them a reward program, such as, "My company won't let me give free tickets away to friends, but a special thing I can do for you is give you tickets 50% off each time you have someone else buy at full price." That way, your friends feel special and are more likely to work hard to promote your business and you've don't have to lose money in the process. It's a win/win situation and eliminates the tension that can build without stating anything at all.

Money Martyrs

I've met a few money martyrs over the years and I'm not sure if it's a syndrome plaguing women exclusively or not. I see more female culprits due to the fact that my material is generally geared towards women and they usually make up my audiences, but I can say, I haven't met even a fraction of the men who are proud to proclaim themselves money martyrs as women.

Why is it that women are compelled to serve their community, will solicit the support of friends and family (some go as far as to harass and guilt) to raise money for breast cancer runs, their kids' school trip, promote another's business, and so on. But, when it's time for her to ask for money in exchange for her efforts, either directly or in the form of a raise, she simply remains quiet?

Martyr (as defined by the *Canadian Oxford Dictionary*)
a. A person who suffers for adhering to a principle, cause, etc.
b. A person who suffers or pretends to suffer in order to obtain sympathy or pity.

I recently spoke at the University of British Columbia's campus in Kelowna. A lovely forty-something, very well dressed and put-together looking woman and her friend came to talk with me afterwards. I'll call the woman Pam. Pam said my talk on prosperity resonated with her and just about broke down as she shared how she couldn't financially support herself and her two children. She said she was bouncing cheques every month, not making minimum payments, and thought even bankruptcy couldn't help her.

As I'm not a financial counsellor anymore and had only a few minutes to chat with Pam and her friend before flying out, we quickly brainstormed as to what she could tangibly, and specific to her situation, take away from our meeting to possibly improve. I asked her a bunch of questions to determine if she had assets of any sort that could be worked with. She didn't. I tried to drill down and identify any excess spending we could trim. There wasn't anything. She was as budgeted a possible and didn't have any room to move within her company at that time anyway.

I quickly threw out a few of options that wouldn't take a great deal of time away from her family after work that could bring in some extra income for her. One of those ideas was an ebook or a book. She quickly beamed and excitedly told me that she did in fact have an idea for a book. She shared that she had an awful divorce and originally, her husband was awarded custody of her kids. She told me it was devastating, but that he was very wealthy and she wasn't. She lost everything financially fighting for her children, but eventually won. She said it was a real passion of hers to educate other women and men on how to work within the court system during a custody battle, their rights, financial shortcuts, and so on. I told her how valuable her information was and would certainly help others. Plus, the great thing is she could also potentially bring in some extra income into her life by selling an ebook on the Internet or possibly by finding a publisher.

As soon as I mentioned the money aspect, her shoulders slumped and her beaming smile disappeared. "Well," she said, "I certainly wouldn't be doing it for the money. I would like to write this as a book, but wouldn't charge. After all, it would be for the well-being of other parents so that they wouldn't have to go through what I had to."

I hear this tragic story, although with different details, from women on a weekly basis. They have a passion, something they want to share, some way of changing the world or someone's life—but heaven forbid they get paid for it. How boorish, they think.

If this concept sounds like you, put away the Mother Teresa act even if it is sincere. There is nothing wrong with serving others, the world, and the market you've identified where you can make a difference *and* getting paid or rewarded for it. Please carefully re-read the last sentence. I'm not asking you to become cold and mercenary. Simply consider—if your contribution is truly of service to the world, why can you not also be rewarded for it? There are times to be sure that your contribution is simply altruistic. You might volunteer your time for many organizations, sing for those in palliative care, and knit mittens for the homeless. But, do you have other talents that, at times, could bring more cash flow to your life and allow you to make a positive impact to others *and* yourself? Perhaps it's time to give yourself and other women you know permission to let go of the martyrdom in exchange for a mutually beneficial exchange.

How do you do it?

The next most common question I receive from women on this topic is, "OK, I buy into the fair exchange concept or asking for money from friends for a business I'd like to start or a raise for my boss, but *how* do I do that?" If you're one of those rare women that does not have a problem asking for money in any way from others, I applaud and admire you! You can skip this section. But for the rest of us (the vast majority), we either have some minor or major issues with asking for money or some form of fair exchange from others.

Like the memory expert, I can assure you, only good old fashioned practice works and, of course, some courage. You simply start. Take a deep breath and ask. "I'm having a barbeque this weekend—would you like to come? Oh, and if you could bring an appetizer and any alcohol you might like, that would be great." And when someone offers you something, money for dinner, to chip in for the family gathering, you simply say, "thank you." I personally don't find it easy to ask and simply say thank you when something is offered. I don't always succeed at all and fall back to my old habits. But I'm proud of myself when I do, am less disappointed, and find each time a little easier. I also find that others are quick to assist when I openly ask them for what I need. Sometimes they are not, but that's more an exception than the rule.

In my other books, I describe the concept of setting up a mini-economy with your friends and family. The idea is that you might wish to overtly practice this asking and accepting of money, favours, and exchanges with others. Oftentimes, those close to us are the hardest to ask and accept from. You might find it easy to ask a stranger for payment on their account, but wince when a friend is 60 days in arrears.

If you're game, call or e-mail a number of friends and explain the concept I have outline above. You can also find the rules of play with a pre-written invitation and explanation at *www.kelleykeehn.com* or e-mail me at *wealth@kelleykeehn.com* or in my books *The Woman's Guide to Money* and *The Prosperity Factor for Kids*. You'll explain the concept to your friends and either online, but hopefully in person, you will determine the products and services you and they have to offer. You might be a great canner and always have lots left over that you could turn into products for sale. Perhaps a hobby of yours is to paint, create one-of-a-kind handmade greeting cards, or specialty cakes. There are thousands of other products that you might enjoy constructing that could be turned into cash.

The exercise provides two major benefits. First, it allows you permission, in a mutually acceptable environment, to ask for payment and to offer payment to friends for your and their wares. The second benefit, but just as significant, is you might just find a side passion that could also generate extra income in your life that you hadn't thought of. Practice asking and receiving from your own network; it does get easier and easier over time.

Kelley's anti budget

Personally, I hate budgets. Rarely do they work. I know, not what you expected from a financial expert. Bet you're pleasantly surprised though. Who needs more rigidity in their life? We want to enjoy our money and have the freedom to spend as we wish, not a spouse or financial planner forcing our purchases into a pre-determined monthly amount.

As a former financial professional, and an author of several books on finance, I'm asked about this financial imprisonment frequently. During my professional career, most of my clients fell into the category of ultra wealthy. As you might guess, this select group doesn't need to budget; they have more money than they could ever spend.

However, unless these people had recently come upon a windfall, the majority of them did carefully analyze and were aware of what they spent each month. How can anyone create a guideline of what they're *going* to spend if they haven't monitored *what* they typically spend?

For instance, I can tell you that you should spend no more than $550 on groceries, dining out, and lunches at work. But if you and your spouse are currently dishing out more than $900 monthly on food, a reduction of $350 is unrealistic.

The key to enjoying your money while curbing unnecessary waste is awareness. Start today and for at least the next 30 days just write down every dollar you spend. Purchase a small notebook that will fit in your purse or suit jacket (yes, write this one down too). Log every dollar spent, including pre-authorized payments and bank service charges.

At the end of the month, tally up your expenditures. Look for opportunities to cut expenses such as ATM bank fees or late payment charges. These can add up significantly and don't do anything to improve your quality of life.

After you've found patterns in your spending, determine if you can reduce areas by 10% or save an equivalent amount by being creative, such as taking your lunch to work or purchasing flats of water for a few bucks instead of spending several dollars per unit while at work or on the road.

I love spending as much as any woman. I'm not going to tell you to give up the essentials such as your morning latte or after work cocktails. Life is about savouring your hard earned dollars, but also paying attention to the details. Watch those wasted pennies. They really do turn into loonies. Happy anti-budgeting!

Chapter 6

Financial Basics for the Savvy Female CEO

I applaud you for making it this far in the book and for investing in your most lucrative investment—You! And, now, You Inc. Don't stop here. You can never truly be independent and free as a woman without being financially independent. You may actually rely on your spouse or someone else to support your income needs if you're for example, raising the children at home. Perhaps you'll never be the money manager of the family. But as I've stated several times in this book, you can never totally trust money matters to anyone. Your financial future is too important to opt out. You don't need to become a math geek, accountant, or financial wiz. But you need to know enough to hold your professional advisors accountable, what questions you should ask, and to know what you don't know.

Too often, I hear so many lame excuses as to why women don't see money, money management, and the topic of finances as within their ability to deal with. I also hear horror stories and tragic occurrences of women being ripped of by ex-spouses and lovers, family members squandering funds and more, simply because they "opted out" of this aspect of their lives. You cannot opt out of your finances. They're part of you and your life, unless you've found a way to work in this world without money. Until then, you need to pay attention.

Here are some excuses I've heard across the country and worldwide from readers and others on why women are not taking control of their finances today and for their financial futures:

Excuse #1: I'm not good at math.

The rebuttal: Oh, please. If you've ever said this, please stop it. Reading your bank statement, the pages of this chapter that follow, and checking your bank accounts online have absolutely nothing to do with math. Knowing when your credit card payments are due, taking the initiative to set up an auto debit program at your bank, and actually saving that 10% of your income each month requires absolutely no math skills whatsoever. The few times you might want to project what you need to buy a house or figure out if you can afford that mortgage payment, assess if your savings are on track for retirement, and so on can all be solved easily through the many free calculators on the Internet. Sure, if you know how to use a financial calculator for these scenarios, it helps too, but with all of the free calculators on the Internet, you don't even need to step into a bank or financial planner's office. You can, but you'll also find everything you need with a few simple search words on a search engine while you're having your morning coffee.

Excuse #2: I'm just not interested in that financial stuff…or it bores me, or I don't get it.

The rebuttal: Girlfriend, get interested. You might not be interested in your health either, but if a doctor told you that you had a major disease and you'd better get healthy or risk death, I'm sure you'd get interested. The risks of "not" looking after your money aren't always as tangibly clear. This aspect of your life is too important to not care. Plus, once you start putting your finances first, respecting that you deserve to have a bright financial future, and deciding that you're worthy of holding on to money, you'll find the world of finance and money management more interesting. You might even find it fun! You don't need to become an expert, but you need to start getting involved and do so today!

Excuse #3: My spouse, government, parents (I'm expecting an inheritance) or someone else will look after me or is taking care of the finances.

The rebuttal: This excuse bothers me on so many levels. I hear countless stories of women blindly signing mortgage documents they didn't read, thinking things were being taken care of, giving money to a lover thinking their intentions were true, or worse, being forced into bankruptcy because of the lack of proper money management by their spouse, whom they were trusted. And for those who are absolutely counting on that inheritance and therefore not lifting a "financial finger" until it happens—a word of caution—it's not guaranteed. I've witnessed situations where the children spend their entire adulthood with a flippant attitude towards money thinking their parents were bequeathing them their fortunes but they were sorely mistaken. Think of the numerous major movie stars who hit the press each year because they are broke and have to file for bankruptcy. Mike Tyson comes to mind. He earned hundreds of millions of dollars and still had to file bankruptcy. How does one squander millions or hundreds of millions and end up worse than they started? I think it's by not paying attention and letting someone else look after what you and I should be doing ourselves. We're not likely to earn as much as Tyson and others in the entertainment business, but the lesson is the same. Trust no one entirely when it comes to your money, your financial future, your credit rating, and protecting your finances in general.

Excuse #4: I'm overwhelmed, am scared, am too far gone financially, etc.

The rebuttal: If the above excuse applies to you, take a deep breath and take a baby step. Everything counts! I'm reminded of a client that was nearing 300 pounds, had gained 50 in no time, and kept falling off her diet wagon. Chatting with her one night, she described how her cravings got the best of her and she ate an entire pie and tub of ice cream that night, proclaiming, what's the difference anyway? That attitude certainly won't help the situation and is a Catch-22 of sorts. As you take small steps to look at your financial statements, make an appointment with a professional who can help. You'll find that small steps will assist in reducing the overwhelmed feeling and open a light at the end of the tunnel. To stay in a defeatist attitude will only make the situation worse. Remember, they're only numbers. They won't "get you" and you can take control of your financial life! Start now with one small thing.

Excuse #5: One day I will...

The rebuttal: The "one day" syndrome is like an insidious disease. Each day, month, or year of procrastination makes your financial life more difficult. You must start today. Try creating a bill folder in your kitchen. Instead of throwing them in a pile, open them as they come in. Review credit card purchases and your utility bills—you might even find discrepancies that are costing you money. Create a chart inside the folder and write down due dates and amounts as your bills arrive. Do this every month. At tax time or when you'd like to review your expenses, you'll have everything organized in one file per month. What other action could you take today to secure your own financial independence? I promise, it feels good to take any steps towards it. Could you call your pension officer at work and discuss how those investments are doing and what the plan details are? Could you set up an appointment with your banker or a financial planner to help you understand where you are and where you need to go? Don't wake up in retirement or life still waiting for one day. That day has come and it's called *today*!

For adults without an affinity for finances, this chapter might be a bit difficult to grasp at first. When possible, include your spouse and children in a monthly financial meeting. As your family's financial IQ increases, it helps get the entire team on board. Any new area of learning can be a bit overwhelming in the beginning stages, but once you've been exposed to even the bare minimum of information, you'll find you're more open to news and stock reports and other financial terms in the future.

I am, however, at the disadvantage of not knowing *you* personally. I can't assess your level of financial education and experiences so as to custom tailor the information to you. I've identified a number of major terms and financial concepts that I think are important for you to simply be aware of rather than be an expert in. I've attempted to explain these concepts simply and in my own terms. Please read and research further after completing this chapter if you like. There's an abundance of free financial information on the Internet.

The purpose of this section is not to define and analyze investments and the many facets of the financial markets. I intend to give you a concise overview so you'll be able to define them easily when you need to deal with or understand the subject. There are many wonderful books on the market that devote their entire text to the explanation of asset classes and our economy as a whole. If you're keen on learning more, visit *www.kelleykeehn.com* for a list of recommended advanced reading and a chart showing how all of these financial instruments fit together. All of the financial descriptions are not intended to provide advice but instead a brief and simple overview. Always consult a professional before investing and shop around.

What are GICs and TDs?

Two of the most basic investments beyond that of a savings or chequing account are GICs and TDs, which can be purchased at a Canadian bank and many other financial institutions.

A GIC (guaranteed investment certificate) represents a kind of loan to a bank. You are now the lender and are giving the bank your money for a term of usually one to five years. In return, the bank promises to give you the money back that you invested (also called your *principle*) in return for a set percentage for the term. Generally, the longer the term, the higher your interest rate will be. GICs can be redeemable or non-redeemable. The latter is most common and pays a higher rate of interest, but you're not able to get your money back until the term is up.

A TD (term deposit) works similarly to a GIC in that your principle and interest rate are guaranteed for a set period of time. The main difference is that a TD usually has a term of one year or less. A GIC has a term of one year or more.

GICs are suitable for investors who are not in the position to risk their original investment or those who need all or a portion of their money earning a set rate of return. The current disadvantage to GICs is that interest rates are relatively low, which makes these investments unattractive compared to others on the market.

GICs generally pay a percentage or two above current rates of inflation.

During times of high inflation, such as during the '80s, GICs were paying nearly 20%. The problem was that inflation was nearly 18% at the time. However, if an investor locks in for a long-term certificate when interest rates are high and they subsequently fall, the investor wins, as their after-inflation rate of return would be substantially higher. The reverse is also true. If an investor locks into a long-term certificate when rates are low and then interest rates start to rise, so does inflation. Therefore, the major risk with GICs is that inflation may increase to a level higher than the interest that you're being paid during the period you've locked into.

What is a bond?

Somewhat similar to a GIC at a bank, a bond represents debt owed to the investor; it is for this reason that this asset class is often called a debt instrument. Think of it as a loan. You're the lender and the company owes you the money you've invested. Plus, the interest rate of the bond is commensurate with the issuer's creditworthiness. For example, a Government of Canada bond with a very high rating will pay a lower interest rate (coupon rate) than a municipal bond. The lower the risk of the bond issuer, the lower the coupon rate.

Bond issuers can be federal, provincial, or municipal governments; they can also be corporations. Bonds can also be issued in foreign currencies. A Government of Canada bond will pay the least percentage rate of any other Canadian bonds, but since they are the safest, their creditworthiness is the strongest (within our country). The idea is that a government can just print more money to repay their debt to bond holders. So if you own a Government of Canada bond, you are the lender and the government is the borrower, and in exchange, you receive a coupon or yield for your money (the interest or investment return).

Unlike a GIC at a bank, the primary difference with a bond is the liquidity flexibility. If you sign in for a 5-year GIC, unless you elect certain options, you must hold that investment for the full five years. With a bond, you're able to sell it on a bond exchange at any time even if you had purchased a 20-year bond. You could of course hold the bond to maturity as well.

Bonds are very complex investment instruments and it's been estimated by many experts that the bond market represents over 70% of investments in North America; stocks make up 30%.

Is a Canada Savings Bond a *bond?* Sort of and not really. A Canada Savings Bond (CSB) works more similarly to a GIC at a bank, but with more flexibility. You still have your principle guaranteed by the government and a promise of a set interest rate in given years. The major difference being that a CSB is not tradable on a bond market.

What is a stock?

A stock represents ownership in a publicly traded company. For example, ABC Bank would like to raise more money for current projects. In return, they offer a partial ownership in their company. Depending on the type of share class, the holder of the stock may have voter rights and be entitled to a return of annual profits (called dividend payments). The level of risk for an individual stock might be rated from medium to extremely high. The chance for a stock's investment return (or loss) is based on the growth (or lack thereof) of the company. It is possible to lose some or all of your principle investment within a stock.

What is a recession?

A recession is a time of economic downturn, constriction, and the temporary decline of stock markets and the economy as a whole. It generally starts with climbing inflation. As the markets heat up, things start to cost more. Employees expect higher wages to keep up with the higher costs. Corporations' earnings must grow to satisfy investors who are always willing to sell their interests.

When interest rates are low and the economy is strong, people as a whole feel confident about the future. Low interest rates allow them to purchase homes, cars, and other goods at reasonable rates. As inflation rises due to demand, the federal government steps in to increase rates so we don't see a repeat of double-digit interest rates like we did in the '80s. If you remember that time in Canada, many homeowners were walking away from their real-estate holdings, handing the mortgage and obligation over to the bank or lender. Rates became so high and unmanageable that many people couldn't make their payments.

In today's environment, the federal government will try to stave off out-of-control inflation by raising rates slowly. In doing so, they intend to stabilize the economy before it gets out of hand. The hope is that if interest rates go up, consumers will spend less and demand fewer goods and the economy will then stabilize itself. It's sort of like pruning your trees. It's necessary to trim back the growth at times for a more robust tree in the future.

There are many factors and economic indicators that may turn down an economy, including war, catastrophes, unemployment, and much more. Basically, when a society feels poor due to low demand for products and services, the high cost to purchase cars and homes on credit, and a fear of low job security, this has a ripple effect on the country as a whole. The opposite is true when markets are swinging upwards and interest rates and inflation are low.

What are bulls and bears?

Bulls and bears are the mascots of the direction of a stock market or how an expert feels about a particular stock.

A bull market is on the upswing. When financial professionals feel bullish about a stock or the economy, they believe a positive move forward is imminent and would suggest buying.

A bear market is moving downwards. Financial professionals feel bearish about a stock when they believe it's ready to tank. In this case, they would suggest selling.

What are the NASDAQ, Dow Jones, and TSX?

We often hear on radio reports during our drive home from work or on the evening news the point gain or loss of these indices. I've included below a few simple definitions as many hear these same reports without understanding their relevance or what they mean. I should note that the word *indices* is simply a finance term to describe many indexes.

The Stock Exchanges

An exchange is really just that. It's a financial medium for investors to buy and sell their investments with intermediaries and some consumer protection, such as securities commissions and requirements for prospectuses to be filed.

Each exchange will have thousands of stocks represented and available for buying and selling. The TSX 300, for example, is not necessarily the best 300 stocks on the Canadian exchange, but the 300 most actively traded. When an index is up or down by a certain number of percentage points, it's a fair indication of how that country and sector of stocks is performing.

- TSX 300—This index represents the trends of the Toronto Stock Exchange by tracking the prices of the 300 most actively traded and influential stocks.
- TSX—Canada's largest stock exchange (known previously to many as the TSE) is headquartered in Toronto and is the third largest financial centre in North America. The TSE was changed to the current TSX because "TSE" is used by the Tokyo Stock Exchange.
- NASDAQ—With approximately 3,200 companies, this index is the largest electronic screen-based equity securities market in the US
- S&P 500—This index contains the stock of 500 leading US corporations. After the Dow Jones Industrial Average, the S&P is the most widely watched index of large cap US stocks.

What is a mutual fund?

There are nearly 6,000 mutual funds on the Canadian market and the entire concept can be confusing and misunderstood. Of the stocks, bonds, and other short-term, safe, and guaranteed investments that were outlined previously, a mutual fund can comprise any and all of these assets.

Many individuals have preconceived notions, either good or bad, about what a mutual fund really is. Some feel that they can be risky, expensive, and better suited for *other investors*, but mutual funds can actually be safe or extremely risky, reasonably priced or very expensive, and are suitable for most investors.

Consider stocks and bonds for a moment. Each investment is as risky as the bond or stock itself. A mutual fund is a pooling of investors' resources. Some funds have only stocks within them and can be global, domestic (just Canadian stocks), or a mix of the two. A balanced fund, for example, will have some cash in it, some bond component, and domestic and/or foreign stocks.

The benefits of mutual funds as opposed to purchasing the individual stocks, bonds, or other securities are many. Mutual funds provide professional money managers whose full-time job is to buy, sell, and monitor the fund's assets on a daily basis. Funds, unlike many stocks, can be bought or redeemed any business day. If you remember the Bre-X scandal of the '90s, there was a time when the company's stock was at an all-time high of $286.50, an amazing feat considering it started out as a penny stock. Due to the fraud findings, the stock was halted. That meant no buying or selling by the investors. Many holders of Bre-X stock watched their fortunes dissipate as the stock value plummeted and there wasn't a thing they could do. A mutual fund's units can be sold any business day.

Another benefit of mutual funds is the low initial investment. Many funds allow you to invest with as little as $500. Many investors would never be able to purchase a blue chip stock at such a low investment. Furthermore, funds provide diversification not possible with a small portfolio. One balanced mutual fund could have dozens of bonds, money market investments, and dozens or even hundreds of stocks within it. An investor would need to have a large portfolio to buy those securities individually.

Mutual funds can also be thought of as safer, in some ways, than purchasing stocks directly. With many stocks within a given fund, the likelihood of an investor losing 100% of their investment is slim. Mutual funds are not guaranteed (in either the principle invested or the rate of return), but with diversification, risk can be reduced. Many Canadians, and certainly most Albertans, remember the fall of Principle Group just a decade and a half ago. CDIC (Canadian Deposit Insurance Corporation) insures most amounts invested from GIC purchases up to a maximum amount, but in the Principle

Group case, many weren't paid for over ten years. The principal protection was a godsend to many. However, considering inflation and the loss of purchasing power, being repaid just the principal was a great loss of potential growth over the span of a decade. What many Canadians don't realize is that the Principle Group Mutual Funds are still around today (to the best of my knowledge). Another management company bought them out. When you purchase a mutual fund, you actually own the stocks and bonds that the fund company is managing on your behalf. If they fold, it's only the management that is affected, not the underlying securities.

Last year, a former client of mine was in a panic to purchase gold. She didn't just want a certificate showing that she owned a certain amount of gold, she was fervent about owning and housing the bullion directly. After counselling and suggesting that she purchase a precious-metals mutual fund that had a gold component within it, she totally disregarded my advice and opened a discount brokerage account. Due to the difficulty and logistics of housing gold bullion, this former client decided to start day trading gold, silver, platinum, and other metals. She started with a modest amount, and within a few months, had profited over $20,000. She told me that she "couldn't lose" and was almost considering day trading as a full-time job. She often informed me of her successes so as to point out that her returns would only have been modest in the mutual fund I had recommended.

After few bad trading days and within a few more months, the former client had lost all of her profits. Over the course of a year, she was up and down as she roller-coastered between highs and lows. At the end of the year, she was $25,000 in debt from her trading and had invested countless hours, causing her company to suffer in her absence.

The moral of the story is that individual trading is a risky game, especially with a short-term frame of mind. If this former client had purchased a precious-metals fund as recommended, the mutual fund managers, with their years of experience and education, could have mitigated her losses and even helped earn her a profit.

A disadvantage of mutual funds is that their management fees and commissions charged by financial advisors are often high. Times have changed, however, and fees are generally negotiable, so one must shop around. A further caveat is, for large dollar amounts an individually constructed portfolio can often be more advantageous than investing in mutual funds. Another criticism of mutual funds is that during a bullish market, one might be better off to invest in a stock index directly and save on fees. All arguments are valid, both for and against mutual funds, and should be carefully examined to determine the suitability for you.

Purchasing Investments Individually

- Cash type e.g. T-bills and other money market instruments
- Canadian stocks
- Foreign stocks
- Specialty stocks e.g. resource, green friendly
- Canadian bonds
- Foreign bonds
- Real estate
- Precious metals
- Index investments e.g. HIPS, TIPS

Mutual Funds

- Cash type e.g. T-bills and other money market instruments
- Canadian stocks
- Foreign stocks
- Specialty stocks e.g. resource, green friendly
- Canadian bonds
- Foreign bonds
- Real estate
- Precious metals
- Index investments e.g. HIPS, TIPS

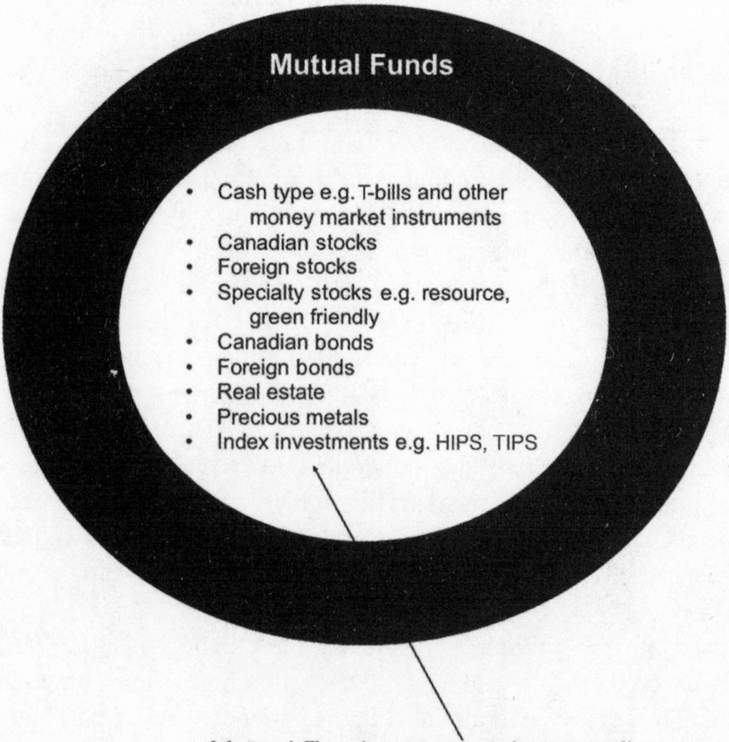

Mutual Funds can contain one, all, or any combination of securities as listed within the circle.

What is an RRSP?

An RRSP (Registered Retirement Savings Plan) is a Canadian tax shelter. Any growth or earned interest from your investments is generally taxable on an annual basis. If these investments are held within an RRSP, the tax is deferred and you therefore have more money earning compound interest. At retirement, death, or other disposition, however, the RRSP withdrawals are taxable. Another attractive feature of the RRSP is the tax deduction for contributions made within a given year.

Don't confuse an RRSP with an actual investment. It is only a shelter. Think of it like a garage. It generates a tax deduction the year the contribution is made and allows your investments to defer taxes. You still need to put cars into the garage. Your RRSP could have GICs, stocks, bonds, mutual funds, and other investments within it.

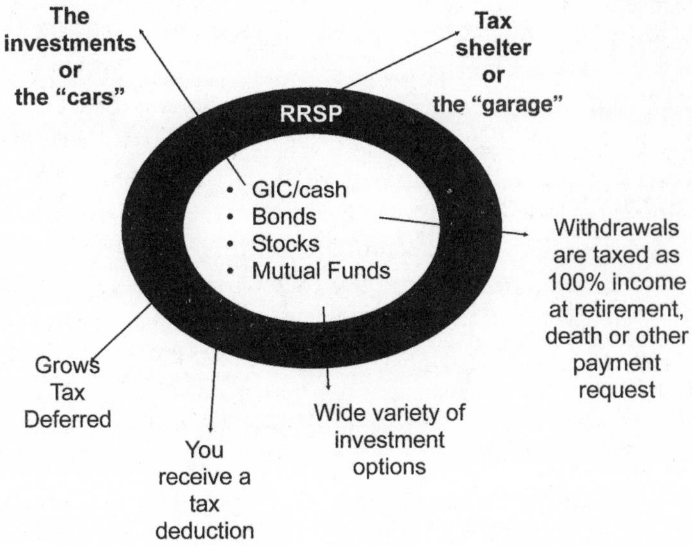

Why are interest rates important?

Interest rates tell us a great deal about what's happening in the economy and what could happen in the future. When rates are low, consumers feel more prosperous and will generally consider spending more if their job is secure (among other factors). If rates are low when it's time to purchase a home, you'll be able to get into a bigger home, have a smaller mortgage payment, or need a smaller down payment than if rates are high. Since a home is likely to be your largest lifetime purchase, knowing which direction interest rates will go is extremely important, even though it is impossible to guarantee accuracy.

I've purchased two homes in my lifetime and have guessed wrong on interest rates both times. As a seasoned financial professional and having researched and carefully examined the economic indicators that drive rates in the future, I still guessed incorrectly. A rule of thumb that sometimes works (but don't stake your house on it) is that the bank usually offers consumers what is in the bank's best interest, not yours. For example, if a bank feels that long-term interest rates are going to rise in the future, they don't want consumers to lock in now to a five-year or longer mortgage. Think of it like this: if today's five-year mortgage rate is 7% and the bank thinks that in two or three years the rate will be 10%, it's in their best interest to deter you from locking in as you would have enjoyed a few years at a rate lower than the market rate. Like any of us, banks don't have crystal balls either and aren't always correct, but they generally know more than the average consumer as to which direction rates are heading.

In today's lending environment, secured lines of credit (SLOC) and equity takeouts are all the rage. For a number of years, banks have been promoting the option of a SLOC as opposed to a conventional mortgage. This offers maximum flexibility because the borrower can pay off their SLOC any time without penalty, can use the "room" again just like a credit card, and receives a rate of interest at the prime rate or slightly below prime (the rate set by financial institutions based on the cost of short-term funds and on competitive pressures). The interest rate fluctuates with the prime rate; it increases or decreases along with it.

A conventional mortgage works similar to a GIC but in reverse. The bank is the lender and you are the borrower. You choose the term (open to five- to seven-year, and some banks now even have ten-year terms). The term is the amount of time that your interest rate is locked in, for better or worse, and the time period that you are locked in with that lender. The amortization of a mortgage is a bit trickier to understand. The amortization can be up to 25 years and, with some banks, 30 years. The longer the amortization schedule used, the lower your payments. If you pick a shorter amortization, your payments will be larger, but you'll also pay your principle off quicker and pay less interest in the long run. The amortization is simply a schedule used by the bank to determine your mortgage payment.

Let's use an example of a 25-year amortization on a five-year fixed rate mortgage of 7%. You would be locked in to that bank with a mortgage term of five years. If rates declined in that five-year term, you would lose out. If they increased during that time, you would benefit.

The 25-year amortization is only an estimate of what your payment would be if you took 25 years to pay off your mortgage if your rate remained constant over that time period. You are not locked in for twenty-five years; it's simply a schedule. When your term expires at your bank, you can renegotiate your mortgage or even move it to another financial institution. You can then recalculate your amortization and shorten or lengthen it depending on how quickly you'd like to pay the mortgage off.

What's better—a mortgage or a secured line of credit?

There's no simple answer to this question. It depends on your situation and which direction rates are heading. Experts in favour of a secured line of credit point to the fact that in the long term of ten or more years, having a mortgage at a prime rate will generally benefit the consumer (more than a fixed rate) even with fluctuations. Furthermore, many banks now have some downside protection for consumers should interest rates start to rise and they don't have a fixed rate. Keep in mind that as prime increases or decreases, so does your monthly mortgage payment. That could mean a difference of a few hundred or few thousand dollars in a year.

If you're the type of person who needs the security of knowing that your mortgage payment is fixed for, say, five years and perhaps your budget couldn't handle a sudden increase of a couple hundred dollars in a quarter, don't choose a secured line of credit no matter what the perceived benefits. Consult your banker for the advantages and disadvantages of both lending options.

Using lending products

Bank loans

Consumers seek bank loans for a variety of reasons. It might be for a car or to renovate a home. A loan has a term over which one must pay back the principal borrowed along with interest. Some loans may be paid off early, with or without penalty. The bank may or may not require collateral depending on one's security of employment, level of income, and creditworthiness. Collateral is some asset of value that a lender might require for security against your loan. In the case of a mortgage, the collateral is your house, but in the case of a loan, it could be your car, cash assets secured against your loan, or other such assets. Collateral assignments might be necessary for granting a loan and might even be required by the lender. In cases where the lender doesn't require security (e.g. an unsecured line of credit), the borrower may still choose to back their loan with collateral that will reduce the interest rate resulting from the bank being fully protected.

Credit cards

A wide range of financial institutions in Canada issue credit cards. They offer the holder an amount of credit that can be used for purchases. The entire balance can be paid off each month without penalty or just a minimum amount each month (usually 3% of the outstanding balance). Credit cards have extremely wide variances for the interest rate charged for unpaid balances, which can range from 10% to nearly 29%. That doesn't include other charges such as annual fees or penalties for being over an established credit limit.

Credit cards are a useful tool to the disciplined holder. A major benefit to making purchases on a credit card is that it can act like a purchases monitor, keeping all expenses in one handy consolidated statement each month. Another valuable feature, which can be found on many gold or platinum cards, is a reward-point system that many companies offer that can be applied to anything from flights to various purchases. Other benefits included in some premium cards are travel protection, theft/loss protection, and much more. However, many consumers don't take the time to learn about these benefits and, if they are not used, the cost of the annual fee could easily outweigh their value. Always check the fine print and know the interest rate, fees, and entitlements of your card.

Mortgages

As discussed previously, a mortgage, in its simplest terms, is a more detailed and structured loan requiring a chattel against a home. Most banks will not lend funds or provide a mortgage for undeveloped land.

A mortgage has a set interest rate for a given term (six months to seven years depending on the financial institution). Payments consist of principal repayment and interest. During the early years of a mortgage, the majority of the payments go towards interest. During the later years, most of your dollars are paying off principal. Most mortgages allow you to increase your payment (so you can pay your mortgage off quicker) and also an annual or semi-annual lump sum payment (that is applied directly to the principal) without penalty and usually to a maximum of 10 to 20%.

Should you fall into an unexpected amount of money and have the available cash to fully pay off your mortgage before its term, you will pay a penalty to the bank called the interest differential. The bank will calculate this amount for you upon request. Should interest rates fall dramatically since the time you locked in to your mortgage rate, paying the penalty could be more advantageous than staying in at a higher rate.

Lenders and the mortgage terms they offer are more flexible today than ever—you can pay your mortgage off sooner, decrease the length of your amortization and make extra payments as set forth by your lender. These extra payments are penalty free and can add up to substantial savings since they are applied directly to the principal. Conversely, when individuals are stretched with their mortgage payment or would like to own a more expensive home sooner, they opt for the longest amortization period available to get the lowest payment possible. This latter group can still benefit throughout the term by paying down on principal during anniversaries or by increasing monthly payments where permitted.

Most financial institutions encourage consumers to make their payments bi-monthly as opposed to monthly to pay off the mortgage more quickly. (With a bi-monthly schedule, you'll actually make one extra payment per year.) Depending on when you receive your paycheque or direct deposit, you may wish to structure your payments to coincide with your cash flow.

Secured Lines of Credit (SLOC)

Like a mortgage, a SLOC is secured against your home via a chattel, but unlike a mortgage, it offers the consumer flexibility. Let's assume that you purchased a home for $350,000 by putting $100,000 down and choosing a SLOC for $250,000 to pay the rest. Think of this amount, or credit limit, as that of a credit card—just without the card. As you pay down the $250,000, you're free to run the amount up again, which, depending on your discipline, could be a good or bad thing. A SLOC also provides some contingency planning as you only need to pay the interest costs per month, which would be less than that of a mortgage (which forces you to pay principal as well).

For example, with an equal amount borrowed, a mortgage payment might be $1,200 per month (forcing you to pay interest and principal) where a SLOC may only require an interest-only payment of $700 per month. By paying only the interest on the SLOC, the balance would never be paid down. This is not an option with a regular mortgage. However, in a month of financial crisis, having an interest-only low-minimum-payment option as a temporary fail-safe could be an appreciated feature.

Remember that a SLOC's rate fluctuates with the prime lending rate of Canada, so if it's important for you to have a set monthly mortgage bill for five to seven years, opt for a conventional mortgage.

Equity Takeouts

An equity takeout simply means that your home has either risen in value or you have paid down your mortgage enough to build up excess equity in your home. Assuming you have a conventional mortgage, let's estimate that with your mortgage payments and property value increases, your mortgage is now only 62% of the appraised value (starting from 75% for example). With an equity takeout, the financial institution may rewrite your mortgage or offer other options to use the 13% equity in your home.

Unsecured Lines of Credit (USLOC)

USLOC is similar to a credit card in that your limit and use is revolving (you can run it up to the maximum, pay it down or off, etc.). The difference is that you may or may not have an actual card attached to the USLOC. Maximum amounts are usually much greater than that of a credit card, but not exclusively.

An USLOC is not secured by a home or asset. The lender approves the USLOC on the borrower's creditworthiness, employment security, servicing ability, amongst other criteria.

As prefaced in this chapter, many assumptions were made as to your familiarity and experience with a broad group of financial terminology. In one chapter, it's nearly impossible to explain every money management technique or product. However, I chose those that I think are the basis of a solid foundation. Please visit my website at *www.kelleykeehn.com* for an extensive listing of books and Internet resources should you wish to study the subject further.

A muddled industry

The financial industry is filled with men and women who are honest, ethical, experienced, educated, and truly wish to change peoples' lives by assisting them with their finances. However, like any industry, there are always a few unethical individuals that ruin the reputation of others in the same business. The financial industry is also extremely regulated with many checks and balances; today, so much more so than when I started in the industry. Clients are often frustrated with all of the paperwork that is actually there to protect them with disclosure. However, I'm really not sure how, but each year and sometimes more than once, some shyster misappropriates or outright absconds with their clients' money and it hits the front of the business section. More times than not, the client could have prevented the theft by always reading their paperwork and never totally trusting anyone with their money.

For the average consumer, the financial profession can be extremely confusing position. There are so many titles, designations, and companies with unique positions. Whether it's a wealth manager who really specializes in life insurance and life insurance investments or the ever-nebulous financial consultant, which can be anything from a broker to a banker, you need to empower yourself before entering into a relationship. If you currently deal with someone and aren't sure if they're the best advisor for the job, shop around. There's nothing wrong with letting your current advisor know that you're making it a priority to educate yourself about your finances and although you might not have formally interviewed them before, you'd like to do it now. Be sure when you're looking for an advisor or evaluating your current one, that you always, I can't stress this enough, shop around. You can't compare the competencies, expertise or your comfort level with such a trusted position until you feel satisfied with your level of knowledge. Advisors are in business. Don't take the relationship personally and stay with someone who under performs continuously, makes you feel uncomfortable, or simply doesn't value your business because they're a friend, you've been with them forever, or it's your nephew. Your money and financial security is a business matter for You Inc. as well. Do ensure you're comfortable with your professional, but other than that, check emotions at the door.

You also need an interview checklist for your current or new advisor. Use the following as a start and ask your friends and network what questions they ask of their advisors. If your advisor is taken aback by this questioning (they should actually be offering a checklist of their own before you ask) or if they don't answer any of your questions or provide some vague response, don't go back. It's that simple.

Questions to ask before you invest

Purchases and sellers of financial products and services have definite responsibilities. Remember, your potential advisor has prepared before meeting you. You should also be prepared before making the important decision to invest. To assist you in the decision-making process, the following is a list of questions that you should ask when interviewing a potential or current financial professional.

What are the credentials, education, and training of the advisor and the support team? What experience do they have in the financial industry? Have you met the support team? Who will look after your account on a daily basis—the advisor, an assistant, or another? Who is the alternate contact to your advisor?

Is the advisor free to shop the market for investments, or is he/she limited to the products of one company? What products is the advisor licensed to sell (i.e. mutual funds, life insurance products, securities, a combination)?

Ask specifically what their bias and limitations are. A mutual fund representative will not be able to sell individual stocks and bonds and will have a bias towards the benefits of mutual funds (which is fine and likely suitable). However, you should know what their licensing limitations are and their personal biases so you can make an informed choice. Likely someone working for a closed shop type firm or even some bank representatives will only recommend, and at times can only recommend, their own products. This fact is not good or bad. You need to know what their limitations are and not assume it's solely their advice, but also know their bias, which will affect their recommendations.

Ask if you may show his/her recommendations to other advisors (lawyers, accountants, etc.). Will you be provided with a written report outlining recommendations?

What has the advisor's track record been? How did he/she respond on behalf of their current clients during volatile markets in the past? Can you contact a couple of clients for feedback and testimonials?

How is the advisor compensated? What are his or her fees? What commissions, fees, or hidden fees are associated with the investments that he or she offers (front or back load mutual funds, management expense ratios, etc.) If you leave your advisor or your investment, what fees will be incurred?

Are there any guarantees associated with the investments recommended? Will any guarantees be provided in writing?

How often will the financial institution provide reports on your investments? How often will the advisor contact you for a review?

What are the responsibilities of the advisor in the proposed relationship (full disclosure of facts, fees, etc.)? What are yours as a purchaser?

Are your needs and risk profile discussed first, and then the products, or vice versa? Are products only recommended after your situation has been carefully assessed?

This questionnaire unfortunately does not render you impervious to scams, bad or unsuitable investments, and advice from those blatantly trying to deceive you. It does, however, fortify you and will hopefully weed out the unscrupulous individuals or those not suited to your needs.

The bottom line is your financial future is your responsibility. You need qualified professionals to help you along the way as they specialize in their respective fields. You also need to make the "fine print" your friend and never, ever, fully trust someone with your money or financial well-being. After all, if you don't care enough about your finances to take the time to tend to and monitor them, why should anyone else?

Your financial team and products

I encourage you to assemble your financial team now and as your needs arrive. Generally, it does not cost you anything for an initial consultation that you should at least consider, even if you think the product or service does not apply to your current situation. Shop around and if you need a referral, ask friends and family who they're using. Also, if you have at least one of the following professionals that you use (i.e. your banker), ask them to introduce you to their preferred advisors. You'll find them quick to assist with a list of names and they likely have many experiences with the quality of those professionals. Just remember, referred or not, use your "questions to ask" questionnaire and always shop around.

Banker – for your day-to-day banking, lending, and (possibly) investing.

Financial advisor – should equip you with a written financial plan. May charge for this if you do not invest with them or if you do, will likely provide a plan for free. This professional could work at a bank, brokerage, independent firm, or life insurance company.

Life insurance agent – will, at no charge, provide you with an insurance analysis. It would behoove you to examine life insurance coverage, critical illness insurance, and disability insurance.

General insurance agent – for your auto and home policies. If you're self-employed, inquire about errors and omissions and/or liability coverage.

Lawyer – look for a legal professional who specializes in what you need. Seek counsel for your estate plan at any stage in your life. There are many legal professionals who only work in the areas of estate planning. You'll wish to use their skills to design your will, powers of attorney, living wills, and more. If you're self-employed, consult a lawyer and accountant as to the benefits of incorporating your company.

Accountant – depending on the complexity of your financial situation and whether you're employed or self-employed, you may need the services of a qualified accountant. However, if your tax situation is simple, a tax preparer might suffice.

Chapter 7
Understanding Credit

Credit

As a now financially savvy woman (or at least one that's ready to be), one of the most important elements of your financial future is your credit, whether it's protecting or re-building it. You may be surprised that I didn't cite the stock market, your mortgage or some other instrument as the crux of your financial future. Think of your credit this way. It's much easier to build a brand new home than fix a house ready to fall apart from a weak foundation, mould, and in massive disrespair. The same theory applies to your financial "house." It's easier to "build" than repair. If you have a great credit history, I want you to keep it that way, free of debt mould. However, if your credit "house" is in need of a renovation or demolition, don't despair. With some discipline, courage, and a deep breath, your credit can be repaired in time.

If you're one in the five percent of Canadians (I'm sure the numbers are similar for our friends in other countries), you have great credit. Chances are as you read this, you're somewhere else in the remaining 95%. So why would you need to care at all? First, you want to ensure that it stays strong and healthy. To do this, you must be aware of your credit rating and check it at least once a year, but I would recommend once every six months.

With today's Internet and credit card fraud, one must ensure that nefarious actions haven't taken place simply because we hope or assume all is well. Furthermore, most Canadians have not checked their credit report in the last year and many have never seen one at all.

The debt doldrums of Canadians

If you doubt the importance of understanding your credit report and the level of debt in Canada today, you might be shocked that, according to the National Bank, Canadian consumers now owe $752.1 billion (2004), which is up 36% in the past ten years when adjusted for inflation. Consider that our country as a whole has never faced more prosperous times. As a buy now, pay later generation, understanding and taking control of our debt is paramount.

Debt is one issue plaguing the average Canadian, however, it's only half the equation. Personal savings rates are also at an all time low. According to a recent study conducted by Ipsos Reid on behalf of the Bank of Nova Scotia, 75% of Canadians have less than three months' worth of savings in the bank. And less than half (44%) of Canadians "feel in control of their financial affairs," fewer than three in ten (28%) say they "accomplish the financial goals they set for themselves," and 16% say they "always stick to their budget, which includes savings."

I hope these numbers have you taking note. But it's not all doom and gloom. Awareness is the first key. Matters of money need to be understood, at the very least in their basic form, by every individual. The best part is that it starts with small and simple steps.

Now that you've learned the basics of being a financial savvy CEO in chapter six, let's ensure your financial ship stays strong and afloat by breaking the taboo of talking about credit; the good, the bad, and yes, even the ugly.

What is a credit report?

A credit report is basically an account of your current and past credit history. There are three reporting agencies in Canada—the top two and most used are Equifax and TransUnion (see the end of this chapter for contact information and resources). My personal and professional dealings have been nearly exclusively with Equifax, so for illustration purposes and my specific information to follow, I will be referring to an Equifax credit report. However, TransUnion should be very similar, if not identical. I have found, though, that creditors report to each agency at different times, so your score could be slightly higher or lower with one of the reporting agencies in a given month.

Your credit report is what lenders (bankers, car dealerships, credit card companies, and the like) use to determine your credit worthiness – that is the criteria for a good portion of their decision to extend credit to you. They're a business like any other and want to know how you've maintained your credit in the past. Are you often late, always on time, maxed your cards to their limits, or do you have a spotless record? Of course, other factors are considered by lenders such as employment income, number of years you've lived in your current residence (statistics show that people that move around often are sometimes not as stable), your net worth, and other factors.

The importance of your credit report and score

The lending landscape in Canada has changed significantly. When I started in the industry in 1994, there were a few trust companies that have now been gobbled up by the big guys (Canada Trust, National Trust, Montreal Trust, etc.), a few smaller lenders, and a handful of Schedule I banks. Schedule I banks are not subsidiaries of foreign banks and examples include the "big five"—RBC, BMO, Scotiabank, CIBC, and TD.

Today, the financial industry is quite different indeed. We simply need to look at the fact that the largest bulk of our population, the baby boomers, are aging, nearing retirement, and have paid off much of their debt. But lenders still need to lend. Hence, many of the stringent loan requirements that even Schedule I banks had to adhere to have changed.

For instance, back in the early 90's, if you were self-employed, it was very difficult to get a mortgage or a loan from a bank. Most small entrepreneurs write off nearly everything they can, thus their net income is very low. Back then, banks weighed heavily on your net income and declined individuals who would likely obtain a mortgage today. Banks have recently relaxed a great deal of their rigidity, some even offer zero down payment options and turn a more favourable eye to the self-employed with little income (perhaps some positive net worth is needed) so long as one's credit is impeccable.

So terrific credit might still not get you a loan or mortgage, but it certainly will improve your odds.

It's also important that your credit be and remain above average as it puts you in a better position to negotiate. For instance, did you know that you could ask your lender for a rate discount on your mortgage? There's what's called a "posted rate," which every lender has. They can be easily found on the Internet or in your major newspaper's business section. They're usually pretty close if not identical between the big five banks. Some banks, if they want your business enough, depending on their flexibility at the time and your individual lending criteria, will discount their posted rates anywhere from a quarter to a full percentage point, sometimes even a little more. Always ask! It could save you thousands of dollars during the life of your mortgage or loan.

Will my mortgage be on it?

Generally, any credit you've had in the past six years. After six years, reports from creditors drop off. Thus, a blemish (or many) can take many years to fully clear up. The great news is that with simple strategies I'll cover, you can dramatically improve your score in less than one year.

Your personal information including your date of birth, past and current employment, past and current residence are listed at the beginning of your report—essentially, the information you would have given to a lender when you sought credit.

Your mortgage can be, but usually is not, on your credit report. Herein lies the dilemma that many Canadians face during tough, short-term cash flow crunches: Should they pay the mortgage or the minimum balance on their credit card? Whenever I ask this question of an individual or group, the consensus is usually to "of course, pay the mortgage." When asked why, most will reply, "I never want to put my house in jeopardy." However, what most don't realize is that if the credit crunch is severe or long lasting, one's house might be in peril due to creditors demanding repayment on loans or credit cards. As your credit card payment or lack thereof is reported every month and most mortgages not at all, it might be prudent to miss a mortgage payment instead of one that's reported (i.e. your late credit card payment).

Before you e-mail me about the blasphemous suggestion that you not pay your mortgage on time, I'll clarify that that's not what I'm suggesting. But if an individual is facing a short-term crisis, to preserve their negotiating power in the future, they must understand what will affect them negatively. To miss or be late on a mortgage here and there is one thing, but if your credit is hurt in the short term and you then go to your lender to access your built up equity for example, they likely won't help as your short-term cash flow crunch would be transparent.

An extremely important caveat to this controversial and grey area is in the case of a non-Schedule I bank mortgage. If your mortgage were held with a small company of sorts (say a Citi Financial, Wells Fargo) or even a private mortgage company or person, missing one or two payments, sometimes even being late, can be extremely cost prohibitive and could land the mortgage in default.

Read the fine print of your mortgage documents and never, never simply trust what the person explaining the document tells you. If you don't understand the lingo, read it over again and call their support center. This is where knowledge really is power.

How do you obtain a credit report?

There are three ways you can obtain a credit report from either Equifax or TransUnion. The first is by writing to them and they will both send you a free report. If you have Internet access, you can download the form that you'll need to submit to them for such a request.

The second and third options cost something. Again, I'm quite familiar with the process and costs of Equifax, so will use them as an example. You can receive the same report that they would mail you for free instantly on the Internet for $15.95. For $24.95 you can instantly purchase and download your credit report complete with your "score" and an explanation of the entire document. (These figures are from 2008.)

What is the FICO score?

The most widely used score today by lenders is the FICO score—FICO is the acronym for the Fair Isaac Corporation. FICO scores are usually intended to show the likelihood that a borrower will default on a loan. A separate score, the Bankruptcy Navigator Index (BNI), is used to determine the likelihood of a borrower's declaring bankruptcy.

Although the Fair Isaac Corporation's Web site offers to sell borrowers "their FICO score," as if it were a single number, the company uses different scoring methods to rate a borrower's suitability for three types of credit—mortgages, automobile loans, and consumer credit—reflecting the loan default risks inherent to these different types of lending. It is not unusual for these scores to differ, by 50 points or more, for the same borrower. The score also depends on what credit reporting agency the data is obtained on, since not all creditors report to all three. The score Fair Isaac sells to borrowers is their consumer credit score, and the borrower can choose which agency the data is obtained from.

Your credit score is a measure of how lenders see you. It's a benchmark analysis of how your score compares to others across Canada. If your score is low, it's more likely, statistically speaking, that you'll default on a loan or will make late payments in the future. If your score is high, it's more likely, on average, that you will not default on a loan, declare bankruptcy, or make late payments in the future.

Lenders, bankers, and credit extending agencies are all in business. They, like any business, want to turn a profit each year and strive to mitigate risk. As such, their criterion in extending credit to an individual in large part is based on the credit score. If your score is high, for example, you might be able to negotiate a discount on your mortgage with your banker. Let's assume you've applied for a computer lease. The rate for which a computer is advertised is usually only offered to those with excellent credit scores and other required criteria (income, etc.). If the score is low, the computer lease company will charge a much higher rate and the purchase will become much more costly over time.

A caveat is, of course, that lenders do not simply use your credit score as the criteria for whether or not they will extend credit to you. Your job security, monthly cash flow, other expenses and debt, net worth, and more are all factors. However, the better your score, the more negotiating power you have.

A general guideline for evaluating your score is as follows. Each lender uses slightly different categories, however, it will give you a good idea of where you are credit wise:

750-840 excellent
660-749 good
620-659 fair
400-619 poor

With each point category up or down the line, you can expect your rate on lending and the actual cost for your debt to be commensurate with your score.

This can cost or save you thousands of dollars over the lifetime of a loan or mortgage. You score, coupled with your employment cash flow and other assets and lending criteria, is the critical factor in a lender saying yes or no to your request.

How do I improve my score?

There are a number of things you can do to dramatically improve your score:

Always pay your minimum payments on time.

Know when your minimum payment is due and add it to your calendar so you'll never miss it. If you bank online, you can even pre-set your minimum payment to be made each month, thereby letting your bank do the remembering for you.

Don't go over 30 days.

If you are going to be late with any loan or credit card minimum payment, do not go over 30 days. On your report, companies disclose how many times you were 30, 60, or 90 days late. The more late filings you have and the longer it took to pay them (i.e. 90 days late), the more damaging this is to your score.

Keep your maximums down.

Let's suppose that you have a credit card limit of $10,000 on one card, $2,500 on another, and a small Internet purchasing account with a $250 limit. The closer you are to your "limit," the more you impair your score. For example, if you had a balance of only $5,000 on your highest limit card, a balance of $2,300 on your card with the $2,500 limit, and a balance of $240 on your smallest card this would actually pull your score down. In this situation, you would be better to have more on your highest limit card and even out the percentage split. For optimal credit scores, do not exceed 75% (ideally even below that) of your credit limit (i.e. don't have a balance of higher than $7,500 on a $10,000 limit card).

Don't seek credit.

Just because credit card companies keep sending you applications in the mail, call you during dinner with their low interest enticements, or harass you at the airport, just say no! Although having a number of cards with low balances might not wound your credit score per se, it may affect how a lender looks at your situation. For example, having five credit cards with a total credit limit of $20,000, but only $2,000 balance total owing might bode well on your credit report. However, a lender considers the available credit (the $18,000 you haven't accessed) as already used. Why? Because you could, in theory, go out tomorrow and use up the entire limit.

Hard Hits Hurt: There are hard and soft hits on your credit report. The hard hits are recorded when you apply for new credit—a loan, car lease, credit card, and so on. These absolutely affect your score. Hard hits show that you may be seeking credit. Perhaps you're in the market for a new mortgage. You shop around at three different banks and they each pull your credit report before they can tell you what deal or rate they'll be able to offer you. By the third hit, your credit, all things remaining equal, will be adversely affected. Why? The third lender will assume that you were not able to obtain a mortgage from the first two banks or that you're seeking too much credit all of a sudden and both can be red flags. Many times it's simply their system—unlike a decade or two ago where it was up to a person to make a lending decision—today, it's mostly up to a computer. So if you are shopping around for a new car or home and you're seeking financing, be sure to print a copy of your own credit report and bring it along with you. It will give the lender a good idea of what type of rate they can negotiate with you. They still will need to "pull" a report when you decide on financing, but each one won't do this until you've decided to conduct business with them.

Soft Hits Hide: Your report also shows all soft inquires made of the last six years. If you have a loan or credit card with a company, likely in the fine print you agreed to allow them to periodically check your credit. They might do this to increase your limit or if your account is in arrears, they might be checking your worthiness to pay your account or possibly "call" your credit line, as they're worried about your stability. Revolving credit (meaning that you're not locked in to a specific payment amount and there's no fixed period for paying the amount owing like with a loan), such as a credit card, can be called at any time by the creditor. This means that what you owe at that time is payable at the creditor's call. Other soft hits that do not affect your score would include you personally pulling your own report as well.

Mortgage brokers or do-it-yourself

As discussed, the lending landscape has changed dramatically over the last decade in Canada and the US. We have more small, non-bank type lenders opening up around every street corner in every major city. We only need open a newspaper today to read about the bankruptcies and foreclosures of our friends to the south.

When the big banks say no to a mortgage request, it would behoove the seeker to reflect on why and be extremely cautious when the desire to own a home supersedes the common sense of what one can truly afford. After all, if one cannot afford to keep up with the home and it's forced into foreclosure, the risk of ownership becomes too great.

Mortgage brokers comprise men and women who I believe are offering what they think is a valuable product and service. And to many it is. I caution though your use of a broker for a few reasons.

Our desire in this century to have "now" what would have taken our parents and grandparents a lifetime to acquire has led to financial troubles for many. Home ownership for example, is a very worthy goal and one all Canadians should strive for. However, with many owners seeking a bigger house, smaller down payments, and barely being approved for a mortgage, the notion of being house poor is rampant and quite frankly, not a great deal of fun. For many, renting and saving up for a few more years could provide the cushion that makes home ownership more comfortable in the long term.

There are basically two main reasons a seeker of debt (usually a mortgage) would use a broker:

Their marketed advantage that they will shop the best rates for you.

They have access to alternative lenders you might not be aware of.

First, it is true that a broker will shop a number of banks and lenders on your behalf. This concept is valid since if you were to simply seek approval from a number of lenders in a short period of time, this could greatly reduce your credit score (see previous page). However, what a broker won't tell you is that you can shop around yourself. As mentioned, purchase your current credit report, bring it into an initial interview with your lender and discuss the likelihood of your approval, interest rate, and terms. Be upfront with them that you're simply shopping around and not consenting to them pulling your credit report. If you do choose to move forward with that lender, they will eventually need to pull your report, however, they'll have been able to give you a good estimate as to the probability of your approval. If you were unlikely to be approved, there's no sense in getting them to put a direct hit on your report, therefore reducing your score further.

Second, if a major bank, which usually has more stringent lending criteria, won't approve your mortgage, this is where a broker will come to the table, but usually for a significant fee.

I've personally met a number of caring and helpful brokers who simply want to help their clients get into a home when it seems nearly impossible or less likely using a standard lender. However, you have to ask yourself the question, at what cost?

In advance, I can't stress enough, always ask for the fine print in advance. No one works for free and nor should they. Even before signing on the dotted line—before anyone pulls your credit report, ensure that you've seen and read the fine print of fees, interest rates, hidden administration costs, and more. Too often, by the time someone is faced with signing the papers, sure the facts are disclosed, but it maybe too late to back out. (If someone is signing a sub-prime mortgage document moments before their keys are given to them, after the entire process has been put into place, and they're told it will cost them thousands of dollars in lenders' fees, it's unlikely the individual would back out.) Whatever you decide in life financially, just be sure to know what your risks and rewards are.

Sidebar:

I recently shared my bias on mortgage brokers with a financial planner I highly respect. He was my CFP (certified financial planner) instructor years ago and is extremely respected in the industry. Spending quite a bit of time recently in the United States, my bias has deepened further as so many of their mortgage troubles south of the border were precipitated and exacerbated by unscrupulous mortgage brokers.

My friend and colleague disagreed strongly with me. He asked if there was a way he could guarantee saving me, for example, $2,000 a year for 25 years, would I be interested? Of course, I answered. He explained that that's what a reputable mortgage broker can potentially do for a consumer shopping for a mortgage. Because of their ability to negotiate with a number of banks on behalf of their clients, they can save them considerably on the interest rate of their mortgage.

My rebuttal was two-fold. First, as a consumer, you can negotiate yourself with a bank. By simply asking for a rate reduction, you'll get it if you're a desirable customer (as mentioned, you have the credit rating, cash flow, down payment, etc.). Second, if an individual isn't credit worthy according to the big five banks, the mortgage broker will do whatever it takes to get that person into a mortgage, even if it's with a sub prime lender charging a much higher interest rate and a large number of hidden fees.

My friend did agree that the latter happens and it's disappointing. However, he also pointed out that in his past years as a VP for a major Canadian bank, most individuals would rarely negotiate their interest rate with their banker for a variety of reasons.

So, there you have two biases to consider when dealing or not dealing with a mortgage broker. If you're the negotiating type and would be comfortable with simply asking your banker for a better rate (and why not, they want your business), then you likely don't need a broker. If you wouldn't ask or the entire process of getting your own credit report and negotiating on your own behalf sounds too complex or intimidating, then, by all means, consider using a broker. However, if a sub prime mortgage is being offered, please be ultra careful to read the fine print and be prudent in determining if you can really afford that home. If the big five won't approve your request, there is usually a reason: you can't afford it!

How often and when should I pull my credit report?

There's no hard and fast rule. Some creditors report regularly and some infrequently. Generally, your creditors will report monthly and usually around the time of your statement or monthly due date. It's important to keep track of this if your credit is at the maximum limit. If you had a card with a $10,000 limit and you're right up to the maximum, your minimum payment might be $300 due on the 10th of the month. You pay it and it brings you down to $9,700. What you might not realize is that your interest due the next week could be $320 thereby bumping you over your limit by $20 right on the date that the creditor will report your history. If you find your credit cards are nearly maxed out each month, ensure that you pay a little more than the minimum.

What's on the report? What's not?

As discussed, your name, date of birth, employment status and so on will show on your report. Depending on what credit you've applied for recently, that information is collected by the reporting agencies (Equifax and TransUnion).

Any credit you've applied for or currently have will show up on your report. After six years, your information starts to drop off. This can be advantageous if your older activity is tarnished and less attractive and you're currently facing difficult times.

Generally your mortgage, utilities, and other such "bills" are not reflected on your report. However, if you had a phone or cable bill go to the collections department of that company or even a third party collection agency, that may show up on the "collections" section of your report. Bankruptcies and public filings of personal insolvency are also reflected on your report.

As mentioned earlier, your hard and soft hits, and the companies you're seeking credit with show at the end of your report.

How do I dispute something on my report?

You can dispute or make a comment on your credit report directly with Equifax or TransUnion. See their Web site for instructions. If something has been wrongly reported, you may wish to contact the company in question for a letter stating the correct information. If you're applying for credit while this process is in place (it can take up to six months to have something corrected on your file), obtaining a letter directly from the company that reported the incorrect information will generally suffice for most lenders.

How many credit cards should I have?

As discussed previously, don't accept those offers in the mail, over the phone, at the airport, or a department store card. Limit the number of cards you have and ensure you carefully read the annual costs and other hidden fees for the cards you do have. Generally, you should have two to three cards.

OK, I'm in trouble. What should I do? Is there hope for me or do I have to seek bankruptcy?

Bankruptcy is a serious process that one should not enter into lightly. The trust of a lender or service provider is broken when all payments cease. To be absolved of this responsibility can potentially have damaging consequences for one's self-esteem. I have counselled a number of clients who had no option but to file for bankruptcy. The blows to their self-esteem were long sustained, not to mention the negative impact bankruptcy will have on their ability to borrow in the future. What I was surprised to learn was that the clients I counselled who were least bruised emotionally by the process were the ones who were slowly paying back their creditors even though they didn't need to. For them, their word and repayment of what they had promised years before were important to them. Although their insolvency afforded them a second chance, they took responsibility for honouring their promises.

I don't aim to support the process of bankruptcy nor condemn those who fall prey to overeager credit providers or unfortunate life circumstances. Take time during your financial meetings to consider the emotional and credit impact that bankruptcy can have and that it should be a last-resort solution should troubles arise.

First, figure out where you are. You might not be in as much trouble as you think. So many individuals file bankruptcy for small amounts of debt.

Second, what assets do you have? Are you able to consolidate your debts with your bank thereby reducing your interest costs and monthly payments?

Depending on your situation, you could cut your costs by as much as half or more by fixing your high interest rate credit card debt to a mortgage (assuming you have equity in your home). A consolidation can be a mortgage or simply a loan at a lower rate that forces you to make payments of interest and principle, whereas a credit card would simply require you to make interest payment only. Consolidation should be a one-time occurrence. Unfortunately, too many individuals who consolidate their credit card debts run them back up again in a short period of time. Consult your banker, financial planner, or the credit counselling agencies in your specific province (listed at the end of this chapter) before visiting a bankruptcy trustee.

You may wish to go directly to your creditors for help. Most do not want you to default on your agreements and will usually work with you, especially if your cash flow situation is temporary. If you have a gold credit card and your balance never seems to be paid off, your bank might have a lower rate credit card that you can switch to or a loan with a much lower rate and forced principle repayment options.

I've had something recently go to collections. Will that show up on my credit report?

It may or may not. If you have a collection agency contacting you, it's in your best interest to clear this up as quickly as possible. Simply ask the agency if they've already reported the occurrence on your credit report. Many won't if you act swiftly. And ensure that you keep excellent records of such payments. Some companies have been known to try and recollect years later leaving you to prove that you've paid the outstanding amount. Although you're in the right, it may take you some time to remove such an error from your credit report.

How long does something stay on my report?

Six years. A credit transaction will automatically be purged from the system six years from the date of last activity, according to Equifax.

The importance of building credit in your own name or building from scratch

Many stay-at-home parents, divorcees, and widows/ers are vulnerable to a non-existent credit history. Let's assume that you have a credit card secondary to that of your spouse. In this case, you are not building credit. Should your spouse die or you divorce, you may lose all current credit privileges.

It's essential that you build credit in your own name and with a company that regularly reports your payments and good history. A general rule of thumb is, if you didn't have to apply or be approved for the credit you have, then you're not building credit. If you have a supplementary credit card based on your spouse's account and it simply came in the mail without your having to fill out forms or apply in any other way, you are not building credit in your name.

In such an instance, how then does one start to build credit? Although I generally would never recommend applying for a department store card, they are usually somewhat easy to obtain. If you do currently have a supplementary card in your name, you can present that card at the department store for automatic approval of their card. They will likely only grant you a small amount of credit (say $300), but it's a good start. Then, purchase only items from that store on your new card that you can absolutely pay off each month. Do this for six months to a year, and you'll create a solid foundation to building positive credit in your name. Once you've done this, you can apply for a standard Visa or MasterCard with your bank and continue to cautiously use or cut up your department store cards (as they tend to have much higher interest rates than Visa or MasterCard).

If you're assisting your child in building credit as a young adult, the same process can work. You can have a supplementary credit card in their name, but on your account. Your child can then obtain a department store or other similar credit card in their own name based on the card they have from your account. A note of extreme caution—only do this if you're confident in your child's ability to act responsibly with your card. When giving a supplementary card to your child, spouse, employee, or any other person, your account is vulnerable and the responsibility to pay all charges is yours. I would not suggest you do this with a high limit card. If you choose this option, you may wish to get a separate, low limit card from your bank, say $1,000, so you know the worst damage the individual could do is rack up a grand on your card. Don't assume, whether it's your child, spouse or any other person, that they will act responsibly with your credit card.

When you should establish credit even if you don't need it

To paraphrase Mark Twain, a banker is there to lend you an umbrella when it's sunny and will take it away when it's raining. It's paramount that you apply and secure sufficient credit while your financial situation is solid (if possible). Although I cautioned you earlier about taking on too many credit card accounts, there's a delicate balance between too many and not enough.

Here's an example. You're currently an employee and have worked for your company for some years. Your general financial picture is solid. You decide to leave your company of employment and open your own business (or perhaps leave to have more children, etc.). Six months into your business, not receiving a salary, you realize that you could really use an operating line of credit to get you through that tough first year. Now when you apply for credit, the lender will look at your current income (which is none in this example), see that you're on a new, perhaps risky venture and your employment history will not be fully considered. Many in this instance would not be approved without collateral or some other strength.

Ideally, in the above example, if you knew you were leaving your stable career as an employee, you would apply for a line of credit *before* you left that position. If you wind up not needing the credit, it won't cost anything to apply for and keep the line of credit open. However, should you need it later when your financial situation is less stable, it will be there for you without the need to apply for it.

Case Study: Where one person's credit was and how quickly we were able to improve it

The following is a credit case study on an individual I'll refer to as Ethan, which of course is not his real name. Ethan came to me for help in 2004 and has agreed for me to use his information and situation as a case study (provided his name was changed and his situation described generally). Ethan was in severe need of credit counselling some years ago, was one small step away from bankruptcy, and, within a relatively short period of time, turned his financial future around.

When Ethan had first come to see me, the business he had recently opened was struggling relentlessly. He jokingly commented on several occasions that his receptionist worked one third of the hours he did and was taking home twice the amount of pay. Each month, his financial situation worsened. He used one credit card to pay the minimum payment on another, was behind 30 to 90 days on every one of his loans and most days, didn't have the courage to even check his bank accounts and how many NSF (not sufficient funds) charges were going through. He didn't know if there would ever be a way out.

The following is a chronological look at how Ethan, in a step-by-step fashion, rebuilt his credit, life, and financial self-esteem.

February 1st, 2004

Ethan knew he was in trouble. He just didn't know how bad it was. He also knew he should pull a credit report, but didn't have the courage on his own. With a little figurative handholding and a deep breath, we ordered an online report. The news wasn't great. To give you an idea of how brutal his situation was only when Ethan filed his 2004 taxes, did he realize that he had incurred over $1,700 in NSF charges for the year.

Score as of 02/01/04: 530.

It could have been worse, but at a score of 530, things were bad. According to Equifax Canada, only 4% of the population had a score as low as Ethan's. At that score, 60% will default on a loan, file for bankruptcy, or fall 90 days past due. The only group score worse than Ethan's is that of 490 or less; that group constitutes 78% of all delinquencies. Certainly, not the ideal candidate for a consolidation loan with a major bank. Ethan had even applied for the highest rate credit card offered to him weeks before coming to see me, hoping to use it to pay current monthly bills, and was yet again declined. His sheer willpower and vow never to declare bankruptcy kept him focused on the financial repairs he needed to make.

His situation in 2004:

He wasn't quite ready to pack up his business and throw in the towel. He had sunk every dollar he had into his company, spent 70-80 hours a week for the past two years trying to make a go of it, and desperately hoped things would turn around.

He had three credit cards (maxed out balances of $7,900, $2,900, and $650).

- The startling issue with the last card that was maxed out at $250 (his limit) was its total balance of $650. How is this possible? Some cards, and usually the non-traditional bank credit cards, have many hidden fees. As Ethan was continually late with his payments and the monthly interest and penalty fees kept bumping him "over limit," in approximately six months, without actually using the card further, Ethan went from owing $250 to over $650 on this particular card.
- One of his bank issued cards had some surprising fine print as well. Ethan's annual interest rate was 18%. However, as we were carefully reading his most recent statement, there was a small paragraph that stated, since he had a history of not making his minimum payments on time, his current annual interest rate was 24%. Once he made his minimum payment on time for at least six months, his annual rate would then drop back down to 18%.
- Ethan's other personal debts included:

  A car lease at $480 per month;

  Two loans with a small lender at 28% interest with monthly payments of $800;

  A first mortgage with a Schedule I (big five) bank;

  A second mortgage with a private lender with payments of $250 per month.

  He had no department store credit cards, collection on his credit report, or bankruptcy/or other blemishes.
- Other factors affecting his score:

Credit card one: two over-30-day late payments;

Credit card two: no late payments, but over limit;

Credit card three: no late payments, but also over limit

Loan one: four 30-day late payments and one 60-day late payment;

Various past credit (loans and credit cards) paid off, up to date, and no further reported late payments.

A macro recap of Ethan's situation and credit score are thus. Due to the number of current late payments, over limit situations on his credit cards, and the number of current debts, Ethan's score was brought near to the worst possible.

At this point, he was seeking help, but really needed to know how severe the situation was. He was barely keeping his business afloat and had no idea how he was going to pull himself out of his situation. His company was not making enough for him to cover his personal monthly obligations, let alone those of his business.

Despite my advice (which we've already looked at in other chapters – e.g. what other cash flow could he bring into his life, considering a career change, self-esteem and prosperity principles), Ethan decided not to do anything for the moment. For the sake of brevity in this example, I'll forego detailing the extreme emotional issues Ethan was dealing with at this time and the indirect counselling and advice. The purpose of this example is simply to illustrate one individual's credit score and with simple actions and steps, how quickly it improved.

November 2005

Ethan came back to see me with his updated credit score. He hadn't done much at this point from the last time I'd seen him. His company was still struggling, as was he personally. However, being much more aware of his situation, he tried to pay his debt obligations on time, but with a sketchy cash flow at best, he still juggled with which bills to pay each month.

What was different for Ethan this time is that he'd opened a second business that was starting to produce a profit. He was very committed to turning his life and financial future around and seriously wanted to do whatever it would take to improve his score and fate.

Ethan had a home with considerable equity in it, but, as his score had been undesirable to lenders and his income over the past year near nil, no schedule one bank wanted to consider lending on that equity. Since he couldn't magically change the fact that his income was near nothing, the only thing he could do was improve his score. His goal was to obtain a new mortgage in the spring and consolidate all of his debts, if possible.

Ethan's score November 2005 – 653

At this point, his score had improved slightly from his situation in 2004. He still had a number of current late payments and two of his credit cards were still over limit. He hadn't been seeking credit, which was good, and his hard hits were all fairly old.

At a score of 653, Ethan was in the 12% FICO score range. The delinquency rate for the group range 600-649 was still 23%, thus a conventional lender would still likely consider him a high risk and limit his options for new credit or a consolidation loan, which he so desperately needed at this point.

Ethan's score January 2006 – 658

Ethan was really trying at this point. His score hasn't moved up much at all since November. He wanted to be in the next batch of scores, over 699. He was working hard to keep his balances under the maximum and had even gone as far as to swallow his pride and borrow a few hundred dollars from family members to ensure he paid his minimum payments on time.

February 2006

Ethan finally made contact with a lender at a Schedule I bank. The lender isn't thrilled with his lack of reported income over the past three years or the number of late payments on his credit history. However, with the percentage of equity in his home and the recent climb in his credit rating, she was willing to try.

Ethan had hoped to obtain a mortgage for approximately 75% of the value of his home, which is still a conventional mortgage, not requiring him to obtain CMHC insurance. (CMHC stands for the Canadian Mortgage and Housing Corporation and insurance is required if you have an unconventional mortgage—i.e. less than 25%. It's an insurance premium purchased at the time you take out your mortgage to provide the lender protection if you default on your obligation.) His goal was to acquire enough financing so that he could pay off all of his debts and perhaps even a little more to renovate his home or invest in the stock market.

For Ethan to fully pay off all of his high interest rate debt, he would need a mortgage of about 60% of the value of his home. At the time of his application with the bank, they were only willing to lend him up to 50% of the appraised value. Although somewhat disappointed that he wasn't able to pay off all of his debts, Ethan was thrilled that he would be able to pay off his extremely high interest debts. The mortgage specialist also informed him that if he took care of his credit over the next six months and improved his score, he could likely come back and obtain a line of credit if he chose. As far as I know, Ethan did just that.

My last visit with Ethan

March 2006. Credit score – 723.

As you can imagine, Ethan was simply thrilled with his new score. In just over a year, and with a reasonable amount of effort and minimal pain, he was able to take his score from unsavoury by the standards of the lending industry, to a viable candidate. By paying down and eliminating many of his loans, credit cards, and the second mortgage, his score had jumped considerably in just one month.

Ethan vows to never again purchase more than he can afford, fail to meet his minimum monthly obligations, or allow his business to put him further into debt.

At this score, Ethan shares his spot with 32% of the population. His score is still below average, however, many lenders would consider this satisfactory. The delinquency rate for those residing in this score range (700-749) is only 5%.

Protecting your credit cards

10 ways to protect your credit cards

You may think these ten rules are unnecessary. But if you ignore them, you make it easy for the wrong people to use your cards.

- Never leave your cards unattended at work. There are more credit card thefts in the workplace than in any other single location.
- If your credit card is programmed to access an Automated Banking Machine (ABM), protect your Personal Identification Number (PIN) or security code. Don't write it down, memorize it.
- Don't leave your credit cards in your vehicle. A very high proportion of credit cards are stolen from motor vehicles.
- Always check your card when returned to you after a purchase. Make sure it is your card.
- When travelling, carry your cards with you or make sure they are in a secure location.
- Report lost or stolen cards immediately. Most fraudulent uses of cards takes place within days of their being lost or stolen.
- Sign the back of a new card as soon you get it. Destroy unwanted cards so no one else can use them.
- Make a list of all your cards and their numbers. This key information is helpful when reporting lost or stolen cards.
- Always check your monthly statement. Make sure the charges are yours.
- Never give your card number over the phone unless you are dealing with a reputable company. The only time you should give it is when you have called to place an order.

- Treat your credit cards like cash.
  Source: Canadian Bankers Association

And I would add that you should *never* respond to calls via e-mail or telephone from any bank or institution. Credit card companies will never contact you this way, if at all. If you're technically savvy, this may go without saying. However, I'm always shocked at how many very intelligent and experienced individuals will conceded that they've been scammed by someone in the past even when, and in their words, they should have known better. When in doubt, call your bank or credit card company directly.

Resources:

Safeguarding Your Money is part of CBA's program of *Building a Better Understanding* with Canadians. For more information on the series of free publications offered by the CBA, visit their Web site at *www.cba.ca* or call toll free 1-800-263-0231.

Credit Counselling Agencies in Canada

British Columbia

Credit Counselling Society
Toll-free: 1-888-527-8999
Tel: 604-527-8999
Fax: 604-527-8008
www.nomoredebts.org

Alberta

Credit Counselling Services of Alberta
Toll-free 1-888-294-0076 (AB only)
Calgary Tel: 403-265-2201
Fax: 403-265-2240
Edmonton Tel: 780-423-5265
Fax: 780-423-2791
www.creditcounselling.com

Saskatchewan

Provincial Mediation Board Credit Counselling
Toll-free: 1-888-215-2222
Regina Tel: 306-787-5387
Fax: 306-787-5574
Saskatoon Tel: 306-933-6520

Fax: 306-933-7030
www.creditcounsellingcanada.ca/saskatchewan.html

Manitoba

Community Financial Counselling Services
Tel: 204-989-1900
1-888-573-2383
Fax: 204-989-1908
www.creditcounsellingcanada.ca/manitoba.html

Ontario

Ontario Association of Credit Counselling Services
Toll-free: 1-888-7IN-DEBT (1-888-746-3328)
www.oaccs.com/main.html

Quebec

Credit Counselling Services of Eastern Ontario
Toll free: 1-866-202-0425

Newfoundland & Labrador

Credit Counselling Service of Newfoundland and Labrador
Tel: 709-753-5812
Fax: 709-753-3390
www.creditanddebtsolutions.ca

Prince Edward Island, Nova Scotia, and New Brunswick

Credit Counselling Services of Atlantic Canada, Inc.
Toll-free: 1-888-753-2227
www.solveyourdebts.com

Yukon

See British Columbia Credit Counselling Society
Toll-free: 1-888-527-8999

Northwest Territories

See Alberta and British Columbia
Credit Counselling Services of Alberta
Call collect: 0-403-265-2201
Credit Counselling Society
Toll-free: 1-888-527-8999

Nunavut

See British Columbia and Manitoba

Credit Inquiries and Reporting Agencies

Canada's two main credit agencies used by lenders:

1. Equifax Canada Inc. - Credit Information Services directs
you to a local credit reporting agency
Toll-free: 1-800-465-7166
www.equifax.com/home/en_ca

2. TransUnion Canada (for all provinces, except Quebec)
Consumer Relations Centre
Toll-free: 1-800-663-9980
TransUnion (for residents of Quebec)
Toll-free: 1-877-713-3393
www.transunion.ca

Not as widely used, but one of Canada's credit reporting agencies:
Northern Credit Bureaus Inc. - National Data Centre
Tel: 819-762-4351
Toll-free: 1-800-532-8784
Fax: 819-762-0675
www.creditbureau.ca

Additional Online Resources for Youth:
There's Something about Money
The CBA's interactive money management site for youth that provides information on budgeting, credit, compound interest, and much more.
www.yourmoney.cba.ca

The YourMoney Network
A one-stop online resource that offers non-commercial financial information for youth. The YMN hosts 54 partners, which provide information from all walks of the financial world on more than 800 resource areas.
www.yourmoney.cba.ca

Conclusion

Many authors suggest that if a reader retains simply one nugget of useful information contained within a book, then the time and money spent was worthwhile. Although a valid thought, I expect more out of the books that I invest in and know that you do as well. As such, I poured as much information into these pages as I possibly could. Also unlike many other authors, I have nothing more to sell you. No tapes, workshops, or coaching, just the information, expertise, and resources that I've acquired over the years. As I wrote *She Inc.*, I realized that I have more to offer you my reader and will no doubt follow-up with articles (you can read those for free on my Web site) and, I hope, with another book. But what I have, I've offered it to you wholeheartedly. It is my desire that it changes your life.

As I've concluded in my other books, knowledge is power, however, missing the element of action, it will only affect your life in a minimal way. Accountability is key and I'd like you to use what you've learned in *She Inc.* now and until it's absolutely revolutionized your life, as it has mine. At the onset, it will take faith. Faith that this perspective shift of thinking of yourself as a corporation will actually pay dividends one day. And it will if you believe today and act now.

The six-week challenge:

I invite you to e-mail me right now at *wealth@kellykeehn.com*. Please include in the subject field: "The Six-Week Challenge" and I will send you a list of tangible, easy, and practical exercises and reminders to reinforce the material you've learned. Then, each Monday for six weeks, I will send you a new list and so on. That way, you'll develop a firm foundation for putting these principles into action.

I hope you've enjoyed your journey to self-discovery and how thinking of your personal and professional life in a larger context can revolutionize your finances, create greater clarity, and assist you in breaking the proverbial glass ceiling in your industry.

I wish you continued success, happiness, and blessings in all of your adventures and look forward to hearing from you personally one day soon.

Until then,
Live prosperously!

Index

Acknowledgements

There are not enough pages in an entire book to list those who I am forever grateful to for their love, support, and endless cheerleading that has allowed me to get to this point in my life.

For the sake of brevity and my publisher's printing budget, I will limit my thanks to those directly responsible for the manifestation of this book.

To my mother Kathy. Without your endless love, generosity, and lifelong support, I never would have had the courage to live one day of my life. You are the angel of my life.

To my love Wyatt. No thanks could equal the countless hours of feedback, ideas, research, and input you have provided over the past seven years. It's no wonder I joke that my books are more yours than mine.

To my amazing family. As large in breadth and too many to name individually, in general, I thank you all! Specifically, to my brothers David and Randy, and to Randy's wife Elaine and their fantastic children. With a support system like mine, it makes writing about prosperity an easier task.

To all of my friends. This is where the pages of this book could surely be filled by the names of each of my friends and those I've met along my career path that made this adventure possible. My heartfelt thanks to each of you.

To my publisher Mike O'Connor and editor Gillian Urbankiewicz. For having someone who believes in your work enough to publish it and to have someone so gifted in editing that my work is actually readable, I owe the team at Insomniac the highest of praise and appreciation.

To my readers and audience members. It is really only you that make this journey worth taking. Writing a book can, at times, seem like an overwhelming project. And then, a reader follows up with how her life was changed because of a new concept or how an idea influenced her and her interpretation of her situation. That is the delight factor that I held on to each moment of writing the words in this book.

Last but never least, my humble thanks to God. Being born at a time and in a country where a woman has a free voice is truly priceless and one thing that money can never affect or buy.

About the author

Kelley Keehn, financial expert, speaker, media personality, and author of six books, including *The Woman's Guide to Money* and *The Prosperity Factor for Kids.* As a former financial professional for over a decade overseeing the management of hundreds of millions of dollars, she's witnessed first hand the problems individuals have with money and has developed a number of fun and practical guides to making changes to our money mind sets at a fundamental level. Kelley discovered that whether someone had a billion in the bank or was a million in the hole, everyone has money problems!

Kelley is a regular, sought-after media guest appearing on TV and radio around the globe and has had many regular columns and published articles. Recently, Kelley was invited to meet with Warner Brothers, CNBC, and auditioned for the position of host with HGTV and the W Network. Kelley travels extensively throughout North America as a faculty member with the Canadian Initiative for Elder Planning Studies, as a sought after corporate lecturer, and for her upcoming book tours.

Kelley's mission in life is to make you feel good about money and you!

Visit Kelley at *www.kelleykeehn.com*